# School Governing Bodies

# School Governing Bodies

Maurice Kogan (editor), Daphne Johnson,
Tim Packwood and Tim Whitaker

 Heinemann Educational Books · London

Heinemann Educational Books Ltd
22 Bedford Square, London WC1B 3HH
LONDON   EDINBURGH   MELBOURNE   AUCKLAND
HONG KONG   SINGAPORE   KUALA LUMPUR   NEW DELHI
IBADAN   NAIROBI   JOHANNESBURG
EXETER (NH)   KINGSTON   PORT OF SPAIN

© Maurice Kogan, Daphne Johnson, Tim Packwood and Tim Whitaker 1984
First published 1984

**British Library Cataloguing in Publication Data**

School governing bodies.
   1. School management and organization—
Great Britain   2. School boards—Great
Britain
   I. Kogan, Maurice
   391.1'531'0941     LB2901

ISBN 0–435–82512–7 Pbk

Typeset by Inforum Ltd, Portsmouth
Printed in Great Britain by Biddles Ltd, Guildford, Surrey

# Contents

# Preface

The authors of this book are greatly in debt to the many people who helped them get the research under way and assisted it with friendly but critical monitoring *en route*. Our first debt is to the Department of Education and Science which generously gave a grant to enable three of us to undertake the substantial fieldwork which underpins our writing. The Department appointed a steering committee, at first under the chairmanship of Clive Saville and later of Roger Morgan, whose expertise and commitment to the importance of the subject sustained us throughout the period of researching and testing our materials. We express our gratitude to the members: S. Davey (Headmaster, Shene School, London), M. G. Duncan (Board of Education, General Synod of the Church of England), A. Evans (Senior Education Officer, National Union of Teachers), T. M. Hinds (Second Deputy Chief Education Officer, Cambridge Education Department), D. A. Howell (Institute of Education, University of London) and Miss A. C. Millett (HMI).

None of the work would have been possible without the expert secretarial and administrative services provided by Mary Furnell.

Perhaps our greatest debt, however, is to the schools and local authorities which, although they must remain anonymous, allowed us to observe the ways in which their governing bodies work, the ways in which they fit in with the working of the larger political and administrative system, and the ways in which government bodies struck up working relationships with the schools. To the governors, heads and teaching staff of the schools, and the officers and members of the four local authorities concerned, we express deep gratitude.

This book is written to be consistent in theme and style, but each of us has taken different chapters as our main responsibility. Maurice Kogan edited the book and was responsible primarily for Chapters 2 and 9. Daphne Johnson, who was the project convenor and the mainspring of the whole study, wrote Chapters 1, 6 and 7. Tim Whitaker wrote Chapters 3 and 4, and Tim Packwood Chapters 5 and 8. But we take collective responsibility for the whole work which is based upon commonly worked-through perspectives and acquired knowledge. For the first year of our study Cathy Bird was a full-time member of the team and we should like to acknowledge the contribution that she made in conceptualising the issues and in opening up the field work with us.

Finally, we should like to thank our colleagues in the Department of Government, Brunel University, who provided the friendly colleague-base in which this work could be undertaken.

# 1 Are governing bodies important?

Built into the Education Act 1944 is a carefully balanced system of checks and balances involving the Secretary of State, the local education authorities, the managing and governing bodies of the schools, parents, headteachers and teachers. Through this flexible system schools are accountable to the elected representatives of the community and to parents. The powers and duties variously defined are sufficient to provide adequate means of obtaining reliable information about the performance of the school system as a whole.

(National Union of Teachers, February 1977)

When this Canute-like statement was made, the waves of change were already lapping round the feet of the teachers' associations. Regional conferences, part of the Great Debate on education, were only weeks away. Within four months the Taylor Committee were to present their report, *A New Partnership for our Schools*.[1] By November of the same year the Secretary of State had made known her ideas about the nature and extent of information to be made available to parents.[2] All seemed in readiness for a new Education Act which would substantially shift the fulcrum of the system of checks and balances with which the teachers had claimed to be so satisfied.

Three years and a change of government later, the Education Act 1980 came onto the statute book. Its opening sections gave pride of place to changes in school government. The shift in the balance of power was, it seemed, to favour school governing bodies. These little known, semi-invisible, institutions would move into prominence, making school governors a force to be reckoned with in the control of schools.

Have school governing bodies, then, become important? Are they now recognisable, consistent, solidly-based institutions which have an unequivocal and influential part to play in the education system of England and Wales? This book will examine these questions in the light of new research.

## The Education Act 1980
In the event, the 1980 Education Act proved to be a less than radical piece of legislation. The changes in school government contained in the Act were small-scale, cautious and to become prescriptive only in the unspecified future. The body of managers constituted for primary schools by the 1944 Education Act was henceforward to be known as a

governing body, like that of a secondary school. In addition to governors appointed by the local education authority, the governing body of every county, voluntary or special school maintained by a local education authority would include at least two parents of registered pupils at the school. In the case of a voluntary school, one of these parents should be a 'foundation' governor, but all other parents on governing bodies, elected by parents of registered pupils at the school, would be known as parent governors. Each governing body would include at least one teacher governor (in a school with less than 300 registered pupils) and at least two such governors in larger schools. Teacher governors would be elected by their colleagues at the school. The headteacher of every school, unless he decided otherwise, would become a governor by virtue of his office. Schools, other than two primary schools, might not be grouped under a single governing body, except with the approval of the Secretary of State. (The full text of Sections 1–5 of the Education Act 1980, concerning school government, is given in Appendix II.)

The requirements listed above would apply to any Instrument of Government made after the coming into force of the Act, but would not otherwise become mandatory until an order was made by the Secretary of State.* The Act therefore set the pattern for future developments in school government, in terms of individual governing bodies for all schools, and the inclusion of parent and teacher governors, but did not require existing governing bodies to fall in line.

While the Instrument of Government establishes the composition of a governing body, it is the Articles of Government which specify its powers. The 1980 Education Act has not been followed by the issue of Model Articles. The existing powers of most school governors look back to the Model Articles issued in 1945, following the Education Act 1944.[4] Some would claim that all the powers governors need to play a useful role were already embodied in the 1944 Act and its attendant Model Articles. Governors, it is asserted, have failed to use those powers systematically and imaginatively, and so they have fallen into disuse.[5] Certainly, the 1944 Education Act still sets the main parameters for school government in the 1980s and consideration must be given to what that Act had to say, and why, about school governing bodies.

---

* The Education (School Governing Bodies) Regulations 1981, made under the Education Act, came into force on 1 August 1981. These regulations concern such matters as governors' tenure of office and the election of chairmen. In December 1983 the Secretary of State announced that the provisions of the 1980 Education Act would become mandatory for the government of maintained special schools from 1 September 1984. In January 1984 he announced that the government of all remaining maintained schools must comply with the new arrangements by 1 September 1985.[3]

## The Education Act 1944

The chief contribution of the 1944 Act to the history of the development of school governing bodies was the requirement that there be 'for every county school and for every voluntary school', 'an instrument providing for the constitution of [a] body of managers or governors of the school' (Section 17(1) ). The notion of individual schools, individually governed, is thereby firmly enshrined in the Act. Even though subsequent clauses whittle away at the intention of Section 17(1), and provide ample possibility for dissenting practice in the form of grouped governing bodies, the individuality and uniqueness of each school as an institution have been given statutory recognition. Students of the history and philosophy of the Act claim that the individuality of schools was acknowledged chiefly to pacify those interests in the independent and voluntary sectors of education to whom such individuality was paramount.[6] Baron and Howell[7] comment that supporters of the older public schools and grammar schools were at this time concerned to stress the possibility of those schools' most desirable features being more widely diffused. The notion of the individual, unique school, and the attendant notion of the need for an individual governing body for each school, were two such features which found their way into the Act.

Whatever the reason for introducing the idea of individual governing bodies, and whatever the weakness of commitment with which the notion was in fact put into practice for county schools, the 1944 Act triggered new thoughts about school government and raised new expectations about its potential form and scope. Like many an educational statute before and since, Section 17(1) provided a platform for use by protagonists of many widely varying educational purposes and concerns.

### School governing bodies in the 1960s

Twenty years on from the 1944 Act, actual practice with regard to school government varied throughout the country. Field studies carried out by Baron and Howell in 1967 showed that the number of county boroughs which had individual governing bodies was almost exactly matched by those county boroughs which had only one governing body for all schools (21 and 20, out of 78). But the remaining 37 county boroughs surveyed all had grouped governing bodies of some kind, most of these (25) being for small groups of two or three schools. In the counties, however, 22 out of 45 had individual governing bodies throughout, and 20 had a mixture of individual and grouped governing bodies. These figures applied to secondary schools, but a similar pattern of practice was found in the counties for the management of primary schools. In the county boroughs, however, primary schools were, more markedly than secondary schools, found to be governed in very large groups.

'History and inertia', Baron and Howell concluded, were important contributory factors to the diversity of the pattern of school government which existed in 1967. Authorities claimed they had always (or never) had individual governing bodies, and saw no reason to change. Another important factor was the attitude taken by the Chief Education Officer towards school government, and the extent to which he could get his own way with the Education Committee.[8]

Some of the justificatory themes which authorities brought forward in support of practice show the variety of ideas seen as relevant to governing body arrangements, during the 1960s. These themes included:

(i)  the primacy of the elected member in local government arrangements;
(ii)  the difficulty of recruiting lay governors; and
(iii) the need for predictability in the behaviour of individuals and groups with whom education officers work.

These three themes were employed in support of grouped governing bodies, controlled by elected members.

But other themes were brought forward to justify individual governing bodies, namely:

(i)   the uniqueness of the school as an institution;
(ii)  the autonomy of the head (and the need for him not to be at the mercy of the local education authority);
(iii) the need to give county schools parity of status with denominational schools in county boroughs where 40 to 50 per cent of children went to church schools.

### Ideas about school government in the 1970s

The 1970s proved to be a decade of active public opinion about schools, and their control. Many publications[9] have chronicled the sequence of events which included the establishment of the Assessment of Performance Unit, the public inquiry into events at William Tyndale Junior and Infants Schools,[10] Prime Minister Callaghan's call for wider debate on educational issues, the ensuing Great Debate, the enquiry into local authority arrangements for the school curriculum,[11] and the Taylor Report, reviewing the arrangements for the government of maintained schools in England and Wales.[12]

The background of concern during the 1970s had a number of elements. Apart from uncertainty about general educational standards, there were more specific doubts about whether schooling was adequately preparing young people to meet the needs of a technological society, and also whether 'the wishes of their parents' were in any effective sense influencing the education which children received, as the 1944 Act required. These elements of concern were not exclusive to the United Kingdom but were also apparent in the USA. In particular, the demand for increased influence by clients of the schools was emerging there. Parents in the depressed areas of New York City, but also in many other parts of the USA, were dissatisfied with the system of education administration which seemed to exclude the expression of wants and needs by parents and clients.[13]

Just as American parents were pressing for increased decentralisation of educational decision-making to local community school boards, so, in the UK, school governing bodies were increasingly seen[14] as one way in which new influences could be brought to bear on schooling. Already, many local education authorities were changing the composition of governing bodies to include parents. The survey which the National Association of Governors and Managers carried out in 1975 showed that parents were represented on the school governing bodies of 70 out of the 82 LEAs which responded. In 62 authorities teachers were also represented.

Giving teachers an official role in school government was in some ways a more radical development than the introduction of parent governors. The Model Instrument, following the 1944 Education Act, had explicitly ruled out teachers from participating in school governing bodies.[15] The turnaround in practice which had taken place by the mid-1970s can be interpreted either as the teachers insisting on an equal and neutralising presence on school governing bodies, countering the introduction of parent power, or as a development within the teaching profession of notions about participation in management[16] which were also being promoted in other occupations. Bacon[17] sees the appointment of teacher governors as a pale copy of developments in industrial democracy. He judges teacher governors to be but feeble and disadvantaged protagonists of worker power on the governing bodies of their own institutions, inhibited from representing the shopfloor by the presence of the headteacher. Others would preserve the more traditional view that clients of a public institution are less able to review its work if those being reviewed sit on its governing body.

Bacon's overall view of the outcome of an early example of school governing body reorganisation (in Sheffield) is a pessimistic one.[18] In 1970, as an act of 'political altruism' by the incoming Labour administration, school governing bodies in Sheffield were completely reorganised, bringing in new voices at the expense of the former council domination of school government. The rationale for the constitution of the new governing bodies was one of partnership in the control of the schools and of education policy. Bacon claims that the 'partnership' rationale was rapidly and effectively countered by the cooption of new governors to an 'establishment' view. Parent governors, in particular, accepted the notion of education as an arena for depoliticised public service, in which their role was to support and legitimate the policy-makers (education officers and senior teachers) at school and LEA level.

Bacon's study demonstrated some of the operational weaknesses of the 'new voices in school government' argument, showing that new participants simply swelled the ranks of a consensual 'educational lobby'. By contrast, other researchers working during the 1970s took the view that schools could be and were responsively accountable to a range of interested parties. Elliott and his colleagues on the Cambridge Accountability Project perceived two notions of accountability as having some currency. 'Public accountability' they defined as a strategy for transferring power over educational decision-making from the professional staff of schools to the state. This they associated with a 'productivity' model, which responds to powerful interest groups but neglects underprivileged minority groups. They contrasted this with the alternative notion of 'responsive accountability', where the school retains control over decisions, but becomes more responsive to those whose interests are affected by those decisions; it was this latter model which they pursued in their action research.[19]

Academic researchers are interested in the values which underlie institutional arrangements. Committees of enquiry tend to place their emphasis as much on the institutional mechanisms which are meant to achieve 'good practice'. The Taylor Committee, appointed in 1975 to review the government and management of maintained schools, took the view that their recommendations should be compatible with:

(i) the roles of central and local government in the provision of education, as specified in the 1944 Education Act (which, they felt, were likely to remain unchanged);
(ii) the possibility of future changes in local government structure (in view of which their recommendations should be flexible and capable of adaptation to different circumstances);
(iii) the need to avoid unjustifiable public expenditure (so proposals must make maximum use of existing facilities and resources).

The Taylor Report is chiefly remembered for its recommendation that governing bodies should be made up of equal numbers of local education authority representatives, school staff, parents (and, where appropriate, pupils) and representatives of the local community. However, the goal which they set themselves in determining their recommendations should also be recalled. This was 'a school with enough independence to ensure its responsive and distinctive character, taking its place in an efficient local administration of an effective national system.'[20] Bearing in mind the arguments at the time of the 1944 Act about the uniqueness of the school versus the notion of the school as a unit in a system, it can be seen that the Taylor Committee hoped to integrate and reconcile the best of both worlds.

## A summary of the arguments put forward as relevant to arrangements for school government

The themes of argument about school government which we have discussed in this account of developments over the forty years preceding the 1980 Education Act together make up a battery of viewpoints of which our own research and writing has had to be aware. We summarise them as:

(i)    the 'new voices in school government' argument (of which the 'partnership' argument is a sub-set, and the 'parent power' lobby a particular example);

(ii)   the 'local circumstances' argument (school government as responsive to the needs of a local community);

(iii)  the 'circumstances of the particular institution' argument (each school a unique institution);

(iv)   the 'school as a unit in a national system' argument (of which the 'mobile society' argument, necessitating consistent educational provision, because of frequent geographical relocation of families, is a sub-set);

(v)    the 'education lobby' argument (this argument stresses the potential of governing bodies as a collectivity, espousing the 'education' interest within authorities working on corporate management lines);*

(vi)   the 'efficiency' argument (public accountability and/or the requirements of new technology for particular outputs from the schools);

(vii)  the 'primacy of the professional' argument (responsive accountability); and

(viii) the 'hard times' argument.

This final item may need some elucidation. In the light of what Kogan has referred to as the 'downward spiral of demography, of resources available to education, of an economy to provide employment

---

* Bacon presents a sub-set of this argument. He claims that governing bodies offer no substantial challenge to the existing structure of power, but can play a key role in defending and legitimising policies and practice developed by the leaders of a school system – full-time education officers, senior members of the teaching profession and leading local politicians.

opportunities for those who pass through the education system, and of expectations',[21] some have considered it inopportune to elaborate and diversify school government. Fulton, in his Minority Report from the Taylor Committee of Enquiry, saw the pressures of the time as creating a need for a greater degree of central planning, rather than devolution to 'non-elected, non-accountable bodies'.[22]

## School governing bodies in the 1980s

Since the publication of the Taylor Report in 1977, the question of school government has been at least touched on during research into more general aspects of educational policy and administration.[23] The Open University has run a course on governing schools, and evaluated its impact.[24] Scottish school councils, the over-the-border cousins of school governing bodies, have been examined,[25] and a small-scale enquiry, focused on the role of parent and teacher governors, has been made.[26]

Our own research began in 1980. The School Governing Bodies Project, the second major study of school government to be funded by the Department of Education and Science,[27] has involved the authors in a three-year study of school government in four local authorities, which we have named Lorrenshire, Mead, Robart and Stapleton in this book, for anonymity. Our research has been qualitative in mode, and intensive in its focus.* It complements the broader survey work of Baron and Howell by making an extended observational study of two governing bodies in each of our four case-study local authorities. Like the Taylor Committee, we have tried to keep a balance between our interest in the uniqueness of each institution, and in the part it plays in the local education system.

Our research had four complementary objectives:

(i) to document a range of school governing body practice immediately following the 1980 Education Act;

(ii) to make a descriptive analysis of a small number of governing bodies, examining each governing body in the context of the school it governed, interest groups in the local community, and the client group of parents with children at the school;

(iii) to advance understanding of school governing bodies as institutions within the education system, affected by the central–local relations of that system;

(iv) to advance practitioners' and policy-makers' understanding of school governing bodies as a form of educational governance, and provide pointers to future policy-making about school government.

---

* A full account of our research methods is to be found in Appendix I, together with a brief description of the local authorities and schools concerned.

In this book our case-study work is the data base for a discussion of the role presently being played by school governing bodies in the balance of powers which govern education. We analyse the forces at work and the arguments being employed in school governing bodies as we have observed them. Governing bodies exhibit great variety in their composition and operation, and have not yet become the consistent, solidly-based institutions postulated at the beginning of this chapter. Our book attempts to show the episodic, multi-modal, sometimes quixotic style of school governing bodies' operations in the early 1980s, and draws out the implications of all this for the interplay of powers which, in Archer's terms, determine the 'definition of instruction'.[28]

Chapter 2 discusses and defines some of the concepts most frequently employed in the discussion of school government. Chapters 3, 4 and 5 take up three themes which affect and explain the behaviour of governing bodies – the link with the local political–administrative system; the nature of the school as an institution; and the existence of the professional dimension within school government. The empirical work in our research then emerges more fully in Chapters 6 and 7, where we use our evidence to analyse how governing bodies work, and the aspirations brought to their work by the governors themselves. We then turn to themes directly related to policy. Chapter 8 outlines the characteristics of governing bodies which might be best suited to fulfil particular purposes in school government. Finally, Chapter 9 debates the policy implications of all that we have found, and suggests that at the present time school governing bodies are 'Sleeping Beauties' still awaiting the kiss of politics.

We now outline, in Chapter 2, some of the concepts used and tested in our research.

## Notes and references

1. Department of Education and Science, *A New Partnership for our Schools* (Taylor Report), HMSO, 1977.
2. DES Circular 15/77, *Information for Parents*, HMSO, 1977.
3. The Taylor Committee had recommended that legislation should give effect to their proposals within five years from the publication of their Report in 1977.
4. These Articles look back to those issued in 1908 for the then newly-established county secondary schools. See Baron, G. and Howell, D., *The Government and Management of Schools*, Athlone Press, 1974, Appendix I.
5. Wragg, E.C. and Partington, J.A., *A Handbook for School Governors*, Methuen, 1980.
6. Warwick, D., 'The local government of middle schools: governing bodies and the problems of middle school identity', in Hargreaves, A. and Tickle, L. (eds), *Middle Schools: Origins, Ideology and Practice*, Harper & Row, 1980.
7. Baron and Howell, *op. cit.*

8. Ibid.
9. See, for example, Kogan, M., *The Politics of Educational Change*, Fontana, 1978; also Lawton, D., *The Politics of the School Curriculum*. Routledge & Kegan Paul, 1980.
10. Report of the William Tyndale Junior and Infant Schools Public Inquiry (Auld Report), ILEA, 1976.
11. DES Circular 14/77, *Local Education Authority Arrangements for the School Curriculum*, HMSO, 1977.
12. Taylor Report, *op. cit.*
13. Berube, M. and Gittell, M. (eds), *Confrontation at Ocean Hill – Brownsville*, Praeger, 1969; and The Bundy Report, Mayor's Advisory Council on Decentralization of the New York City Schools, *Reconnection for Learning. A Community School System for New York Schools*, 1967.
14. In the previous decade interest in the potential of school governing bodies had already been shown by the Campaign for the Advancement of State Education (established 1961). The Plowden Committee, in their report, *Children and their Primary Schools*, HMSO, 1967, advocated a strengthening of their role.
15. Ministry of Education, Education Act 1944. Schedule to Administrative Memorandum No. 25, issued 26 January 1955. Model Instrument of Government for a County Secondary School, clause 4.
16. Regan contends that the Weaver Report on the *Government of Colleges of Education*, DES, 1966, was a major influence on the demand for the greater participation of teaching staff in the government of schools. Regan, D.E., *Local Government and Education*, Allen & Unwin, 1977.
17. Bacon, A.W., 'Co-management of the school system – a case study of teacher representations on school governing and managing bodies', in *Educational Studies*, vol. 3, no. 1, March 1977.
18. Bacon, A.W., *Public Accountability and the Schooling System*, Harper & Row, 1978.
19. Elliott, J., Bridges, D., Ebbutt, D., Gibson, R. and Nias, J., *School Accountability*, Grant McIntyre, 1981.
20. Taylor Report, *op. cit.*, Preface, para. 2.
21. Kogan, M., 'Should governors govern?', *Address to Annual Conference of NAGM*, 1981.
22. Fulton, P.O., *Taylor Report*, p. 126.
23. For example, Becher, T., Eraut, M. and Knight, J., *Policies for Educational Accountability*, Heinemann, 1982. Also Elliott *et al.*, *op. cit.*
24. Open University, *Governing Schools*, Course No. P.970. Also George, A., *Resource-based Learning for School Governors*, Croom Helm, forthcoming.
25. Macbeth, A., Mackenzie, M. and Breckenridge, I., *Scottish School Councils: Policy Making, Participation or Irrelevance?* HMSO, Edinburgh, 1980.
26. Taylor, F., *Accountability in Education: the role of elected parent and teacher governors of schools, and their relationship with their constituencies*, CIS Commentary Series, NELPCO, 1983.
27. The first was, of course, the Baron and Howell study, *op. cit.*, which was for a decade almost the only available reference on school governing bodies.
28. Archer, M.S., *Social Origins of Educational Systems*, Sage, 1979.

# 2 Relevant concepts in understanding governing bodies

Governing bodies of schools form part of complex social and political systems which can be described in several forms of language and analysis. They are, at one and the same time, legally part of a school yet organisationally at its boundary. They are part of the system of educational government, and a zone of political activity and movement. They may be part of the wider governing managerial structure and yet be a means through which there can be participation and representation of the community and client groups and action taken by educational professionals. Within government and politics there are no absolute autonomies; any group or institution which exercises its influence, power or authority has linkages with at least one other institution or group.

This book depends mainly on concepts drawn from political science. At the same time, however, it seeks to create its own idiom derived more closely from the phenomena which the researchers observed in their fieldwork. In this chapter we outline concepts which are relevant to understanding school governing bodies and which are referred to elsewhere in the book. But to state the concepts against which experience can be judged is not to proclaim the existence of all the phenomena which concepts can help analyse. For example, when we describe theories of élites in politics we do so that the reader may judge for himself how far élites exist and, if so, how far they help explain the interaction of local authorities and governing bodies. Again, when we describe rationalistic models of policy-making, we do so in order that the reader can see how far the actions of the governing bodies which we have studied fall outside this traditional model of action. We hope thus to enable readers to see what governing bodies are not, as much as what they are, as well as to help build up the range of choices about what governing bodies might become when we turn to potential models and policy implications for governing bodies in the later chapters of this book.

## A traditional description of educational government
We start with a traditional description of British educational government before referring to concepts which can be used to criticise some of these more traditional assumptions. It is based on the law of education

which enables and constrains governing bodies, and their relationship with local education authorities. A traditional description is essentially that of a liberal, top-down model. It begins with the legally and electorally legitimated local education authority which is required by statute to provide education in its area and in doing so is authorised to make certain key decisions. These include the need to maintain schools; to employ teachers; and to make decisions which affect, if they do not determine, the curriculum which is primarily created and administered by the schools. In running such a system, a local education authority is legitimated by the facts that its members are elected by universal suffrage and that it acts within nationally-created law. It delegates authority both to its permanent officials and to its employees within the schools. Here it would be possible to use the language of systems theory. In running a system, in allocating resources, and in making other decisions the local authority 'reduces interests' and aggregates the value preferences endorsed by the ballot box. Its outcomes are the sanctioning of activities undertaken by its professional employees in the schools.[1]

The traditional liberal, top-down model takes account, too, of the accepted paradox of British educational government. Local authorities are authoritative in the decisions they make but they have, traditionally, conferred great discretion upon the head of a school. Within the prescriptive framework established by local authority decisions, the head has authority to lead the school in the creation of its curriculum and to allocate resources within the school boundary.[2] The head is authorised, too, to maintain, extend or preserve the boundary between the school and its environment, its clients and other institutions.[3]

**Modifying the traditional model: models of structure and process**
Other theoretical descriptions of political systems elaborate, modify and challenge so simple a model. Concepts drawn from political science, recent administrative theory, and sociology challenge the extent to which the relationship between a local authority and a school possessing such great discretion can be viewed in terms of a simple hierarchical relationship. Theory challenges traditional managerial models by asking, and providing vocabulary enabling the observer to question, whether policy-making originates solely from within the local authority's authorised channels, or whether values are generated more diffusely. It asks whether the processes of arriving at policies take place more widely within the policy-making system and also among those groups who press upon that system.

Our study of governing bodies begins by assailing the assumption that there is a simple managerial relationship between the local education authority and the school. The structure is in fact diffuse and complex. Ultimately and legally, the school is subordinate to the local authority. But, as Chapter 4 shows, that notion is conditioned by the implicit power of the education professionals (Chapter 5), by the nature of the school's tasks, and by the place the school and its governors hold in the local political–administrative environment and system (Chapter 3). Policy is made or modified by the interaction within a network of organisations and groups which each fulfil functions in local education governance. Conflict is possible and negotiation becomes necessary.

Within the political–administrative system, patterns or relationships and modes of behaviour criss-cross and condition each other. The local authority itself is no static entity and has increasingly become subject to strong political modes of control; the degree of that control affects the relationships struck up with governing bodies. The stronger the control of the ruling party the more formal and centralised the policy-making usually is. The system may accommodate itself to the pressures placed on it by interest groups. In so doing it may regard the governing bodies as an extension of its own system for policy-making and consultation, or as some of the pressures which it must absorb or resist. The structural relationships are also communicated more insidiously through its political culture which is made up of attitudes to participation and consultation, and its administrative culture which conveys customs and attitudes on relationships between schools and local authority officers and advisers.

The political–administrative system and its decision-making processes have been subject to several qualifying extensions of theory. The simple top-down model fits most easily into what has been typified as a rational pattern of policy- and decision-making. This evokes a system that is able to establish objectives, to order them according to collective desirability, and to settle upon a course which will maximise objectives or minimise the cost of possible failure.[4] Some local authorities do, indeed, assume that it is possible to plan and implement policies rationally. They also assume that they are able, in setting and implementing objectives, to engage in 'forward mapping'.[5] The ability to plan ahead from a statement of goals also assumes a hierarchical pattern of policy-making where those at the top of the hierarchy can largely control the factors that influence implementation. An alternative construct assumes that policy-making must take account of what resources already exist, and what those who actually deliver and receive the services think it is possible to do. This involves a kind of 'backward mapping' in which the service-givers – in our case the schools – generate the knowledge and the motivation which eventually form part of a collective plan.

The notion of the political–administrative system does, in fact, fall in with other models of the policy process and particularly the 'organisational' and the 'political'.[6] The organisational model assumes that the decision process is disjointed amongst many individuals. As a result, processes come into play which take account of the fact that sub-systems rank objectives differently from other sub-systems. Individuals within the system are concerned with personal goals such as security, professional identity and their professional links. If, however, the decision-making process is disjointed, decisions are ultimately centralised through the establishment of organisational routines. Again, this model may well serve as a plausible metaphor for the way in which individual schools, professionals, local authority, politicians and administrators produce the policies within which governing bodies are engaged.

A further model which helps explain aspects of the political–administrative system is political. A political bargaining model allows for collective positions, but these result from bargaining in which outcomes are determined by the relative resources devoted by each participant to the achievement of a satisfactory solution.[7] Participants may calculate rationally or observe organisational criteria, but the outcome depends upon the interplay of the participants.

If the political–administrative system is diffuse and variable this allows choices in the way it constructs the role of the governing body. It could be part of the extended political system and be regarded as a form of legitimate pressure-group; alternatively, the governing body could be part of the policy-making and decision-making system acting on delegated authority from the local authority. Whatever the answer, a major empirical finding of our study is that it is the local authority which effectively sets the framework for governing bodies' functions, powers and modes of behaviour. Thus far, whilst they differ greatly in what they do and how they do it, the key formative variables are the Articles, instructions and resources handed to them from above. At the same time, however, our evidence justifies current thinking in political science and organisation theory which shows how no form of authority fails to be modified by the actions of those to whom it is applied.

So, on the face of it, there must be conflict between the notion of a pressure-group and the notion of the governing body as an arm of educational government. But recent writing tends to soften the distinction between the 'institution of government, representing the authority of the state, impartiality, and even a judicial temperament' and groups which 'represent special interests seeking some preferential treatment from government for their members'. It has been noted how government and pressure-groups cooperate well and often in making public policy because 'they need each other'.[8] Administrators may need the support of some of the pressure-groups in their relationships with other political institutions. They need the information they can supply. They need their support in furthering budgets. There is a series of legitimate interactions, including required consultation and the involvement of pressure-groups in implementation. There are other forms of close relationship in which an interest group might become the natural expression and representative of a given social sector and develop close kinship or other ties with government or the dominant political party.[9]

This brings us to questions of how power is distributed in the system, and the extent of exchanges and dependencies within it.

## The distribution of power within the system

The different models of decision-making seek to describe *how* decisions are made. A related question is *who* has the power to make decisions: the predominant explanation has been pluralist. This emphasises the interplay of organised interests or interest groups amongst whom government acts as a final arbiter. Decisions are unpredictable and, as we have seen, dependent upon the resources each participant is willing or able to devote to its cause. But among such groups there are those with greater access to the decision-making arena than others. Newton[10] distinguishes between established groups and the remainder, as does Kogan between the legitimated and non-legitimated.[11] Power may be tied to issues so that the degree of pluralism depends upon the state of the policy area in question. Thus within education, it has been argued,[12] interest groups were quite institutionalised as long as there was consensus. A greater degree of conflict has emerged between groups as consensus has been eroded. Issues can be fleeting or persistent, provoking coalitions among interest groups and citizens ranging in their duration from momentary to semi-permanent. There can be unexpected configurations of forces, or the unexpected assertion of the right to speak from hitherto quiescent or barely existent groups.

Pluralist theory thus accommodates the notion of both an authoritative system and of reciprocity between it and groups in a more pluralist world. Reciprocal relationships can exist between leaders and constituents or groups representing particular elements of constituencies.

Élite theory, at the other end of the spectrum, which presents public institutions as largely dominated by ruling groups, has been applied to our field by Bacon's account[13] of the dominance over Sheffield's governing bodies of political and administrative élites. In between, a neo-pluralist perspective[14] displays central institutions as allowing considerable power to lower levels of political authority as well as to the professionals employed by the public. The Marxist perspective, so far not applied to school governing bodies, assumes that political interests are concerned to substantiate the existing social and economic order. More recently, Marxist thought has allowed for the interplay between different institutions and government, and for concessions to be made by the capitalist state to the working classes in order to sustain stability.

It is not easy to be certain where governing bodies, as a generalisable class, belong among these definitions. For one thing, both pluralism and élite theories assume that their subjects have real power and authority, and this, as we show, is arguable in the case of governing bodies. Thus two constructs become possible. One is that governing bodies are allowed real authority within a system which is essentially élite, but is prepared to let some of its authority out on licence, as it were, if only to maintain élite dominance. If, however, governing bodies are not part of an élite system which delegates authority, they could form part of a pluralist model to the extent that power is diffused through them and they are able to contest the decisions of the authorities.

In this book we have leaned towards the eclectic use of theory – or at most modified pluralism – because that is where our evidence has taken us. If the local authority is the dominant partner, that does not of itself substantiate élite theory because it is also part of a network of influence and power-making which is dependent in part on the people over whom it is dominant. The strength of the centre is eroded by the presence of ambivalent roles, such as those of the chairmen of governing bodies, perhaps gaining power from leading a sub-system of giving support to the centre as part of its élite. Simple models must be elaborated by the concept of the educational professional (see Chapter 5) who emerges as shielded by professional status and as an assertive force, 'a challenging interest', and thus modifying the power of the local authority's political and administrative leadership.

### Exchange and dependency theory

Yet a further modification of notions of simple hierarchy, of top-downness, can be found in exchange theory to which recently there has been a vigorous return of interest. The principal source is the work of Peter Blau (1964)[15] which in the context of educational politics has been taken up and furthered by Margaret Archer[16] and Stewart Ranson.[17] Essentially, it views social and political actions as a process of exchange within a political model in which relationships between levels of government form a complex network of institutions, interest groups, and the like. The groups live in an environment of uncertainty produced by the scarcity of resources. They pursue interests and acquire strategic resources by creating dependencies among other actors. Authority and power provide critical bargaining levers to manipulate exchange relationships in the network. Where there is an inequality in exchange, power develops.

Working through a system of exchange, the operation of the inter-governmental network is shaped by the pattern of resource ownership and the structure of dependencies. This model of exchange and power is known as resource dependency theory.

As applied to education it could be said that schools, and teachers in them, have been able to expand their power and discretion because they possess critical resources available only to members of the teaching profession in as much as they are the sole owners of a complex professional expertise; or if that view is challenged (see Chapter 5), they do at least possess DES-controlled qualifications without which it is not possible to teach. But local authorities possess legal control of policy implementation, finance and other resources. On the face of it, therefore, schools and local authorities are potentially in an exchange relationship because the one cannot do without the teachers' expertise and commitment, and the other cannot do without the resources and legitimacy conferred by the local authorities. Indeed, even when hierarchical relationships are more explicit, as between heads and teachers, mutual dependencies arise since the cooption of teachers to the school's policy is necessary if good teaching is to result.

Within such a framework it is possible to ask what might be the exchanges between governing bodies and their schools, and governing bodies and their local authorities. The schools and their governing bodies can confer support and deeper, if more informal, legitimacies than those allowed by the ballot box. They can provide local testing of local authority policies and, in return, might be given a share of decision-making and influence. Our evidence points, however, to such exchanges as potential rather than actual. In later chapters we show how governing bodies lack control over resources which would make them partners in an exchange with the professionals. We have no convincing evidence either that they are able to exchange their support of the local authority for status or power. They must therefore rely upon access to other sources of power rather than employing their own.

## Outcomes of the political system

So far, the concepts discussed have concerned the different models of policy-making, the conceptualisation of ways in which power is distributed within systems, the nature of negotiations, as through exchange and dependency theory, and all of these to be played against the concept of a system which becomes increasingly more determined in its use of political power and yet accommodates institutions with strong boundaries. These structures and the processes are inputs affecting the pursuit of objectives. The examples of outcomes discussed below – accountability, participation and representation, legitimation and cooption – can all in their different ways be seen either as primary goals or as ways of securing such other goals as a more efficient, more democratic, or more professionally run form of education, leading to better teaching and learning.

*Accountability*

The notion of accountability has been the subject of many empirical, analytical and normative accounts.[18] Its literature is, indeed, strewn with dichotomies. Thus Elliott and his colleagues have distinguished between accountability for results and accountability in terms of professional codes of practice.[19] Another distinction drawn is that between accountability and responsibility. Accountability is formalised as part of the political or administrative system; practitioners may be called to account for their performance or results. Responsibility, however, denotes personal and professional codes and ethics which may or may not lead to more formal accountability. Elliott, too, distinguishes between 'being accountable' and 'calling to account'. The teacher and school may be required to give an account of their performance. In the other case, the school and the teacher may be required to render accounts in the sense that they will be expected to work within policies set elsewhere. A further distinction is made by Elliott and his colleagues. 'Public accountability' is concerned with transferring educational decision-making from the schools to the state in the interests of productivity; 'responsive accountability' allows the school to retain control which, Elliott assumes, make it more responsive to those whose interests are affected by the decisions. Yet other dichotomies refer to the source of demands for accountability. The demands for it can come from parents and local community groups who want there to be local and direct answerability by teachers. In other developments, accountability is demanded of teachers by system managers who may ask for tangible evidence of the connection between costs and educational gains.

Yet, in viewing accountability in its many and contradictory meanings, at the level of the school and the governing body we must again note that the sharpest issues are as yet being taken off-stage. The role of the governing body is immanent rather than actual and is to be conjured forth in the occasional acute crisis, and then only if particular configurations of forces are present, as in the William Tyndale case.[20] The Taylor Report formula would have made the school largely accountable to its governing body.[21] But as the reformed governing body struggles to life none of the many formulations seems wholly to apply: governing bodies for the most part make no systematic evaluations and have not, therefore, control over the first line upon which to require heads and teachers to be accountable to them in any of Elliott's senses of the word. The governors in our research did, however, form judgements about the school, which they voiced in interviews, but these rarely emerged in governing body meetings. The line of accountability still flows from the school, through its head, to the education committee and its officers.

## Power

If that is so, it is appropriate to examine constructs which will enable us to describe more analytically the present relationship between the school and governing body. Here some help is to be gained from examining the uses of power as a concept. Lukes' description concerns the making of key decisions which might involve conflict. Power can be viewed in a conflict-centred approach, or in a conflict-avoidance approach, or in its unconscious use. Power may be used not only directly to assert the will of one group, but also unconsciously, or to avoid conflict.[22] And in determining how issues come on to an agenda, Bachrach and Baratz[23] have maintained that power is exerted when a person or group can sustain social and political values which determine which issues enter the arena. There can be 'mobilisation of bias' or there can be 'non-decision-making' which results in suppression or thwarting of a challenge to the interests of the decision-maker. Again, Parry and Morriss[24] distinguish between types of power in terms of their intention: to initiate routine political procedures; to maintain these routines once established; and to use consequential power based on the routines.

The analysis of power moves between attempts to depict which groups set or are able to maintain or oppose value positions to the modes by which a grip over decision-making is established. This book produces several examples against which conceptualisations of power can be tested. We show that the local education authority determines the boundaries within which governing bodies work. The very terms of reference of the governing body may be subject to interpretations put on them, sometimes by the local authority through its appointed clerk to the governors and otherwise. The operation of the governing body is deeply influenced by the mode of operation of the school as a provider of education and as an organisational form. In both cases educational professionals have a gatekeeping role. Such roles as chairman to the governors can be analysed in terms of their proximity to the sources of local authority power. Conversely, the lack of power of certain groups, parents, or representatives of particular community groups, can also be analysed in terms of their ability to affect the values set within which the school works, or the agenda of the governing body, or its ability to move one way or the other.

## Participation and consultation

The adjacent concepts of participation and consultation are concerned with categories that make power operational.

If holding schools and their teachers to account draws upon conceptualisations of educational government and of the distribution of power, so too do the many notions of participation. There are several models of participation. One broad span model is that of Pateman,[25] who distinguishes between 'ballot box democracy' and 'participatory democracy'. Her distinction underpins what was said earlier in this chapter about the move from the top-down, traditional model of educational government which relies upon the ballot box for its legitimation. Participatory democracy assumes, however, that those directly affected by decisions will participate in the fine-grain of decision-making as they perceive the impact of what has been decided.

Some of the main conceptualisations of participation, such as Arnstein's,[26] go through a hierarchy in which the main dimension is the degree of autonomy given up by the principal decision-making body. Citizen power would involve citizen control or delegated power or partnership. A far weaker stage in terms of the power conceded she calls 'tokenism', which is placation or consultation or informing. Non-participation is either 'therapy' or 'manipulation'. Other classifications[27] range from negotiation in which a decision is contingent on the approval of those entering the negotiation, to mere articulation where a group presents its views without being asked, or[28] the promotion of interaction in creating structures for participation as against publicising or giving information.

The important generalisation about these and other models is that all assume a yielding of authority by one body to another and a hierarchy of power at the different levels of participation.

But power may determine the outcome of participation. Participation itself may affect the attitude of decision-makers and the power and motivation of those wishing to participate.

Within the concept of participation, representation is a particularly important component. Pitkin[29] usefully differentiates between an authorisation model in which a representative has authority to act and commit the represented who are responsible for his actions, and an accountability model in which he takes on special obligations and is constrained by re-election. The represented can hold the representative to account after he acts. She also distinguishes between descriptive and symbolic representation. In symbolic representation the body upon which the representative sits is defined in terms of how it is composed and where he should embody the characteristics of those represented. In symbolic representation the representative must be credible as part of a legislative or other body which works to retain the confidence of those it represents.

These categories can come to life as one inspects the problems of governing bodies. They lead us to ask whether individual governors act as representatives of their constituents or whether they acquire a more collective psyche and personality in representing the school in the total system, or whether they act as representatives of the local authority which appoints them. A governor might represent a group, or take on delegated powers, or develop a sense of responsibility in which the school becomes more important than those whom he represents to it. The corporate identity was stressed by the Auld and Taylor Committees.[30] As we recount in Chapter 7, common purposes can be found in the corporate activity of the governing body and, in Pitkin's terms, the majority of parent governors felt they were involved in 'descriptive' representation in as much as they sought to embody the characteristics of and be knowledgeable about those they represented.

## The school and the governing body

Concepts of the political–administrative system and the themes of interest groups, the educational professionals, power, participation and representation running through them lead us, finally, to the school and the governing body and their relationships with each other. Here our evidence (Chapters 4, 6 and 7) reinforces concepts from inter-organisational theory about the way in which the characteristics of the school condition its relationship with the governing body. Where the school is large and complex, but has some definable 'products' (as in secondary education), the relationship may be more formalised and in a sense stronger. The smaller primary school, with its less definable tasks, produces different relationships with the governing body. But whatever theoretical constructs we might apply, the evidence remains clear that the laity, as represented by lay governors, have difficulty in appreciating the concerns of the professionals, whether they form part of an élite or of a pluralistically diffused system, or of a loose-coupled and diffused élite. The school has the potential for political dynamics and conflict within itself and for competition between groups. But that vital element of power, placing matters on an agenda so that they can be discussed and determined, remains distant from the governors. It rests with the local authority, or its governing body clerk, the head of the school or the chairman.

Part of the explanation for governing body actions rests not only in its structural relationship with the local authority but also with its social psychology. The relationship between the school and the governing body becomes institutionalised so that considerable momentum might have to be exercised to cause change in that relationship. Yet the governing body meeting itself provides corporate socialisation of the new governor to the extent that individual governors interpret their roles similarly to their fellow governors, whoever nominated them to the governing body. There are also symbolic aspects of the role which reinforce the degree of corporate identity and the expectations of governors. The governors could engage in symbolic representation whether or not they felt they had power actually to represent constituents and take action. The reservation of seats for governors at school functions, to some extent the provision of hospitality for members at governors' meetings, the reception of governors at schools when they make individual visits, all bestow degrees of symbolic status.

In conclusion, we have been conscious of describing and attempting to conceptualise the states of governing bodies that are not only variable at any one time but, it must be assumed, will continue to develop rapidly over the next few years. We have accordingly attempted, in Chapter 8, to present models of what might be. These are inevitably normative models which do not attempt to summarise the state of governing bodies as they are but to extend their range of possibilities and indicate some of the consequences of pursuing them. The four models we have presented show a range of governing bodies from the minimum to the maximum accountable, the advisory, the supportive and the mediating. These rest upon discussions which will emerge in Chapters 3 to 7, and also depend upon concepts discussed here.

Stated without reservation and without too much example, social scientific conceptualisations rarely can apply in a direct and linear fashion to an institution being observed or one that those with authority to do so would seek to create. It is to be hoped, however, that the concepts and vocabulary outlined here will provide some of the social science context for the chapters that follow. We turn first to a more detailed discussion of the place of school governing bodies in the political–administrative system.

**Notes and references**

1. For an exhaustive application of system theory to education institutions, see Howell, D.A. and Brown, R., *Educational Policy-Making: An Analysis*, Heinemann, 1983.
2. Richardson, E., *The Teacher, the School and the Task of Management*, Heinemann, 1973, Chapters 2 and 12.
3. Johnson, D., Ransom, E., Packwood, T., Bowden, K. and Kogan, M., *Secondary Schools and the Welfare Network*, Allen & Unwin, 1980, Chapter 5.
4. McGrew, A.G. and Wilson, M.J. (eds), *Decision-Making. Approaches and Analysis*, Manchester University Press, excerpts from many of the works referred to in the chapter.
5. Elmore, R.F., 'Backward mapping: implementation research and policy decisions', in Williams, W. and Elmore, R.F., *Studying Implementation. Methodological and Administrative Issues*, Chatham House Publishers, 1982.
6. McGrew and Wilson, *op. cit.*
7. Richardson, J.J. and Jordan, A.G., *Governing Under Pressure*, Martin Robertson, 1979.
8. Peters, B. Guy, 'Insiders and outsiders: the politics of pressure-group influence and bureaucracy', *Administration and Society*, vol.9, no.2, Sage Publications, 1977.

9. La Palombora, J., *Interest Groups in Italian Politics*, Princeton University Press, 1965.
10. Newton, K., *The Theory of Pluralist Democracy*, Oxford University Press, 1976.
11. Kogan, M., *Educational Policy-making: A Study of Interest Groups at Parliament*, Allen & Unwin, 1974.
12. Williams, G., 'Educational planning: past, present and future', *Educational Policy Bulletin*, vol.7, no.2, 1979.
13. Bacon, A.W., *Public Accountability and the Schooling System*, Harper & Row, 1978.
14. Newton, *op. cit.*
15. Blau, P., *Exchange and Power in Social Life*, John Wiley, 1964.
16. Archer M.S., 'Educational politics: a model for their analysis', in Broadfoot, P. *et al.* (eds), *Politics and Educational Change*, Croom Helm, 1981.
17. Ranson, S., 'Changing relationships between centres and locality in education', *Local Government Studies*, vol.6., no.6, 1980.
18. McCormick, R. (ed.), *Calling Education to Account*, Heinemann, 1982.
19. Elliott, J., Bridges, D., Ebbutt, D., Gibson, R. and Nias, J., *School Accountability*, Grant McIntyre, 1981.
20. *Report of the William Tyndale Junior and Infant Schools Public Inquiry* (The Auld Report), ILEA, 1976.
21. *A New Partnership for our Schools* (Taylor Report), DES and Welsh Office, HMSO, 1977.
22. Lukes, S., *Power: A Radical View*, Macmillan, 1976.
23. Bachrach, P. and Baratz, M.G., *Power and Poverty: Theory and Practice*, Oxford University Press, 1971.
24. Parry, G. and Morriss, P. 'When is a decision not a decision?', in Crewe, I. (ed.), *Political Sociology Year Book*, Croom Helm, 1974.
25. Pateman, C., *Participation and Democratic Theory*, Oxford University Press, 1970.
26. Arnstein, S. 'A ladder of citizen participation', *Journal of American Institute of Planners*, vol.35, 1965.
27. Ham, C., 'Community health council participation in the NHS planning system', *Social Policy and Administration*, vol.14, no.3, Autumn 1980.
28. Hampton, W., 'Research into public participation in structure planning', in Sewell, W.R.D. and Coppock, J.T. (eds), *Public Participation in Planning*, John Wiley, 1977.
29. Pitkin, H., *Representation*, University of California Press, 1967.
30. Op. cit.

# 3 School governing bodies and the political–administrative system

## Introduction

The first of our thematic issues is the administrative structure of the English education system in which school governing bodies have a place. It is characterised by a lack of clear relationships between the various institutions and bodies. Recurring questions in the study of this system are: who are the dominant actors, and how is their control achieved and maintained? The 1944 Education Act prescribed a diffusion of power and authority between the elements such that no single body was intended to assume a dominant position, instead, partnership and balance were to be the guiding principles determining the style of these relationships. School governing bodies were therefore vested with certain powers in order to provide a point at which the authority of the individual school and of the local education authority could come into balance. However, as Chapter 1 has demonstrated, despite the formal position of governing bodies, the values and assumptions underlying their role have changed as new expectations have arisen and systems of control altered. In any analysis of their roles they cannot be treated in isolation but have to be viewed as part of the local political–administrative system dealing with the education service.

## The political–administrative system of education

The assumption underlying the concept of the local political–administrative system is of a network of a number of different organisations and groups each fulfilling certain functions in the governance of local educational provision. Because of their common concern with education they engage in interaction with each other. The main institutions and groups involved are illustrated in Figure 3.1. The lines between the different bodies indicate possible linkages rather than formal relationship; they are of course involved with many entities other than governing bodies and the different networks criss-cross each other.

The concept of a policy-making or inter-organisational system is found in the fields of political science, public administration and organisational theory.[1] It developed as a heuristic and analytical tool to portray 'government' as a series of different groups which impact upon each other and therefore form relationships. Implicit in this approach

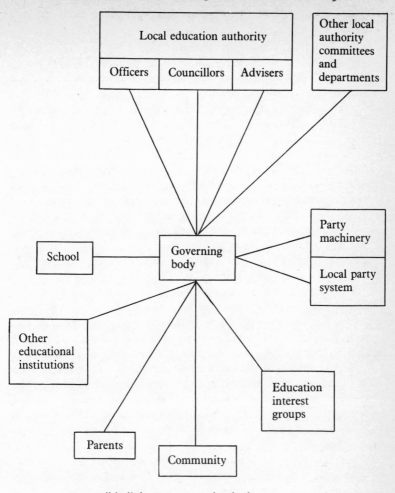

Figure 3.1   The governing body's potential links with the local political–administrative system of education

are, first, multiple linkages involving different types of influence and, secondly, the existence of complexity and at times an ambiguity in these relationships. Although each body may have its own terms of reference, there is overlap between the functions performed and bodies become interdependent. Within the existing literature in this area of study a major theme has been the potential for conflict or disagreement between institutions and the emphasis within such systems on negotiation.[2]

At the level of the local education system there is the distinction between the responsibility of the local education authority and the strength of the school as a prime institution. This notion of the school as a prime institution is important in understanding the operation of the education political administrative system. The prime institution, as defined by Kogan, is 'the lowest level of the system with sufficient discretion for the principal resources to be deployed, for judgements to be made by individual practitioners in their relationship to client needs.'[3] The implication of this level in education is that substantive decisions, such as curriculum issues and the organisation of teaching, are principally the prerogative of the school. Yet the school does not have unlimited autonomy, for it has to engage in important relationship with the local education authority to gain resources. In formal terms the LEA has the specific tasks of determining the level of overall finance and allocating it between schools, building developments, and setting the staffing establishment of the school. Its role is therefore one of providing a coherent range of education in its area and if necessary to initiate development in policies.

The LEA is also part of a local authority with its own electorate and subject to control by the political system; its autonomy is not unlimited and it has to compete with other services to secure new policies and funding. The LEA also has relationships with national government and is required to implement national policies on education.[4] For the LEA there is the question of the balance between the need to maintain and enhance institutional autonomy and to ensure public accountability. Its difficulties in managing and coordinating the system are perhaps accentuated by financial and demographic pressures, and may lead to the LEA exerting a more centralised style of authority and control in the system.

Included in the local political–administrative system are numerous pressure-groups associated with the provision and consumption of education. These may be groups with a formal organisation and established contact with policy-makers such as a Community Relations Council or more informally based groups such as parents' associations. A further distinction may also be made between 'sectional' groups (such as teachers' associations), whose function is to protect a distinct interest in the education system, and 'promotional' groups (such as groups wanting to abolish corporal punishment in schools) seeking to promote a cause.[5] All these types of group may not only exert pressure upon policy-making but may also play a part in the implementation of policies. Their style and strategies will in part depend upon the distribution of power in the political–administrative system.

Within the political–administrative system governing bodies have a place between the LEA and the level of the school. Inevitably they are subject to the pattern of interactions in this system and moreover their role is to a large part determined by the structure of power. This chapter goes on to analyse the main form of interactions between school governing bodies and the rest of the political–administrative system. At the end, an attempt is made to explain the pattern of relationships.

## LEAs and school governing bodies: the formal relationship

In formal terms the school governing body is subordinate to the local education authority because its existence and status are controlled by the LEA. This is important in structuring the potential role of the governing body in the local political–administrative system. The LEA determines whether each school should have its own governing body or whether a single governing body should serve a group of schools. Within this structure the LEA determines the functions and categories of governors.

The formal functions of governing bodies are specified by the LEA in the Articles of Government for all of its governing bodies. The LEA sets the functions and can decide, subject to the approval of the Department of Education and Science, to amend them. The LEA Articles of Government are based upon the 1945 Model Articles of Government and Management set by the DES. Although Articles have a similar format there are significant variations between authorities in the actual functions given to governing bodies. For example Articles differ in the extent to which governors play a part in areas of concern of school management such as the suspension of pupils, the appointment and dismissal of teaching and non-teaching staff, the finance of the school, and determining the use of school premises. Likewise the form of participation delegated to the governing body indicates the extent to which management functions, such as the appointment of staff, are centralised or decentralised and delegated to the governing body. This variation may be seen to reflect the nature of political and administrative control in the local education system.

The composition of governing bodies is determined by the LEA in the instrument of government which it draws up. By this instrument the LEA determines those eligible to take part in school government and may determine the manner of appointment of certain categories of governors. Of importance in setting this structure is the LEA view of the balance between the different categories and in particular the proportion of LEA nominated governors. The strength of this latter category may indicate how strong political control is in the local education authority. In formal terms, then, the governing body is subject to LEA control over its functions and balance of composition.

## LEA views of school governing bodies

The Articles of Government provide a formal statement by the LEA on the specific functions of governing bodies which reflect a division of authority in the political–administrative system. This can be supplemented by 'Notes of Guidance' for governors which provide an interpretation of this role and suggestions about how governors may seek to fulfil their duties. It is likely that Notes will reflect a more recent assessment than do the Articles of their role and indicate current concerns of the LEA. For example, our research shows that in some authorities the formal responsibility of governors in the appointment of teaching staff has been changed by the LEA as the redeployment of teachers has become more widespread. In such circumstances the LEA redefines the role of governing bodies. Likewise, in three of the authorities in the research governing bodies were expected to contribute to LEA policy-making, and yet the Articles of Government did not mention this role. The attitudes and values of decision-makers in the LEA (both officers and councillors) are of key relevance in determining the role of governing bodies.[6] In our research these attitudes reveal more complicated perspectives than those formally conveyed to governors in the Articles of Government or Notes of Guidance, and were likely to place more emphasis upon the form of governing body participation in their areas of responsibility.

The LEAs' statement of views constitutes expectations which may be continuously reinterpreted to governors. Our research reveals a wide range of possible views but there are distinct patterns to be found. They indicate what purposes the LEA sees governing bodies as fulfilling in the different areas of concern in the local education system; their role in local education policy-making; their participation in school management and place in mediating interests between the different elements in the system. The main purposes of governing body activity which were found in our interviews with councillors, education officers and advisers are set out in the following paragraphs. Although they are treated here as separate entities they will of course coexist in various patterns in different LEAs.

### As an intermediary between school and LEA

The role of intermediary is most frequently stated as a purpose by LEAs; it places governing bodies as a form of contact between the LEA and school. According to this view the governing body enables both councillors and education officers to keep in touch with developments in the individual school. The governing body constitutes a channel of communication with the LEA and provides the school with a forum to articulate its interests to the LEA. Through this link the school can be kept aware of LEA policy and receive expectations from the rest of the local education system. It follows from the intermediary role that the governing body should include both governors nominated by the LEA and school interests.

## As an executive body

The executive body role would confer on governing bodies certain statutory functions to perform in school management which it is expected to perform in an efficient and responsible manner. The value of delegating these functions to the governing body is that it is democratic to allow the laity to participate in educational government, and by decentralising decision-making it ensures that decisions are compatible with local needs. For example, on judging appeals against suspensions the governing body, whilst acting as a quasi-judicial body, is expected to reach a decision based upon its knowledge and assessment of local circumstances. Similarly, in the appointment of staff, the governing body can choose teachers who will respond to the objectives of the school.

## As a forum for local accountability

In this approach the governing body is expected to become a forum for the local accountability of the school. The assumption is that the governing body is so composed as to allow the views of the local community to be made known to the school. The governing body aggregates and transmits these different views to the school and provides for a dialogue between the professionals and laity on the governing body. In so doing it may evaluate the school or the local authority and attempt to call either to account for its actions.

## As part of the local consultative network

The governing body in this view is able to provide feedback to the LEA on proposed policies, including those that go beyond the immediate interest of the school. It is part of the LEA's network for consultation which includes formal groups and other pressure-groups. The governing body, in bringing together different interests, acts as another route for community views to be made known to the local education authority. As will be seen, the purposes behind this consultation vary.

## As a system of support

In this view the governing body's main function is as a system providing moral support to the school and other forms of assistance such as relevant expertise to its staff. The assumption is that the governing body will display a strong attachment and loyalty to the individual school. A variant of this view may also be where governing bodies are expected to provide support for the LEA. This might be used to promote the position of the education service within the local authority.

The different views about their purposes found in the four LEAs in our research define selectively for each the main focus of concern of governing bodies and how they fit in with the rest of the political administrative system. These views indicate that the governing body may be expected to embrace different functions. Yet the statements about the role of governing bodies vary in the clarity with which they define the required expectations.

The LEA's perspectives are conditioned by a number of interrelated factors derived from the characteristics of the local education authority. The first and most important is the organisation of education policy-making in the authority. A key dimension of this organisation is the extent of party political control of policy-making in the local authority.[7] Numerous other studies have revealed that the impact of party political activity has increased since the reorganisation of local government in 1974.[8] In terms of local authority policy-making structure several changes have become evident. There is the strict organisation of policy-making on the basis of party allegiance resulting in increased party solidarity, the use of whipping for voting, party control of cooptions to committees, and the majority party control of council business. There is the emergence of the party group composed of senior party members occupying key committee chairmanships which assumes a dominant position in the policy-making process. Associated with this informal arrangement, the policy and resources committee acts as the main committee in the local authority and is able to dominate all other committees. The overall impact of these developments is the production of a more formalised and centralised policy-making system.[9] As one writer has noted with respect to education: 'The policy process for education in local authorities takes place in an increasingly closed system which is characterised by an emphasis on domination and control through party political organisation and direction.'[10]

If in practice the extent of party control varies considerably in scope and intensity between authorities, its effects upon policy-making is pervasive. Authorities in the research characterised by a high level of party political control were more likely to have governing bodies with a large number of LEA-nominated governors who are apportioned strictly on the basis of party allegiance. Majority party-nominated governors may be expected to implement LEA policies in the confines of the individual school and be held accountable to the party political machinery which nominated them. For example, in one authority in the research governors nominated by the Labour Party were allocated to schools by a committee of the local constituency party. Regular meetings were organised for these governors by the local party to brief them on party policy and to discuss their role. The governing body in this context is viewed as a political mechanism existing between the LEA and the school. In such partisan authorities there will be variation in how open or closed is the structure of decision-making. In closed systems party political factors will override other independent views, whereas in open systems it is acknowledged that full control over the activity of governing bodies is neither possible nor necessarily desirable.

At the opposite end of the spectrum there are those authorities with a weaker party political alignment. The LEA-nominated governors are not a majority on the governing body and party membership is not a criterion for their appointment. These governors stated in interviews that they did not see their role as party political, and in many cases they were not members of a party but were nominated because of their standing in the local community. Governing bodies are therefore not viewed by the LEA as party political bodies and are more likely to be independent from the policy-making machinery of the LEA. As such, they are not necessarily concerned with the affairs of the local education system, but are attached to their individual schools.

The operation of party political factors upon governing bodies in the LEA is also reinforced by the political culture and style of political activity in the authority. The political culture refers to the predominant way in which demands are expressed and received in the local authority, and the degrees of cleavage or consensus amongst participants.[11] An expression of this is the way the LEA approaches public participation.[12] In certain authorities an open structure of participation is evident where there are numerous pressure-groups placing demands upon the LEA. In this context the governing body is more likely to be viewed by the LEA as part of the consultative network of the local education system and a further source of pressure. Likewise, governing bodies may be viewed by interest groups as an alternative channel for articulating demands in the local education system and are subject to such pressures either from outside or from governors who represent these groups.

The third dimension of local education policy-making found in the research with repercussions on the activity of governing bodies is the balance between the views of education officers and councillors. So far in this chapter the LEA has been treated as a single body, but this ignores the different value positions that exist between officers and councillors.[13] Different views about governing bodies are apparent between these two groups. Education officers may adhere to certain professional standards which define the way that policies should be made and who should be involved. In terms of Alford's terminology they may be seen as a 'challenging interest' to the institutional autonomy of the school by trying to coordinate the local education system and make schools more efficient.[14] The delegation of management functions to governing bodies may limit officers' administrative control. In a similar vein, our research showed that advisers who share the values of teachers tended to be hostile to what they perceived as the intrusion of lay governors into the sphere of the professional control of the curriculum. Likewise, councillors evince values about issues such as representation and participation which have implications for their view of governing bodies. In some authorities councillors stated that the existence of governing bodies as local representative bodies could detract from the representative role of the councillor. Councillors have their own distinct views about educational issues and the relevance of public accountability. The balance between the views of officers and councillors influences the LEA's view of its governing bodies.

The final factor which affects how the LEA approaches school governing bodies is the style of relationship between the LEA and individual education institutions. This 'administrative culture' consists of the whole style and complex of relationships that exist between LEAs and schools and the views about these from the different participants in the local education system. As has been noted, the underlying assumption of the school as a prime institution possessing discretion to maintain its own organisation has been entrenched in this relationship, but is susceptible to change. Important elements in this relationship are factors such as administrative procedures on finance and staffing, the nature of accountability, past history, and the existence of multiple channels of contact.[15] For example, in one authority in the research where advisory staff had a strong relationship with schools, the role of the governing body as an intermediary between school and LEA was seen to be limited. Also, in some LEAs the use of meetings of head-teachers as a channel of contact and source of policy advice acted as a constraint upon the possible activities of governing bodies in providing a link between the school and the LEA. Besides such organisational factors, if there is a large number of schools an authority may find it difficult to maintain governing bodies as an efficient channel of contact.

Of increasing significance in these relationships is the administrative complexity of the local authority. Accompanying the development of party political control in some local authorities is the rationalisation of policy-making involving the procedures of corporate management. The implication for the education department is that it becomes increasingly linked to other departments of the local authority which provide allied functions such as the control of non-teaching staff.[16] In some authorities, prompted by financial stringency, this has led to a centralisation of local authority decision-making in the local education system and particularly the position of the education service in the local authority. A number of governors interviewed felt that on questions of finance, decisions were being taken centrally in the local authority. The implication for governing bodies is that the locus of power may shift from the LEA to the rest of the local authority which makes it difficult for them to exert pressure.

## LEA–school governing bodies structure of contact

The view of the LEA about the role of school governing bodies and the boundaries set by their composition are reflected both in the tasks they are expected to undertake and the resources made available to them. As has been demonstrated, there are a variety of possible roles for governing bodies which are conditioned by a number of interrelated factors. Within this general framework the most significant influence upon the operation of governing bodies is the contact between governing bodies and the LEA. This determines to a large extent the relationship between individual governing bodies and the rest of the political–administrative system.

In analysing the lines and form of contact there is first the range of tasks given to governing bodies by the LEA. As has been seen, although the Articles of Government frame responsibilities these do not necessarily emerge as salient but are interpreted and operationalised by the LEA. At this stage an important distinction can be made between those authorities which do not directly seek to influence the work of governing bodies and those which consciously shape the direction by influencing the substance of their work. In the former case governing bodies are seen to be school-centred and their mode of relationship with the school is left to the governing body to establish rather than imposed by the LEA. In the latter LEAs, the use of an authority-wide agenda for all governing body meetings determines the sequence and type of work to be undertaken by the governing body. Normally in this case a model agenda is constructed by the LEA which puts forward items to be supplemented by school-initiated items.

Items initiated by the LEA can be of two types. First, specific documents relating to a policy issue may be placed on the agenda in order to consult governing bodies. Examples from our research included such issues as the tertiary reorganisation plans, multi-cultural education, and the use of school crossing patrols. The intention behind this process is to incorporate the views of governing bodies on changes affecting the level of the whole local education system. The decision on which items of policy governing bodies will be consulted is made either by the Education Committee or Director of Education. Items, too, such as DES documents are introduced in order to prompt governing bodies to consider aspects of educational provision such as curricular changes that might be relevant to the school. Here the LEA is attempting to enable governing bodies to perform their role effectively. In some cases in the research the LEA involved governing bodies in schemes for the self-evaluation of schools, where governors were expected to provide an input to this process.

As has been shown earlier, the range of functions contained in Articles of Government varies considerably between authorities. In particular, governors may act as committees to consider appeals against suspensions or to appoint staff. Governing bodies thus vary in their discretion and the autonomy allowed them. The LEA, in controlling the work of the governing body, is able to direct the focus of concern, but this may be subject to the requirements of central government. Indirectly the form of the agenda influences the scope for governors to raise demands. For example, in one LEA a specific item was introduced on the agenda to allow parent governors to have an opportunity to raise issues. In contrast, in another authority some governors stated that the large amount of LEA-initiated items on the agenda of meetings had the effect of reducing the amount of time they had for discussing issues related to their individual school. However, as will be seen, this control over the substance and sequence of work does not automatically lead to the governing body performing the role expected.

The main intermediary between the LEA and governing bodies in most LEAs is the clerk to the governing body. Again there is an important distinction between those authorities which clerk all governing bodies and those which do not provide clerking or which clerk only secondary school governing bodies. In the latter case the clerk is one of the governors or in some cases the school secretary. As will be seen from the more detailed description in Chapter 6, the clerk services the governing body in producing and distributing agenda, reports and minutes and communicating with other bodies in the local education system on behalf of the governors, and by providing a linkage between the LEA and governors. The way clerking is organised is likely to influence the type of contact. Some authorities have clerking sections which service governing bodies and consist of specialised governing body clerks. In other cases the clerking is carried out by an education officer, adviser, or even an officer from another local authority department. The administrative status of the clerk is likely to be important in how he is viewed by governors. In two of the case-study authorities the clerk was accompanied to meetings by a more senior officer to advise on policies and provide a direct line with the authority. Governors in these cases thought that the presence of these more senior officers meant that their views would carry extra weight.

What then happens to resolutions and minutes depends upon such factors as the view of the LEA concerning the importance of governors' views, and the structure of the education department. In some authorities in the research the clerk sent the specific requests from governing body meetings to particular officers in the department for their attention. Also in some authorities the copies of all governing body minutes were circulated to all senior officers. However the extent to which the requests from governing bodies were made known to councillors varied. In some cases it was practice for members of the schools sub-committee to receive minutes and notification of action on specific resolutions. Similarly on issues of consultation it was practice in some authorities for all responses from governing bodies to be collated by officers and presented to councillors. In turn the clerk reported back to the next governing body meeting on the progress on particular items raised by governors. In those cases where no clerk was provided by the LEA this process becomes less formalised because the clerk was not a full-time member of the education department and not necessarily familiar with the organisation and processes of the LEA.

As well as the formal mechanism of transmitting views between the governors and the LEA there are additional informal links which might be used. The LEA-nominated governor can assume a particular significance. The appointment of party-nominated governors is normally in accordance with the party balance on the council. There are a variety of methods of appointment to this category reflecting the nature of party organisation in the authority. In some authorities ward parties put forward nominations to the party group on the LEA and the final decision was made by party whips or senior councillors. In other cases it was individual councillors in an area who nominated governors and party membership was not a requirement. Instead it was expected that governors should have similar values or some specific experience or expertise which would benefit the governing body.

The LEA view of the role of these LEA-nominated governors again depends upon the extent of party political organisation. In certain authorities it was felt important for councillors and, in particular, members of the education or schools sub-committees to serve as governors. The assumption is that by having a member of council on the governing body a direct link to the LEA is provided and the councillors can aid the governing body. Yet it is important to note that councillors from the minority parties do not see themselves as spokesmen for the authority. In certain cases in the research they used the forum of the governing body to criticise majority party policy.

A further line of contact can be provided by the chairman of the governing body. Before the 1981 Regulations[17] it was customary for the chairman to be a councillor or at least a member of the majority party on the authority. This was seen both to provide contact with the LEA and in some cases ensure that governing bodies acted within the confines of LEA policies. The chairman had a dual role of acting for the LEA and as one of the governors. Since then, in many LEAs it is still assumed that it is best to choose a councillor as chairman. The role of the chairman in all authorities was viewed to be a key one, although there were not any specific guidelines by which to define his role and responsibilities. It may be expected that the chairman is a link with the LEA. In some authorities biannual meetings were held for the chairmen of all governing bodies to discuss issues of common concern. In other cases the chairman had the right to meet with the chairman of the education and schools sub-committee. But, in general, this line of contact was likely to be varied depending upon the individual's own status and sources of contacts. Therefore the structures of contact will vary between authorities both in their range and styles. Of particular importance is the degree to which the role of the governing body is strictly defined by the LEA and has to work within a formal, regulated system for governing bodies in the authority. This will influence the range of activity and style of bargaining of the governing body.

## Styles of LEA–school governing body interaction

The first part of this chapter has outlined the formal structural relationship between the LEA and governing bodies and has shown that within certain limits the LEA can control the functions of governing bodies. In particular, opportunities for governing bodies to interact with the political administrative system are structured in different ways. The image is of the governing body as a subordinate body to the LEA and working within defined parameters. The next part of this chapter explores in more detail the actual relationships that exist and delineates the various patterns of interaction.

### Local education authority policy-making

A feature of the policy-making process of many LEAs is the extent to which governing bodies are an element of the consultative process. This is in accordance with the LEA view of governing bodies as a mechanism to keep in touch with the views of the community.[18] A related LEA concern is the need to ensure that governing bodies are aware of LEA policies and knowledgeable about expectations of other parts of the local education system. It is likely that these types of authority are characterised by an open style of policy-making which admits pressure-group activity.

The part the governing body can play in the total education policy-making process is framed by the way that the LEA decides to proceed with consultation. For the LEA, consultation can exist on several levels. First, it may be designed to illuminate a problem and enable them to receive different viewpoints prior to a decision being made by the education committee. For example, one authority in the research undertook a planning exercise for the reorganisation of the schools in an area in which options were formulated at different stages in the whole process with governing bodies consulted at each stage. The entire process was structured, and governing bodies were one of a number of groups engaged in participation.

Secondly, governing bodies may be informed by the LEA once a decision has been made with the intention of keeping them informed of policies and building up support before implementation.

The consultation process designed by the LEA may be classified according to a number of factors. Participation of groups including governing bodies may take various forms. Arnstein's ladder of citizen participation contains eight levels, ranging from manipulation and therapy, through informing, consultation and placation to partnership, delegated power and finally citizen control.[19] The main dimensions of such a ladder are the degree of autonomy given up by the decision-making body and the assumption that the possession of power is necessary for groups to progress up that ladder. Similarly, participation will depend upon the stage of the policy-making process at which the views of groups are sought. This is important because at a later stage of the process the options given to groups to consider may become more restricted. Finally, the extent of participation depends upon information for effective contribution and this will vary in its content and style of presentation by the LEA.

In practice, the LEA's views about consultation and its control of that process were matched by what governors saw as the legitimate scope of concern of the governing body. These views may rule out involvement in issues of wider education policy-making as being beyond the authority of the individual governing body. A feature of a number of governing bodies in the research was their attachment to the affairs of the individual school rather than to the local education system. Which view is taken by the governing body will depend upon the type of governors and composition of the governing body (see Chapters 6 and 7). Governing bodies must themselves be viewed as political bodies composed of various groups with different values. For example, in a governing body with a majority of party political nominees their role may be to formulate and implement party policy. Another relevant factor is the existence of 'community' governors nominated by pressure-groups in the local education system. These and other governors are likely to have links with other status positions in the local political environment to form what Dunleavy terms the 'burgher community'.[20] These linkages make up informal networks of influence which present selected demands to policy-makers and can frame the definition of policy issues. The implication of networks for the position of governing bodies is that they may be used by pressure-groups in certain circumstances as channels in the transmission of demands. (See also Chapter 7.) In this way the boundaries between the different elements of the local political–administrative system become blurred. The linkages will affect the operation of the governing body in terms of its internal style and presentation of demands.

Yet is it also true that governing bodies may be in an isolated position in the political–administrative system because the main political transactions take place around them, rather than through them. Equally true is that party-nominated governors may not be active members of their ward parties, and do not take part in the formulation of party education policy-making so that governing bodies are insulated from the pressures of the local political system. Our research clearly showed that, in general, pressure-groups seek to exert pressure on the LEA which they view as being the main locus of power rather than on governing bodies. However, the political–administrative system changes over time as the configuration of power changes. Governing bodies may constitute a possible pressure channel, which may be used by groups when particular types of issue emerge. An issue such as the possible closure of a number of schools increases the likelihood that governors will display a concern with LEA policy-making and act as a pressure-group upon the LEA. In one authority where there were plans for the reorganisation of its schools, governing bodies were used by the schools to exert pressure upon the authority to protect their interests.

The effectiveness of the participation of governing bodies in LEA policy-making depends upon the overall structure of policy-making and whether the distribution of power follows the élitist or pluralist model. As has been noted, a major factor is the views of councillors and officers about governing body participation. The reasons given for allowing governing bodies to contribute to education policy formation varies from a desire for different viewpoints to be expressed to the need for the legitimation of policies and maintenance of support. But, in general, the ability of governing bodies to formulate or change policies is limited. Both councillors and officers stated in the research that the views of governing bodies could be forecast, and therefore only served to confirm the direction of policy. Only if there was a concerted and unified opposition from governors (which was viewed to be unlikely) would policy change dramatically. On major issues of majority party education policy opposition would be less effective, and in some cases policies were introduced without governing bodies being consulted. In one authority in the research the abolition of corporal punishment had become LEA policy despite widespread opposition from governing bodies in the authority; this was because this issue had been a major element on the party manifesto. In another case a governing body facing the closure of the school was debarred by the clerk from discussing the decision in formal governing body meetings because it was interpreted that the governing body could not criticise LEA policy.

These cases illustrate what Ham has identified as the importance of power in participation.[21]

School governing bodies may thus constitute one element in the education policy-making process. In general, they are reactive rather than proactive, or providing a continuous contribution. They coexist amongst other elements such as teachers' unions, political parties, pressure-groups and headteachers. Although these groups may be represented on the governing body, they see it as just one amongst a number of channels of communication rather than being a prime element.

## School governing bodies and administration

The second main activity of governing bodies as shown by the research is to act as a mechanism of positive support for the school in providing contact with the LEA. This is viewed by governors to be an important function. It is different from participation in policy-making because it involves a more spontaneous and fluid relationship with the LEA and allows the governing body in some cases to be proactive in its demands.

The LEA's view of this function varies. In documents such as the Notes of Guidance for governors it is generally identified as a crucial activity for governing bodies which helps the LEA to keep in touch with the affairs of individual schools. Yet in this concern an important factor is the amount of autonomy in administrative functions possessed by the governing body.

Governors in general see the governing body as an important source of pressure upon the LEA: this is in accordance with what governors see as their responsibility in providing support. It is also recognised that the governing body possesses the authority to assess the needs of the school and to mediate between school and LEA. Although this view was generally found amongst all governors interviewed, it was particularly marked amongst teacher and parent governors. Likewise, head-teachers view the governing body as a potential pressure-group which can exert pressure to reinforce other requests to the authority.

The form of contact with the LEA takes place at different levels. The LEA clerk – where he exists – is most often used as the first formal contact with the authority. In some cases, the clerk has an influence over the exact wording of resolutions making specific demands to the authority, and is able to influence the governors' stance on certain issues. Governors rely upon the clerk because it is judged that he possesses the necessary knowledge of where to send resolutions and the contacts to follow up progress.

When the LEA does not clerk the governing body the chairman or correspondent becomes the main intermediary with the authority. The position of the chairman depends upon the category of governors and their individual statuses. Where the chairman is a majority party councillor this is viewed by the rest of the governing body as a useful asset. The chairman then has contacts with key councillors and senior officers and some status in the eyes of the LEA. But even where the chairman is a key councillor it does not automatically benefit the governing body. In the one case in the research where the chairman of the governing body was also chairman of the education committee, he stated that he owed a loyalty both to the governing body and the LEA, which meant that on certain issues he would defend LEA policy and distance himself from the governors' demands.

Other LEA-nominated governors can be used by governing bodies to influence the LEA. Local education authorities in the research often saw this type of governor as one who would be conversant with its policies and, if necessary, would defend them. However, most governors in this category do not necessarily possess the relevant information about policies or procedures, and do not regard themselves as defenders of the LEA. This was particularly true of minority party governors. In some cases they are able to use party political networks to raise issues with councillors.

In these cases the governing body is acting as a pressure-group. Although in most cases bargaining takes place through using 'key notables' – leading political figures – in some cases governors themselves engage in direct lobbying of the education or schools sub-committee. The style of bargaining and the relative success of various strategies depend upon a number of interrelated factors. As we have seen, the nature of administrative contact between LEA and governing bodies influences the pattern of activity. If there is a formalised system of clerking and processing of governing body requests governing bodies are more likely to have a ready route of access and be used as a mechanism for the LEA to receive issues of concern. But although this channel may benefit the governing body, it can also reduce its scope of action as it becomes incorporated into the administrative process.

Secondly, the type of issue and the way it is viewed by the LEA is also a key factor. Local education authorities in the research had definite views on what was 'reasonable action' and a 'legitimate' demand which influenced how they processed such requests.[22] For example, officers in the research stated that a demand by governors for extra resources had less chance of success in a period of financial stringency. From our research, governors were well aware that their powers of exerting pressure in these circumstances were limited.

A third factor is that governing body activity depends upon the style of administrative relationship between the LEA and its schools. The governing body might not be used as an intermediary with the LEA if the head has his or her own well-established contacts. Also on issues such as building it was customary for some authorities to have a detailed administrative process for identifying requests for repairs. In these cases, the governing body might only be used if the system broke down, or in the case of delay when extra pressure was viewed to be desirable by the headteacher.

Lastly, governing body activity depends upon the composition of the governing body; the governors' own view of the purpose of the governing body; and also on the governors' own contacts elsewhere in the political–administrative system which affects strategies adopted. For example, teacher governors in some cases saw the governing body primarily as a forum of support for the school and raised issues of resource deficiencies in meetings in order that their fellow governors should act upon these and request additional resources from the LEA.

## School governing bodies and the political–administrative system: an assessment

The previous analysis of the role of governing bodies in the local political–administrative system shows how they are conditioned by exogenous factors, particularly the stance taken by the LEA. It shows that their role is multi-modal depending upon the type of issue they face. Yet this analysis should not be viewed as static for it is clear that changes in the local political–administrative system, for example a change from an élitist to a pluralist distribution of power, have repercussions on the possible roles of the governing body. Similarly, the presence of new governors with links with the political system may lead to changes in the roles adopted. Yet an important conclusion from our research is that, in general, governing bodies do not have systematic relationships with community groups, and that such groups are more likely to seek to exert pressure upon the LEA. School governing bodies are not used by community groups as a major channel of contact to exert pressure upon the school and the local education authority. In part this is because they lack visibility in the local education system and also because community groups commonly perceive governing bodies as lacking any real power or purpose. It is the LEA which is seen by these groups to be the major power-holder and so direct contact is the most favoured strategy.

In assessing what part the operation of school governing bodies plays in this system, our research confirms the earlier findings of Baron and Howell that governing bodies operate on the periphery of the network because they do not have links with any structure except the LEA.[23] Yet this should not lead automatically to the view that they completely lack power. This contrasts with the views of other writers. For example, Bacon, in his analysis of school boards in Sheffield, presents an élitist account of education policy-making with the local educational establishment composed of key officers and councillors forming an 'administrative–political élite'.[24] According to this analysis, school boards developed in Sheffield in the context of problems facing the educational establishment in the 1970s – the need to maintain authority and executive control and to ensure public support for the introduction of new policies. In this context school boards aided the introduction of new and contentious policies and provided an alternative way for the local educational establishment to gain information and elicit public opinion. This was achieved through the process of the cooption of possible challenging interests. Therefore school boards did not make any challenge to the existing structure of power.

From our research it is difficult to reach conclusions of such a generalised nature which would be applicable to all cases. Our account presents a more complex view of governing bodies engaging in multiple forms of contact. By using such a framework several important factors become evident. First, different institutions in the local education system are engaged in different linkages with each other. Governing bodies as one such element occupy a unique role because they may constitute the various interests present in the system and such overlapping membership assumes importance. Secondly, because of the different values held by individual governors, governing bodies lack clear organisational identity. Their functions therefore have to be negotiated because they are used by different constituent groups for their own purposes. Of particular importance is the power of the LEA to determine the composition of the governing body, its functions and mode of relationships. These control patterns obviously exist at different levels and allow governing bodies different degrees of autonomous action. The twin notions of compliance and discretion determine the operation of governing bodies. What Bacon and others view as complete control by the administrative–political élite does not completely determine their operation. Our analysis echoes Howell's view that within limits governing bodies can exploit their access to sources of power and can remain a potential source of conflict with the LEA or school.[25] In our research there were a limited number of examples of governing bodies exerting pressure upon the LEA and refusing to acquiesce in legitimating policies. Yet in the end result they were not always successful. Although occupying a weak position, governing bodies are not completely debarred from action of a particular kind, although this is likely to be individual rather than involving groups of governing bodies.

It is possible to construct three ideal-type relationships showing the way that certain political factors (but notably the party political system) influence the context of the operation of governing bodies. These are shown in tabular format in Figure 3.2. These do not represent actual

Figure 3.2  School governing bodies and the local political system

| | Type A | Type B | Type C |
|---|---|---|---|
| Political organisation of local authority | Strongly partisan – centralised party control of education, policy-making and administration. | Partial party control of educational policy-making. | Limited party control extending to main decisions. |
| Style of LEA–SGB relationship | SGBs as a subsidiary element to the education committee. Autonomous functions limited. Independence limited. | 1. Some delegation of functions to SGBs. <br> 2. Involved in LEA consultation and in school. <br> 3. Formalised contact with education department. | 1. SGBs not viewed as political bodies. <br> 2. Isolated from LEA – school-centred. <br> 3. Minimal clerking. |
| Political composition of governing body | Ruling party governors in majority on governing body. Dissension ruled out. | Party governors may be largest single group. Number of governors representing local groups – pluralist composition. | Governors not appointed on strict party lines but as trustees for 'community'. |
| Relationship with local political environment | Formal attachment to local parties and limited contact with pressure groups. Not an independent actor in environment. | 1. Some attachment to local party although party governors are not representative. <br> 2. Contact with pressure-groups. <br> 3. Overlapping linkage between SGB and other elements. | 1. Limited local contact with party but no representation of these interests. <br> 2. Governors isolated from political environment of whole local education system. |

cases, but demonstrate the range of possibilities.

Type A is characterised by a strong party political control of the education policy-making process. All decision-making is centralised in the hands of the ruling political élite. Governing bodies are viewed by the LEA as an extension of the education committee, providing a link with the individual school. They are dominated by a majority of ruling party-appointed governors who provide a link with the local political party. The party governors in this context are part of a 'top-down' linkage. The intention of the governing body is predominantly to implement LEA policy and accordingly its scope for independent action is limited. Moreover, as governing bodies are viewed as extensions of the party political machinery a change of party control in the council will completely change the balance. Policy-making in this context is enclosed within the party group and any pressure-group activity is oriented to the party élites.

Type B is still characterised by party control but there is more likely to be a viable opposition. The control exerted is less imposed and therefore more open than in Type A. There is likely to be a strong ethos of participation in the authority and the political élite involves governing bodies in consultation. In this context education officers play an important part in policy-making. Party-nominated governors may be the largest single group, but they do not have a formal relationship with the party machinery and frequently take an independent line particularly on school issues. The authority has formalised links with governing bodies through the clerk and there exists a process for handling the demands of governing bodies. Pressure-group activity in the authority creates a competitive local political system and governing bodies may have links with various pressure groups. The focus of concern of governors is both with the affairs of the local education system and of the school. In this context the governing body has more of a semi-independent role and has cross-cutting linkages with other groups.

Type C is characterised by limited party control where governing bodies are not viewed as political bodies. LEA-nominated governors are not necessarily party members, but may come from a wide number of groups in the local community. The governors are not expected to represent sectional views but to act as trustees for the community. The governing body is viewed as being primarily concerned with the school and with providing a link with the LEA rather than being concerned with any wider issues in the local political system. This reduces the extent to which the individual governing body is incorporated into the political–administrative system. The LEA has only weak contacts with its governing bodies and the mode of contact is initiated by governors. The governing body in this case is expected to provide ritual support for school demands. The governing body is not used as a channel for different interests because it lacks power and the more important interests bypass it.

## Notes and references

1. For example, see Benson, J.K., 'The inter-organisational network as a political economy', *Administrative Science Quarterly*, vol.20, no.2, 1975; and Archer, M.S., 'Educational politics: a model for their analysis', in Broadfoot, P. (ed.), *Politics and Educational Change*, Croom Helm, 1981.
2. For example, see Leach, S., 'County–district relations in town planning', in Leach, S. and Stewart, J., *Approaches in Public Policy*, Allen & Unwin, 1982.
3. Kogan, M., 'The central–local government relationship – a comparison between the education and health services', *Local Government Studies*, January/February 1983.
4. See Hunter, C., 'Education and local government in the light of central government policy', in Ahier, J. and Flude, M. (eds), *Contemporary Education Policy*, Croom Helm, 1983.
5. Potter, A., *Organised Groups in British Politics*, Faber, 1961.
6. For example, see Lewis, J., 'Variations in service provision: politics at the lay professional interface', in Young, K. (ed.), *Essays on the Study of Urban Politics*, Macmillan, 1975.
7. Jones, G.W., 'Varieties of local politics', *Local Government Studies*, vol.1, 1975.
8. For example, Jennings, R.E., *Education and Politics: Policy-making in LEAs*, Batsford, 1977; and Alexander, A., *Local Government in Britain Since Re-organisation*, Allen & Unwin, 1982.
9. Cf. Hinings, C.R. *et al.*, 'The organisational consequences of financial restraint in local government', in Wright, M. (ed.), *Public Spending Decisions*, Allen & Unwin, 1980.
10. Jennings, *op. cit.*, p. 182.
11. See Saunders, P., *Urban Politics: A Sociological Interpretation*, Penguin, 1980.
12. Darke, R., 'Attitudes towards public participation', *Local Government Studies*, vol.7, no.3, May/June 1981.
13. For example, Collins, C.A. *et al.*, 'The officer and the councillor in local government', *Public Administration Bulletin*, December 1978.
14. Alford, R., *Health Care Politics: Ideological and Interest Group Barriers to Reform*, University of Chicago Press, 1975.
15. For a number of current problems affecting these relationships, see Dennison, W.F., *Education in Jeopardy: Problems and Possibilities of Contraction*, Basil Blackwell, 1981.
16. See Howell, D.A., 'Corporate management in English local government and the education service – an interim report', *The Journal of Educational Administration*, vol.17, no.2, October 1981.
17. Education (School Governing Bodies) Regulations, 1981.
18. See Krause, E.A., 'Functions of a bureaucratic ideology: citizen participation', *Social Problems*, vol.16, 1968.
19. Arnstein, S., 'A ladder of citizen participation', *Journal of the American Institute of Planners*, vol.35, 1969.

20. Dunleavy, P., *Urban Political Analysis*, Macmillan, 1980.
21. See Ham, C., 'Community health council participation in the NHS planning system', *Social Policy and Administration*, vol.14, no.3, Autumn 1980; and Richardson, A., 'Thinking about participation', *Policy and Politics*, vol.7, no.3, 1979.
22. See Dearlove, J., *The Politics of Policy in Local Government*, Cambridge University Press, 1973.
23. Baron, G. and Howell, D.A., *The Government and Management of Schools*, Athlone Press, 1974.
24. Bacon, A.W., *Public Accountability and the Schooling System*, Harper & Row, 1978.
25. Howell, D.A., 'Problems of school government', in *Education in the Eighties: The Central Issues*, Simon, B. and Taylor, W. (eds), Batsford, 1981.

# 4 The school as an institution

**Introduction**

Chapter 3 illustrated the theme that governing bodies are an inextricable part of the political–administrative system and that in particular circumstances they can be greatly influenced by the operation of political factors. Yet equally in analysing governing bodies it is important to explore the way in which they become influenced by the institution they are expected to govern. This chapter moves, therefore, from the context of the political–administrative system to that of the school. The relationships between school and governing body are not immune from these wider pressures, but are influenced by the specific context of the school.

As has been seen in Chapter 1, since the publication of the Taylor Report and the gradual implementation of the 1980 Education Act, the trend has been for each school to have its own governing body. The Taylor Report emphasised that the partnership of school staff, parents, community and local education authority must operate in relation to the individual school.[1] The underlying assumption was that there should be a close relationship between school and governing body and that the unique factors specific to each school require it to have an individual body. The premise of this chapter is that the specific institutional characteristics of the school condition the relationship between school and governing body. These characteristics have an impact upon the work of the governing body and its form of participation in the school. School governing bodies differ from each other in comparison with similar groups such as Community Health Councils because of the nature of the school as an organisation, as well as the variability of the controlling superstructures. Lay participation is possible in education, but the form of participation is constrained by particular characteristics in the field being governed.

In Chapter 3 the school was viewed as a prime institution with the requisite autonomy to be able to determine its own objectives and organisation subject to the parameters set by other bodies, notably the local education authority. A further crucial feature is the ability of the individual professionals to formulate objectives and set arrangements to fulfil these. The theme of the professional dimension and the way it influences the role of the governing body is explored in Chapter 5. But whereas the school is a permanent institution controlled by professionals, the governing body is characterised by lack of corporate identity, as exemplified in Chapter 7, and intermittent contact with the day-to-day life of the school. These circumstances pose four issues in the contact between school and governing body. First, they create problems for the governing body in developing and maintaining its relationship with the school. Secondly, as the governing body is composed of the controllers, providers and consumers of education it may be difficult for it to create its own coherent viewpoint about the school. Thirdly, they emphasise an unequal partnership; the school is likely to be the dominant partner so that its characteristics and style of working play a large direct and indirect part in influencing the role of the governing body vis à vis the school. Finally, lay governors may find it difficult to understand and evaluate the workings of the school and must rely upon professional definitions.

Although the governing body is likely to be influenced by specific characteristics appertaining to its school, there are common types of institutional influences upon the governing body.

## The organisational nature of schools

Throughout this chapter the notion of the school will be approached from the standpoint of various themes in organisational theory which offer a conceptual analysis isolating the most important dimensions and interconnections. This provides a more adequate perspective than that of a straightforward narrative or descriptive approach to schools. The study of schools from a political perspective is somewhat neglected in all but a limited number of studies.[2] This may be explained partly by the fact that schools are viewed (particularly by educationalists) as unique institutions which cannot be grouped with other organisations for analysis.

What are the main elements in viewing schools as organisations? It is necessary to construct a framework which will sensitise attention to the key factors. A starting-point is the notion of organisational goals. Organisations are created to pursue certain goals. Schools are commonly viewed to be 'service' organisations whose prime beneficiaries are the pupils reliant upon the institution to best serve their interests.[3] But further clarification of the nature of the goals is needed.[4] First, a crucial problem is 'whose goals?'; it is unlikely that all members of the organisation will necessarily subscribe to the same goals. Secondly, there are different types of goals. Formal goals may be statements by the organisation which do not accord with what actually happens. Similarly, goals may change over time in reaction to new circumstances or even when they are achieved. New goals may be put forward by groups in the organisation which attain positions of power. Derr and Deal argue that it may be difficult to use a simple notion of goals in educational organisations,[5] and maintain that schools have diffuse and unclear goals. These multiple goals may be conflicting and may be latent. The implication of this, they argue, is that it is difficult to put forward clear criteria to judge the effectiveness of the school in meeting these goals.

Next, the concept of organisational structure is important in differentiating between organisations.[6] By structure is meant the regular patterned activities that occur in organisations. The structuralist approach describes the main dimensions of structure.[7] Specialisation is the way in which the work of an organisation is divided into a number of positions and specialist roles. In all organisations, Salaman argues, work will vary according to its differentiation, variability, complexity and the amount of freedom permitted.[8] This differentiation will involve both horizontal and vertical dimensions. Vertical hierarchy is the number of job levels and spans of control which has then to be matched by the horizontal grouping of positions. Specialisation in the organisation will necessitate some form of coordination. In particular, control will have to be exerted over the nature of work activity – the way it is designed, control over its quality and quantity, the specification of work practices and the manner of its supervision. Centralisation is one such form of control concerned with the distribution of authority to make decisions. Another form of control is standardisation which refers to the establishment of procedures to govern activities. This is related to the extent of formalisation – the extent to which rules, procedures and instructions are codified. These notions are commonly viewed to be the main elements of bureaucracy.

A school's structure may be seen as its formal patterned activities. Certainly, the school does mirror the characteristics of a bureaucracy. School structures includes horizontal and vertical role differentiation (e.g. pastoral and academic structures, specialist teachers, senior teachers, non-teaching staff, etc.), interdependence (e.g. working parties and other forms of collaboration), and mechanisms for co-ordination (e.g. policies, rules and distinctive authority patterns between staff and pupils). A number of writers argue that the form of structure is more complicated that this.[9] Derr and Deal argue that the prevalence of professionalism as an organisational principle in the school has certain repercussions. The main implication is the creation of positions with various degrees of autonomy which do not become subject to hierarchical control. Packwood has reviewed the applicability of the concept of hierarchy to schools and argues that far from being authoritarian and anti-professional it is ubiquitous and more complex than critics assume.[10] He concludes that hierarchy 'provides for the work of many to be integrated and for accountability to be identified and maintained', but that it can 'accommodate professionals and professional freedom'.

A number of writers have argued that certain organisations – particularly educational organisations – do not adhere to the rationality presented by the perspective of structure. Two alternative perspectives have been developed which seek to explain the ambiguity that is seen to exist. Organisational anarchy is used to describe organisations where structure is not related to activity.[11] This is because such organisations have unclear goals, fluid membership, a turbulent environment and uncertain technology which leads to a lack of predictability. Even so, patterns can be identified but activities such as decision-making and policy-making may have different functions from those in hierarchical systems, notably a ritualistic maintenance of stability. The second perspective is of organisations as loosely-coupled systems which describes the lack of coordination in education organisation.[12] The level of interdependence in schools may be low because teachers work independently of each other. Likewise, the goals of schools may be made ambiguous and are not susceptible to external inspection or evaluation. Therefore loose-coupling is a rational response where coordination or external evaluation may lead to conflict within the organisation.

The concept of patterned regularity is only one aspect of structure. Structure also incorporates less formalised features which remain stable and durable. Structure has therefore increasingly been viewed in processual terms. Elger refers to structure as 'a pattern of social relations and social constraints' which 'should be seen as the ongoing product of social processes enacted by organisation members'.[13] These social processes involve negotiation about the goals of the organisation, the way in which decisions are made about policy formulation and the allocation of resources. The problem of this perspective is in analysing the way in which this structuring process occurs. The following section draws upon the main elements of this process as outlined by Ranson.[14]

First, all members of the organisation experience their membership in distinctive ways which are combined into meaning systems. The key point of this action perspective put forward by writers such as Silverman is that action arises from meanings held about situations.[15] This meaning system remains deep-seated and taken for granted until it becomes articulated as values and interests.[16] Values may be defined as specific elements of meaning which become articulated in day-to-day interaction to explain particular problems encountered, and to legitimise action taken. For example, research on disaffected pupils in schools shows that these pupils had their own distinct values which were at odds with the educational and institutional values of the school.[17] The meaning system is also displayed in the interests of groups which are their evaluations of the resources of the organisation, their allocation, and who controls them.

The values and interests of groups of organisation members form the basis of interaction within the organisation. Becher and Kogan show in their study of higher education institutions that the different groups and entities have their own particular values.[18] A number of other studies of educational organisations portray the pattern of activity which Hoyle has referred to as 'micro politics'.[19] Richardson's study of a secondary school shows the internal dynamics of the school with competing viewpoints.[20] Likewise, a number of studies of universities shows them as political organisations involving competition between groups.[21] Conflict between groups, as Bennett and Wilkie argue, is precipitated by factors such as status, the dissatisfaction with the existing allocation of resources, rewards and prestige in the organisation.[22] Although this approach creates the impression that organisations are marked by fluid processes it is apparent that activity is constrained by the distribution of power. Power is defined here not just as the authority vested in particular positions but, as Walsh shows, it derived from the possession of resources (e.g. revenue, manpower, skills, information) and the ability to manipulate the allocation of resources.[23] Likewise, power may also be seen to be exercised where dominant power-holders have institutionalised their own meaning systems in the structure of the organisation which works to their advantage.

Another important dimension of the operation of the organisation is the effect of its environment.[24] The organisation is shaped not only by the constraints of its own characteristics but also from its environment. The environment consists of three main areas: the socioeconomic infrastructure, the existence of other organisations and its 'institutionalised environment'. The first is made up of physical characteristics (such as the geographical location of the organisation); social characteristics (demographic, class and ethnic patterns) and economic characteristics (the type of industry and nature of the local economy). All these characteristics will impinge in different ways upon the organisation and may serve to influence structural arrangements. In educational organisations these set of factors are liable to be very important particularly as reflected in the social characteristics of the pupils in the school. Organisations do not exist in a vacuum but form part of a network of other organisations – its 'organisation set'. The organisation may depend upon these other organisations for its resources – not only material resources, but also the expertise of other organisations, and support. This creates the possibility of the exchange of resources between organisations as each seeks to fulfil its role. A yet further dimension of environment is the 'institutionalised environment' made up of cultural, political and economic values which control and legitimise organisations. One element of this is the way that dominant ideas influence the structure of the organisation. Meyer and Rowan demonstrate that organisations seek the legitimation of their own structural arrangements.[25] As they state, 'elements of formal structure are manifestations of powerful institutional rules which function as highly rationalised myths that are binding on particular organisations.' In respect to schools, Derr and Deal emphasise that schools are inter-penetrated and controlled by their environment.[26] Although they may have a near monopoly of clientele, they are dependent on local communities for support and rely upon public relations to maintain their image.

The environment potentially influences the structure of the organisation. A dominant approach in organisation theory is the relationship between these contextual characteristics and organisation structure. Research has been carried out on the impact of organisational scale, technology and the wider environment on the organisation. The assumption is that if the organisation is to become effective in its performance it must accommodate itself to these contingencies. This approach can, however, become unduly mechanistic unless it takes account of the 'strategic choices' which are made by decision-makers and enables their organisation to select or ignore these contingencies.[27] In schools, the senior staff can engage in 'demand conversion' whereby they select or amend which demands should be faced by the school and how they are dealt with. It is also possible for the school to influence its environment by, for example, shaping the educational expectations of the local community.

Messages from the environment may be contradictory or unclear, and have different implications for different parts of the organisation thus creating uncertainty. Changes in the environment may affect the organisation indirectly rather than directly: for example, the increasing size of the organisation produces problems which may affect existing structural patterns and necessitate change.[28] The task of analysis should be to show the constraints that operate and the choices that are available.

Organisation theory can be used to show how specific characteristics of schools influence the role and activity of the governing body. For the purpose of the analysis in the rest of this chapter the governing body will be taken to be conceptually separate from the school, although this position does vary according to circumstances.

### The type of school

The starting-point in exploring the effect of institutional characteristics upon the governing body is the type of school which is likely to influence some of the internal characteristics of the school. Also, whether the school is primary, middle, 11–16 comprehensive, 11–18 comprehensive, special or community has repercussions for the work of the governing body.

The *primary school* is usually smaller than other schools and has a less complex set of structural arrangements. Specialisation is less evident; teaching tends to take place for the most part in a single class. A distinction, too, may be made between the traditional and progressive styles of education in primary schools which affect the grouping of pupils. The characteristics of the pupil body produce consequent patterns of organisation. Of importance here is the age of pupils and their degree of dependency upon the school for basic socialisation. Related to this is that dependency extends to the parents' relationship with the school and influences their style of interaction with the school. Parents are more likely to engage in individual *ad hoc* contact with teachers at the school than in secondary schools.

These general characteristics affect the governing body's criteria in evaluating or monitoring the school. Governors may not be knowledgeable about the aims of primary school education. For example, in one school in our research governors thought that testing children before their transfer to a comprehensive school would be in the children's interest, but their view was not in accordance with the style of education advocated by the school staff. Governors of primary schools are not faced so acutely as in secondary schools with such problems as discipline, low achievement and attendance. In one infant and junior school in our research it was noticeable that the joint governing body paid more attention in meetings to junior school business. One explanation was that governors saw these issues as more important. A possible reason for this was that they viewed infant schoolwork as caring rather than education. Yet although the small size and lack of complexity in school organisation may seem to aid the governing body in reviewing the primary school, the informal ethos and lack of explicit technology make this difficult. In our research governors commented on the informal nature of primary schools and the fact that governors' visits were limited in scope because they were seen as friends of the school there to provide support. The support of the governing body is viewed to be for the whole school rather than just for the headteacher.

Some of the same characteristics are also apparent in *middle schools*. The lack of clear guidelines about the aims, methods and organisation of middle schools make it difficult for governors to establish clear criteria for judging the school.[29] In both these cases the style and organisation of education lead to governors being viewed as agents of support. Our research shows that governors of these two types of schools will be more likely to adhere to this expected role.

The *comprehensive secondary school* is larger and more complex. It is marked by a higher level of differentiation and specialisation. The wider age range and different abilities of pupils add to this complexity, and there is a more varied curriculum. The comprehensive school has a larger number of 'boundary issues' involving the intake of pupils, relationship with other educational organisations, and the world of work. The school has a larger number of contacts with external agencies – social welfare agencies, careers service, and the like.[30] Decision-making is more complex and structured, involving decisions taken at different levels of the organisation. Because of the social welfare function of the school and the problems of discipline and attendance of pupils there is likely to be a differentiation between the pastoral and academic sides of the school. These characteristics influence the governing body in a number of ways.

First, governors are faced with a wider range of work and problems than in the primary school. The questions of management and organisation assume greater saliency. Again, the different styles of education in the school produce problems for the governing body. But governors are likely to rely upon more specific criteria such as examination success or career destination in their evaluation of the school. The headteacher's report is used as the main source of information for governors. From the research case studies it was clear that the information given to governors was wider than for primary school governors partly because the issues were more numerous and complex. Finally, the governing body can assume a greater significance for the school because the school has a larger number of contacts with the community and also because it is more visible in the community. In general, in our research the governing body was seen by staff and governors alike to be providing support for the headteacher and the management of the school.

In *community schools*, where educational and social provision for the community coexist with formal education for the compulsory years, there are particular problems for the governing body. As the Taylor Report noted, they produce special management implications. They also commented that the interests of the governing body were likely to be wider than that of primary and secondary schools, but varied depending upon the facilities available and arrangements for their administration. The committee also stated that there should be a full range of interests on the governing body, particularly the representatives of the various activities taking place at the school. The consequence for the governing body is the extended scope of its responsibility. Where the community school has organised links with its community, this may rule out the use of the governing body as an intermediary in this communication. Finally, community schools face problems because they frequently come under the jurisdiction of different branches of the education department – schools, adult education and further education.

*Special schools* present unique management characteristics: this chiefly is due to the nature of the pupil population requiring a specific type of education. Teaching is likely to be child-centred. Such schools are likely to be characterised by team-working amongst staff because of the problems of the pupils. A particular feature is that parents do not display collective organisation and their contact with the school is likely to be individual, which reflects a degree of parental dependency upon the school. The role of the governing body in this type of school will be different from that of other types of schools. Governors may be expected to adopt a supportive role because of the nature of the problems faced by the school. It will be difficult for governors to evaluate the school as the nature of special education is uncertain in its balance between care and teaching. There is likely to be an expectation by the LEA that governors should have particular experience relevant to the field of education.

Discussion about the type of school is further complicated by the nature of voluntary aided schools, which produces a number of additional factors influencing the role of the governing body. Under the Articles of Government the school has discretion over certain functions such as its admissions policy, the appointment of staff, and the repairs and development to buildings. This influences the range of formal tasks and responsibilities of the governing body. The governing body will have autonomy over these functions in its relationships with the LEA. It must also, however, work with the Diocesan Board. Secondly, the nature of the school's contact with the local church influences the governing body. Foundation governors (including the local vicar) are in a majority on the governing body and are expected to ensure that the school is fulfilling its role with respect to the original aims of the school laid down by the foundation. There is likely to be a relationship between certain of these aims and some of the main policies of the school. The school's contact with the local church also means that the community of the school may be perceived by staff and governors as being the local parish. In this case the governing body may act as a major channel of contact between school and church.

**Environmental features of the school**
The next set of institutional factors are the geographical, physical and social characteristics of the school. They may be viewed as contingencies deriving from the environment which the school and governing body must face.

The first factor is the geographical and social characteristics of the area surrounding the school. Several elements of this can be isolated. First, the changing demographic conditions of the area. Up to the 1970s the rising school population affected the size and structure of schools. The increase in size led to some use of split-site buildings. But with falling rolls contraction of size may necessitate a change in the structure of the school and the narrowing of curricular options. The need to maintain a viable intake makes public support more necessary. The governing body may thus move towards building up and maintaining support for the school. In one secondary school in the research the head wanted governors to extol the virtues of the school to others in the community. In more extreme cases the imminent closure of a school may lead the governing body to exert pressure upon the LEA.

The socio-demographic characteristics of the surrounding area also affects the nature of the pupil population at the school. Relevant factors here include ethnic and class differentiations. Different sections of the population are likely to have particular views about the nature of education. Inside the school the different needs of pupils present themselves in two ways. The pupil culture consisting of attitudes of pupils can affect the goals of the school. Similarly, the needs of pupils also serve indirectly to influence organisational arrangements. For example, in schools with marked social problems issues of discipline and attendance may become more acute. If exclusions result, appeals can cause the governing body (where Articles of Government permit) to act as a body of adjudication. Social problems also mean more emphasis on pastoral care with resulting adjustments in goals and structure as well as an increased flow of interchanges with external agencies.

Curricular arrangements, too, are affected. In certain cases special curricular needs are met by the provision of additional specialised courses. The process by which this comes about may itself result from a period of negotiation which may or may not include the governing body. The existence of pressure-groups in the community can also create externally-induced change. It is important to note whether the governing body is used as a channel of communication with the school. The implications of this diversity for the governing body are the increase in the range of work confronted and the problems of monitoring the school.

The different socio-demographic characteristics of the community also affect the culture of the parent body which itself influences the pattern of home–school relations, the nature of parental demands placed upon the school and the manner of their articulation. Problems of language or distinctive views about schooling may restrict interaction with the school. Conversely the presence of articulate middle-class parents may induce the school to relate in a particular way to the parent body. In special schools the geographical dispersion of the parent body and the problems they encounter with handicapped children make parental contact difficult. Indirectly, these factors are likely to influence the operation of the governing body. High levels of parental interest in the school may prompt the parent governors to adopt a representative role by articulating the views of parents to the school. Alternatively, a low level of parental interest means that the parent governor becomes isolated.

Socio-demographic characteristics thus constitute an important part of the environment and act as contingencies upon the school and governing body. Some of these pressures are transmitted straight to the school, whereas in a limited number of cases in our research they were mediated through the governing body. As there are different dimensions of the school's environment so environmental constraints may present conflicting pressures which result in uncertainty for the school and governing body. Where the extent of change is rapid (such as with demographic change) this can influence the existing patterns of how the school copes with its environment.

## Internal structure and decision-making

The structure of a school is oriented to the achievement of goals, the performance of work and the maintenance of control within the organisation. Specific characteristics of structure have repercussions for the role of the governing body. In a sense all schools display some bureaucratised features – differentiation of authority and responsibility, task definition, a career structure, and the recruitment of staff on the basis of expertise. More specifically, this is manifested in the extent of specialisation, departmentalisation and formalised rules governing communication, although these features are linked to school size.

Governors are therefore faced with a structure which has been developed as a result of a number of pressures. At its lowest level differentiation occurs as the individual teacher interacts with a single class or a small number of classes over a period of time: to a large extent this promotes autonomy over what they teach and how they teach it. Decisions are made at a higher level about whether, for example, there should be mixed-ability teaching or team-teaching. In one primary school in our research a decentralised system had been promoted by the former headteacher – teachers were responsible for the whole curriculum of their class, controlled the way it was taught, and were allowed considerable classroom autonomy. Although the small size of the school facilitated informal communication between staff, there was no formalised communication of policies or standardised procedures. Teachers worked within the confines of the implicit objectives of the school. Until the arrival of a new headteacher who initiated changes, coordination was not viewed as a major problem.

In larger schools differentiation is promoted by departmentalisation. Departments are introduced because the increasing scale of activity makes more specialisation necessary. There is a division of labour based upon the grouping of teachers according to subject specialism. The need for control is met by faculty structures designed to coordinate departments. In some schools the departments and faculties contribute to planning and policy-making. The pastoral structure of the school is a further element of differentiation. A commonly encountered pattern is a system of form tutors coordinated by a year head. The existence of a separate pastoral and academic structure may lead to conflict in the school.

The implication of the structure of the school for the governing body is that it reflects the underlying values in the school. For example, the existence of a decentralised system of teaching carried out in individual classes may reflect the importance of professionalism as a value governing institutional arrangements though it is not always clear that governors are aware of these structures and their underlying values. Secondly, the differentiated nature of the school requires the governing body to review the school as a complex structure in which decisions are made at many different levels. In one example in the research governors received reports from particular departments to acquaint them with the varied policies of the school. Yet many governors interviewed in other schools in the research did not have detailed knowledge about the activities of the school and were unable to develop a corporate view of its operation.

**Decision-making**

The style of decision-making in the school is important in understanding the role of the governing body. It exists at three levels. First, how are the objectives of the school defined, and who exerts most power in this process? The literature on goal formulation in organisations shows the possibility of a plurality of goals. Goals may be no more than formal and incongruent with what actually occurs in the organisation. For example, the goals of a school contained in the parents' handbook provide a general statement, but this may not accord with the views of different groups in the school – teachers, pupils and parents. At a lower level than the overall goals there are choices to be made about the primary decisions in the school such as staffing structure and financial allocations within the school. At yet a further level are the secondary decisions on the day-to-day life of the school, involving questions of management. These three levels of decisions involve different participants, and display different patterns of interaction. The review of the literature on organisations also shows the need to view them from a pluralistic perspective because they consist of different groups. The notions of values, interests and power therefore have to be brought into the analysis to explain the various patterns of interaction.

The historical context of decision-making in the school is relevant.[31] Governors face a school which is a permanent institution with a historical background. This problem is particularly acute for a newly reconstituted governing body composed of nearly all new governors where the governors must subscribe to policies accepted or condoned by the previous governing body. The institutionalisation of a set of values in decision-making may be presented to governors as an immutable entity. Equally, the process of change presents problems of what part the governing body plays in these negotiations. These twin notions of continuity and change appeared as an important dynamic in our research particularly when a new headteacher was appointed to a school. It is at this juncture in the stage of the life of the school that rapid change may occur. For example, in a middle school in the research there was a distinctive ethos and style of education which had been promoted by the former headteacher. These values were based upon the assumption that the school should be child-centred in its concern, and remain insulated from the community and other educational institutions. Despite the appointment of a new head these values were institutionalised, and many of the staff subscribed to them. The new head attempted to make the school more open, but this had to be negotiated with the long-serving staff. In these circumstances the governing body had only a limited role in the formulation of new goals because change was being negotiated internally in the school. Equally, the arrival of a new headteacher with different ideas of participation could lead to the governing body being kept better or worse informed and consulted on policies. The governing body thus exists in a system where values are institutionalised and decision-making accordingly constrained. Values become enshrined in procedures as well as in policies and require considerable momentum to challenge.

The orthodox view of school decision-making is that it is controlled by the headteacher. This view of his authority has persisted in the public view and was frequently mentioned by governors in our research. Bacon's research showed that it still was the most important position in the school and could wield great power.[32] The position of headteacher is vested with a high degree of both formal authority and possession of power. The Articles of Government give the headteacher responsibility for the internal running of the school, but this is only couched in general terms. The headteacher does in fact have control over the internal organisation, management and discipline of the school. He has the power to define his own role and to a large extent the structure of the school.

It is important to explore further the role of the headteacher and the resulting style of leadership in the school, as in many cases it is the headteacher who acts as the main intermediary between the school and governing body. It will be demonstrated that the style of leadership is a vital factor in understanding the role of the governing body.

From our research three ideal-type styles of headteacher can be identified which may have implications for the school's relationship with its governing body.

### The headteacher as autocrat

Although this conception of the role of the headteacher is viewed to have declined as headteachers face a more open environment there is evidence that their potential autonomy and power are still great.[33] Where this role exists it is characterised by a centralisation of school decision-making. The head has the power to frame the objectives of the school and determines the primary decisions such as staffing and finance. Only in secondary decision-making is there any sharing of control. Staff meetings may take place, but they are primarily used as forums for the provision of information rather than for decision-making. Staff participation is low and there are few opportunities for the expression of views as consultation is of an *ad hoc* and informal nature. Policies are constructed by the headteacher and only subject to limited amendment by other parties.

Our research gives ground for speculation of two kinds of implications for the governing body. First, where governors support, or acquiesce in the objectives and values of the school this style of centralised leadership is accepted as legitimate. Governors are content to be kept informed of current policies and make occasional suggestions. There is likely to be a relationship between the head and chairman rather than the majority of the governing body. In one school in our research this style of leadership and relationship with the chairman was institutionalised and had been apparent for a number of years. There was little motivation for governors to participate in decision-making.

A second implication of this style is that governors may seek to induce change in policies because they disagree with the objectives of the school but fail in their attempt because they lack the power to make changes. Instead the main elements of power (formal position, information, control of resources) are controlled by the head. This state of affairs is also reinforced by the governors' lack of access to the views of the staff in the school. Governors will tend to experience the school from the perspective provided by the headteacher only. The head decides which information should be made available to governors; reports from departments are likely to be edited by him. Because of this authoritarian style of control the role of the teacher governor invariably will be to reinforce the headteacher's viewpoint and so governors are confronted with a strong consensus amongst the professionals.

### The consultative headteacher

In much of the literature on the role of headteachers, it is proposed that the style of leadership become more open to include the views of other groups both inside and outside the school. In this style there is emphasis upon consultation and the sharing of decision-making. Decision-making may be initiated and concluded by the headteacher, but it will incorporate the views of others as it becomes formulated. There are likely to be consultative mechanisms such as staff meetings and a management committee which provide the forum for the expression of views. However staff participation exists at various levels, varying from being limited to responding to the initiatives of the head to a situation where change is proposed from the staff. Many of the schools in the research showed this style of consultation and collaboration, with the acceptance that the head should be accountable to external authority for the decisions made. The intention is both to allow staff a greater share in decision-making and to attempt to manage a complex institution where support for new policies is necessary.

In schools characterised by such consultation the governing body is likely to 'call the school to account' and give views on policy. Information will be provided for governors to allow them to assess the activities of the school. But although there is governor access to the school, and it is presented as a pluralistic organisation, there is still likely to be a united front presented by the professionals on the governing body.

*Headteacher as* primus inter pares

An extension to the second role of the consultative style of leadership is the type of school where there is a democratic style of school decision-making and staff play a large part in decision-making. A network of meetings and sub-committees act together to formulate policy. The formal policy-making body of the school is the full staff meeting which is not controlled by the headteacher. In this system policy-making is a collaborative process and a product of the majority decision of the staff at the school. The role of the head, apart from taking responsibility for some of the secondary decisions, is to provide general leadership and facilitate this structure. However, it is assumed that the head will be accountable for decisions made by the full staff meeting.

The implications for the governing bodies can be various. First, the governing body may be accepted as part of the school policy-making process which will be consulted on policy issues. The governing body provides legitimation from the community and thus becomes structured into the total school decision-making process. Governors review the main policies of the school and provide support. They have access to the school which is presented to them as a professional organisation based upon a rational/democratic mode of organisation. Detailed information is given to the governing body. The headteacher is viewed by governors as the chief executive or team leader of the school. A second possible effect is that the governing body is distanced from the school by this style of decision-making. The governing body occupies a role outside the main structure, and its role is ambiguous. Governors are expected to contribute to policy yet remain supportive. Although they are given full information concerning school policies this is for them to legitimise rather than influence. Policy-making therefore becomes an internal process decided by all staff, and governors lack the power to make an impact.

The style of headship therefore plays a large part in influencing the operation of the governing body. The role of the head can be more complex than any of these three types which constitute a spectrum of roles. Likewise, the relationship between style of the head and the governing body should not be viewed as mechanistic. Also the role adopted may vary over time and be adapted to meet particular circumstances. In some cases the actions of staff at the school or the governing body may promote changes in the head's approach.

## Structural conflict in the school

Although the role of the headteacher and resulting style of leadership exert a strong influence on the governing body there are other aspects of school decision-making shaping the relationship between school and governing body. The literature on organisation theory portrays organisations as pluralistic and composed of different groups engaged in negotiation over goals and distribution of resources. An important feature is the degree of structural conflict in the school. As has been noted, differentiation in the organisation of the school creates the potential for conflict.[34] For example, conflict can occur between the interests of departments over timetabling or between the academic and pastoral structures of the school. There may also be conflict over values in the schools so that the degree of consensus becomes important in understanding the internal operation of the school.

In certain cases conflict remains confined to the school, and governors are not drawn into it, but in other cases of value conflict the negotiation becomes open. In one example there was disagreement over the issues of compensatory education and there developed a division between the head and a section of staff. The disagreement was brought to the attention of governors by the teacher governors. The governing body therefore became a sounding-board for competing viewpoints. In such situations the governing body can bridge the gulf caused by professional dissensus. But equally the governing body faces a problem in monitoring the school when it receives different information or views from those provided by the headteacher. The extent to which change results depends upon the type of issue and strategies adopted. In one school which was in the process of becoming a community school there was conflict, exacerbating existing cleavages in the school, over the effect of this extra provision upon the day school. Staff discontent and confusion were made known to governors by the teacher governors. Although the governing body had supported the scheme, teacher opposition led to its being delayed through pressure exerted upon the LEA. Not only was there a conflict of values but the governing body could also be used as part of a strategy to gain support or to publicise an issue.

**The external relations of the school**
The concept of the environment of the school has so far been discussed in terms of the social and demographic characteristics of the school's community. It has been shown that different types of community present different demands on the school which responds in different ways. But the environment of the school also includes the operation of other organisations which interact with the school. In this section the process of 'demand conversion' will be further explored. It is argued that this process and the nature of the school's external relationships depend upon the internal administrative style of the school and its own view of the nature of its tasks.

*Relationship with the LEA*
The school can be viewed as a prime institution, but although it has considerable autonomy it is dependent upon the LEA for its resources. As was shown in Chapter 3, the structure of administrative relationships promoted by the LEA is a major determinant of the school's relationship with the authority. Relevant factors include the type of policies promoted by the LEA and the administrative autonomy delegated to the schools. But within this structure the school's own view of its status and the scope of the LEA's jurisdiction also govern its style of relationship. Style is reflected in the strategies it adopts in relation to the LEA and influence demands made upon the governing body. In one school the head had his own extensive contacts with the LEA which meant that these direct channels were used when problems arose. Only when they were unsuccessful was the governing body used as an instrument of strategy.

*The school and accountability*
The process of 'demand conversion' of demands from the community depends, first, upon the values in the school concerning the dominant task of the school and orientation to pupils and, secondly, the school's view of its accountability.

The tasks of the school vary between a traditional notion of education based upon a professional–client relationship to a wider concern with the social functions of education. For example, in one school the traditional perspective of the school's tasks (shown by an emphasis upon the values of academic achievement and strict discipline) led to an isolationist policy by the school with respect to the community. In this context it was school policy to use the cultural liaison teacher or education welfare officer as links with the community or parents. The contact sponsored by the school therefore defined its manner of communication.

In contrast, a school which emphasised the social context of learning had a more open relationship with the community. It was thought that support and relevant expertise should be forthcoming from the community and that communication should be a two-way process. In both these cases the different tasks of the school led to different styles of organisation and distinct modes of evaluation were expected from governors. In the former case evaluation would be based upon traditional school outputs, such as examination performance; in the second case the distinctive policies and organisation of the school meant that evaluation would be based upon criteria formed by school policies and processes.

The nature of task-definition is also related to the school's view of its accountability.[35] The first dimension of accountability is to which groups should the school be accountable. This may be primarily oriented to parents or pupils or may embrace other groups such as governors, the LEA and other sections of the community. Secondly, there is the substance of accountability. Accountability may include various areas of the school – curricular objectives, internal organisation, or output. Bridges, in the Cambridge Accountability Project, distinguishes the way that different audiences are involved in communication and decision-making.[36] The 'professional/isolationist' school only occasionally releases information to external audiences and staff are unconcerned with outside views. The 'professional/participatory' pattern is characterised by the school consulting outside audiences in an early stage of the formulation of policy to incorporate different views. The professionals are obliged to be guided by these opinions. Finally, the 'professional/rational' pattern incorporates opinion after practice has been developed. Information is provided and explanation is given because the school is confident in its justification of policies. In our research teachers did not see the governing body as part of the school or as a body to which they were accountable. Indeed, few teachers could name governors. This finding accords with the studies by Richardson and Elliott, which showed that governors were not identified as part of the school nor as a major forum for accountability.[37]

These ideas of task-definition and accountability have a bearing upon the way demands are perceived and incorporated. They have implications for the school's view of the role of the governing body. These two themes will be shown in more detail in the school's relationship with parents and the community.

*Relationship with parents*

The school's relationship with parents may be classified according to the individual or collective modes of contact. The individual contact includes individual meetings between parents and teachers and different sorts of forum, such as year meetings. Both of these are designed to allow communication through an individual 'professional–client' relationship and the transmission of information from teachers to parents. In some primary schools parents enter the school as parent helpers. On the collective level the relationship is with a larger body of parents and is normally mediated by a parents–teachers' association. These types of associations may fulfil a number of functions. First, as a system of support for the school providing direct help such as fund raising; secondly, as a representative forum to allow parents to engage in some form of a dialogue with the school; thirdly, as a method for the school to communicate, explain and legitimise policies. The important point about these types of parents' association is that their existence and role are defined by the school: as such they may not possess any formal legitimacy in the school decision-making process. Also their form influences the manner of parents' collective action with the school. Where there is no PTA parents may be prevented from engaging in this type of collective action.

The implication of these patterns for the governing body, and more specifically the role of the parent governor, is varied. In certain cases the existence of a PTA means that parent governors can use it as a representative forum to collect views and report back on governing body activities. It also provides an alternative channel for pressure upon the school. But it is more likely that the PTA has no links with the parent governors and acts solely as a support mechanism for the school. Equally, where the predominant mode of contact with parents is individual neither the governing body nor the parent governors are viewed as a means to place demands upon the school. In these cases it is likely that the parent governor is not necessarily seen to be a legitimate representative of parental opinion.

*Relationship with community*

As has already been noted, the different types of community place both direct and indirect demands upon the school. The school's contact with the community takes different forms. The nature of accountability and teachers' views of the community are of importance here. In the special case of voluntary aided schools there is a formal relationship with the local church which may contribute to some external influence upon the setting of the goals of the school. The governing body has a majority of foundation governors whose role is to represent and implement the official goals of the school. But in general the school's relationship with the community may be limited to the church. In some cases contact extends to the use of school facilities but it was rare in our research for there to be any impact upon school organisation. The school is able to define its relationship with the community, produce its own contacts and, if necessary, resist demands. In the case of a community school contact with the community may be more formalised and extensive although it is doubtful that it will extend to negotiation of the goals of the school. This contact with the community will influence the governing body in different ways. Where there are low levels of contact with the community the governing body is viewed as an external body and a primary contact with the community. The existence of multiple contacts with the community may mean that the school is more receptive or open to the views of the governing body. However in these circumstances an alternative result may be that the governing body is not viewed as representative of the community and is bypassed by other channels of contact. In our research community groups did not always know of the existence of the school governing body and did not recognise it as a channel of communication with the school. Instead they tended to try to develop contacts with the LEA.

**Summary and conclusion**

This chapter has explored the ways in which the different characteristics of the school influence the role of the governing body. By using perspectives from organisation theory it is possible to disaggregate the school and show how schools have distinctive characteristics which influence the likely manner of participation of the governing body. Using this theoretical background the main characteristics of the school can be outlined and analysed. Figure 4.1 summarises these main elements which have been discussed.

   The influence of these factors should not be viewed as mechanistic but rather as a checklist of factors which come together in particular combinations in different schools. In certain schools some features may have a greater significance for the governing body than in others. The general conclusion is that the governing body is faced with governing a school which is a complex structure with its own distinctive history, dominant values and style of decision-making. These factors will both directly and indirectly impinge upon the way that the governing body performs its role. They will influence its range of work, its participation in school decision-making and its own internal style of operation. This implies that the governing body to a large extent is constrained by the

*Figure 4.1* The influence of characteristics of the school upon the governing body

| Institutional characteristics | Structural characteristics | Environmental characteristics |
|---|---|---|
| type of school | dominant values about accountability | socio-demographic characteristics |
| phase of life of school as an institution | | parental demands |
| size of school | internal school organisation | community demands |
| school–LEA relationships | headteachers' leadership style | |
| pupil characteristics | style of school decision-making | |

Role and Operation of Governing Body

school. However, the role of the governing body is also a product of the different views of the governors concerning the purposes of the governing body which is further explored in Chapter 7. The next chapter explores the way that professionalism is manifested in the operation of the governing body.

## Notes and references

1. Department of Education and Science and Welsh Office, *A New Partnership for our Schools*, HMSO, 1977.
2. For example, see Davies, B., 'On the contribution of organisational analysis to the study of educational institutions', in Brown, R., *Knowledge, Education and Cultural Change*, Tavistock, 1973; Bidwell, C.E., 'The school as a formal organisation', in March, J.G. (ed.), *Handbook of Organisation*, Chicago, 1965; King, R., *The Sociology of School Organisation*, Methuen, 1983; Tyler, W., *The Sociology of the School: A review*, Tyler, 1982.
3. Blau, P.M. and Scott, W.R., *Formal Organisations: A Comparative Approach*, Routledge and Kegan Paul, 1963.
4. For example, see Gross, E., 'The definition of organisational goals', *British Journal of Sociology*, vol.20, no.3, 1969.
5. Derr, D. and Deal, T., 'Towards a contingency theory of change in education: organisational structure, processes and symbolism', in King, E.J. (ed.), *Education for Uncertainty*, Sage Annual Review of Social and Educational Change, vol.2, 1978.
6. Pugh, D.S. *et al.*, 'Dimensions of organisation structure', *Administrative Science Quarterly*, vol.13, 1968.
7. Hall, R.H., 'The concept of bureaucracy: an empirical assessment', *American Journal of Sociology*, vol.69, no.1, 1963.
8. Salaman, G., *Work Organisations: Resistance and Control*, Longman, 1978.

9. See King, *op. cit.*

10. Packwood, T., 'The school as a hierarchy', in Bush, T. *et al.* (eds), *Approaches to School Management*, Harper & Row, 1980.

11. March, J.G. and Olsen, J.P., *Ambiguity and Choice in Organisations*, Bergen, 1976. See also Turner, C., 'Organising educational institutions as anarchies', *Educational Administration*, vol.5, no.2, Spring 1977.

12. Weick, K.E., 'Educational organisations as loosely-coupled systems', *Administrative Science Quarterly*, vol.21, no.1, 1976; and Meyer, J. and Rowan, B., 'Institutionalised organisations – formal structure as myth and ceremony', *American Journal of Sociology*, vol.83, no.2, 1977.

13. Elger, A., 'Industrial organisations: a processual perspective', in McKinlay, J. (ed.), *Processing People: Cases in Organisational Behaviour*, Holt, Rinehart & Winston, 1975.

14. Ranson, S. *et al.*, 'The structuring of organisational structures', *Administrative Science Quarterly*, vol.23, March 1980.

15. Silverman, D., *The Theory of Organisations: A Sociological Framework*, Heinemann, 1970.

16. Ranson, S. *et al.*, *op. cit.*

17. Bird, C. *et al.*, *Disaffected Pupils*, Brunel University, 1980.

18. Becher, T. and Kogan, M., *Process and Structure in Higher Education*, Heinemann, 1980.

19. Hoyle, E., 'Micropolitics of educational organisations', *Educational Management and Administration*, vol.10, no.2, June 1982.

20. Richardson, E., *Authority and Organisation in the Secondary School*, Macmillan, 1975.

21. For example, Bucher, R., 'Faculty politics and power', in Blankenship, R.L. (ed.), *Colleagues in Organisations: The Social Construction of Professional Work*, New York, 1977; Baldridge, J.V., *Power and Conflict in the University*, Jossey-Bass, 1971.

22. Bennett, S. and Wilkie, R., 'Structural conflict in school organisation', in Fowler, G. *et al.* (eds), *Decision-making in British Education*, Heinemann, 1973.

23. Walsh, K., 'Power and advantage in organisations', *Organisation Studies*, vol.2, no.2, 1981.

24. Lawrence, P.R. and Lorsch, J.W., *Organisation and Environment*, Boston, 1967.

25. Meyer and Rowan *op. cit.*

26. Derr and Deal, *op. cit.*

27. Child, J., 'Organisational structure, environment and performance: the role of strategic choice', *Sociology*, vol.6, no.1, 1972. For an application, see Harding, P. and Scott, G., 'Management structures in colleges of further education', *Educational Management and Administration*, vol.10, no.1, February 1982.

28. Kimberly, J.R., 'Organisational size and the structuralist perspective: a review, critique and proposal', *Administrative Science Quarterly*, vol.21, December 1976.

29. Cf. Warwick, D., 'The local government of middle schools: governing bodies and the problems of middle school identity', in Hargreaves, A. and Tickle, L., *Middle Schools: Origins, Ideology and Practice*, Harper & Row, 1980.

30. See Johnson, D. *et al.*, *Secondary Schools and the Welfare Network*, Allen & Unwin, 1980.
31. See Pettigrew A.M., 'On studying organisational cultures', *Administrative Science Quarterly*, vol.24, December 1979.
32. Bacon, A.W., *Public Accountability in the Schooling System*, Harper & Row, 1978.
33. Cf. Bacon, *op. cit.*
34. See Bennett, S. and Wilkie, R., 'Structural conflict in school organisation', in Fowler, G. *et al.*, *op. cit.*; and Walton R.E. and Dutton, J.M., 'The management of interdepartmental conflict – a model and review', *Administrative Science Quarterly*, vol.14, 1969.
35. See Becher, T. *et al.*, *Policies for Educational Accountability*, Heinemann, 1981.
36. Elliott, J. *et al.*, *School Accountability*, Grant McIntyre, 1981.
37. See Richardson, *op. cit.*; and Elliott, *op. cit.*

# 5 The professional dimension in school government

## Introduction
The professional dimension provides the third major determinant of the way in which governing bodies work. The ability and means of 'gripping the activities of professionals' have become a common concern of institutions of representative democracy. In the case of governing bodies, how can the part-time amateur hope to govern the full-time specialist meaningfully? However, governing bodies face a further difficulty in that, following the 1980 Education Act, headteachers and teachers were deliberately incorporated as governors. Therefore, the governing body must itself accommodate the expert and non-expert: the full-time worker in the school and those with a part-time interest in its operation. The presence of professionals as governors thus defines the other members as the laity. This accommodation, complex and sensitive enough in itself, has further to reckon with the diversity of interests that exist within both groupings.

This chapter begins by examining the state of professionalism within education and the occupations that are seen as professional by lay governors, before applying the research findings in analysing the different interests that are subsumed within the professional and lay groupings, and the nature of their interaction within the work of the governing body. The chapter concludes by suggesting ways in which this complex relationship can be conceptualised.

## Professionalism and education
Despite recent recognition of the importance of the parental contribution, education has increasingly become a specialist domain. Furthermore, the educational occupations have, to use Johnson's[1] definition, become state-mediated; that is, the state has intervened in the relationship between service providers and consumers and the majority of educationalists are now employed in large social institutions whose activities are defined and underwritten by government. However, the state has, at least until recently, concentrated on the terms under which education should be provided, and has left its content to the professionals. The growth of state intervention has also brought the professionals a guaranteed clientele as children are legally obliged to receive an education and its duration has gradually extended.

The consumer, then, has little choice in obtaining the services of one professional rather than another, and cannot determine what is provided. Consumers' interests are fragmented and heterogeneous. In Johnson's terms,[2] they lack the power to define their own needs and how these should be met. At the same time, the education occupations have expanded and have themselves fragmented. The intervention of the state has fostered occupational cleavages between service demands and those of management and politicians, so that now it is no longer clear whether the client is the child or the state. These processes have led to a reaction in terms of growing criticisms of restricted public participation and weak accountability.

However, the current uncertainties of the educational environment now threaten the professionals. Education is no longer regarded as a self-evident good to be preserved and expanded at all costs.[3] Doubts about the value of the education system have been accompanied by falling rolls. As a result, education has to fight for its share of resources at government level, and individual schools must struggle to maintain their facilities. The way in which educational matters have been taken up by the media, and have come to be seen as a legitimate area for consumer concern and organisation, have added to these pressures. Robinson suggests that professionals are now faced with having to sell their services to an uncoerced and unconvinced population and thus have to tailor their provision to the views and interests of their customers.[4]

A strong case, then, can be made for public involvement at the institutional level. If, as Macbeth *et al.* argue, professionalism is a local, even an individual phenomenon, it makes sense if checks on professional performance are made at the local level.[5] Kogan, too, comes to the same conclusion, arguing that schools present a public personality and develop their own set of values and objectives, which must be related to the local community that the school serves.[6]

The origins of governing bodies certainly reflected a belief that the public should have a voice in the way in which individual educational institutions were conducted. An early account gives their functions as being to maintain the interests of the institution against domination by personal or local interests and by professional influences or prejudices.[7] They therefore came to represent one of the intersections in the system which brought the professionals and the laity together. As Baron and Howell demonstrated in their study,[8] governing bodies failed to provide the laity with much influence, but recent policy initiatives, both national and local, have been designed to strengthen their role. A prominent element in this resurrection has been to insist that they include members drawn from those local interests who have the greatest stake in the success of a school – parents, as well as teachers and representatives of the LEA. This broadened membership has brought about a new configuration of interests in educational government. At the same time it has brought an added complexity, in that governing bodies are not only expected to review the work of professionals but the reviewers, themselves, must reconcile lay and professional viewpoints. It follows that the professional dimension is indeed crucial in understanding how governing bodies work.

### The education professions

Governing bodies mainly encounter members of three educational occupations – teachers, education officers and advisers employed by the LEA. Most governors see these occupations as professional by virtue of the expertise of their members who, through their work in the educational system, possess knowledge that is not available to the laity. It is in this sense of lay assumptions of expertise in employment that the educational occupations are defined as professional in the remainder of the chapter. Most governors we encountered were under no illusion that they could run the schools themselves, and accepted that they must give due weight to those who do the job.

Clearly, however, none of these three occupations enjoys the status and autonomy that are associated with the archetypal professions, such as medicine and the law. Indeed, in sociological categorisations they do not always qualify: teaching is classed as a semi-profession by Etzioni,[9] a mediated occupation by Johnson[10] and as a bureau-profession by the Parrys.[11] The expertise of the educational occupations lies in their mastery of process. Teachers, advisers and many education administrators have considerable freedom in deciding how best to perform their day-to-day work. Qualified teachers, for example, expect – and are expected – to decide the way to educate the children who enter their classrooms, both as individuals and as a class.[12] However, they also belong to hierarchical organisations and are thus constrained by the managerial decisions of their superiors.[13] These are generally concerned with the application of resource inputs, with the coordination of individual process in the interests of the institution, and with setting policy to determine outputs.

As has been mentioned, all the occupations are largely employed by government, and it is national or local government, rather than the occupation, that determines the conditions of work and controls the numbers and terms of entry. Although there are national or local associations which may develop norms of behaviour for the three occupations, such as the Society of Education Officers, they have no professional council in England and Wales that would allow them to imitate doctors and collectively regulate their own conduct. Teachers' collective activity is most visible as trade unionism, and all the educational occupations experience internal conflict between professional and union objectives and norms of behaviour.[14]

Teachers face a further drawback in the professional stakes in so far as their mystique is reduced by universal experience. Everyone, to a greater or lesser extent, has been educated and therefore knows something about their work. Johnson also points out that in state-mediated systems, such as education, the occupational community is unlikely to be the repository of specialised knowledge, which is more usually developed externally by full-time research institutions.[15] Status is also reduced in that much of teaching, particularly in the primary sector, is seen as women's work which has traditionally carried lower status in our society. Although education officers are generally required to have had some experience of teaching, and advisers will normally have taught for a sustained period and achieved a senior position, their work does not visibly form part of educational practice. They are rather seen as administrators – enablers, providing support to the schools.

To the laity, then, these reservations have the effect of making the educational occupations appear somewhat schizophrenic regarding professionalism. Teachers, for example, may appeal to their professional status with external audiences, while effectively working as part of an organisational hierarchy. Strategies to influence government frequently appear to owe more to union traditions than to those of professionalism.[16]

## Multi-professionalism

Having disposed of the general issues of who are the professionals, we need to look deeper at the different occupations and the way they relate to governing bodies. Professional values include ideas as to the proper relationship with the laity. First, however, it should be noted that the presence of three groups suggests that the laity are not necessarily confronting a solid professional front. Within any system there is likely to be tension between different occupational groups competing for scarce resources. Further, as has already been noted, there is likely to be tension between those occupations concerned with service delivery and those concerned with service management. Our research suggests that education officers and advisers could, in the terminology adopted by Alford[17] with reference to the American health service, be seen as a challenging interest, trying to make the schools more efficient. This brings them into conflict with the teachers who, because of their work, are likely to be more child-centred in their concerns. The governors get caught up in the cross-fire, their seal of approval being sought for the policies desired by both parties.

However, inter-professional tensions and rivalries within the governing body should not be over-stated. Schools and education departments have their own relationships within the education system that by-pass governing bodies. The professional response to local difficulties is typically to employ a confidential and informal approach. A school may have a far closer relationship with advisers or the relevant area education officer than with its own governors. A study of senior educational administrators undertaken by Bush and Kogan suggests that education officers do share the same values as teachers.[18] From our work, they also share the belief that governors are generally unaware of the realities of education. As a headteacher in our study explained, faced with criticism from the governors, a school's first line of defence was to call in an adviser to testify to the wider professional agreement that supported its case.

Governing bodies have to live with the politics engendered by multi-professionalism. On occasion this means that the experts will be pushing them in different directions, teachers saying 'You should be concerned with the school', and the education officers saying 'You must realise the purpose of authority policies that limit (or seek to expand) what the school can do.' Different professionals hold different values and objectives, although in many situations they will speak with a common voice.

**LEA officers and advisers**
In their study of educational accountability, Becher *et al.* found that LEA staff had that strong sense of the need to maintain professional standards which was the hallmark of professional accountability.[19] However, officers and advisers are external to governing bodies. Unlike teachers, they will not be encountered as fellow governors and their work is not usually of direct interest, or likely to be scrutinised. Their concern is seen to be with management of the educational system rather than educational practice. As was discussed in Chapter 3, their influence depends upon the general role the authority has in mind for governing bodies and, more specifically, upon their visibility in terms of whether or not they clerk governing bodies, whether other officers and advisers attend and, if so, how they construe their role and upon their seniority within the department.

Inevitably there is a tendency for officers and advisers to be cast in the role of scapegoat for the LEA; lay and professional governors unite in attributing the ills of the school to lack of resources. However, we found that governors appreciated that their freedom of action *vis à vis* the school was constrained by the general policies of the authority which its officers interpret and maintain. These are therefore in a position to say what is and is not possible and their relationship with governors thus contains a strong element of authority as well as one of support.

## Educational politicians

Before moving into the school we should mention a further group concerned with the LEA who may also be seen as education experts by their fellow governors. These are LEA representative governors who also serve on the education committee of the Council or on one of its sub-committees. As will be shown in Chapter 7, the majority of LEA representatives on governing bodies are not drawn from this source and are not even councillors. However, where such educational politicians are present on governing bodies, they are likely to be seen as experts as far as educational policies are concerned and a powerful source of influence on the school's behalf. This group owe their expertise to their career in politics and their interests are different from those of both LEA officers and advisers and of teachers. We found that sometimes they used their position as governors to make their colleagues aware of the realities – particularly the financial realities – of authority policy, which explains why their presence was sometimes felt to 'stifle action' by other governors. However, and particularly if they represented a minority party, some were happy to see the governing body exerting pressure on the authority. Others who occupied this position, however, felt that the inherent tension between advancing the interests of the authority as a whole and one school in particular could only be resolved by strictly separating the two roles – deliberately not speaking as a councillor in governing body meetings or as a governor when in committee.

## The teachers

It is likely that the teachers will represent the strongest professional influence on most governing bodies for they are appointed to govern a particular school. Thus, with the possible exception of the group of politicians mentioned above, governors have a closer relationship with the school staff than with education officers or advisers. The school, too, provides the largest professional group at governors' meetings with the headteacher and teacher governors and possibly others who have been invited for the particular occasion. The teachers' exercise of professionalism is obviously related to the school in which they work, although some will have wider reference points related to their subject or particular area of expertise.

We found that the majority of teachers knew little about the work of governors and saw them as peripheral to the work of the school. In part this reflects the work and concerns of teachers; awareness of the governors' existence increases with seniority and involvement in school administration. Lack of knowledge also reflects the low visibility enjoyed by governing bodies in the education system. However, the view of governors as peripheral to the school has implications for their exercise of accountability. Robinson has noted how professionals are likely to be strongly resistant to any external judgements of their performance.[20] Certainly, in the Cambridge Accountability Project, Elliott found that the majority of teachers felt neither individually nor collectively accountable to governors or local government officials.[21] In our research this was true of some of the staff interviewed, who believed that governors lacked the necessary knowledge, both of education in general and the activities of the school in particular, to evaluate their performance competently. However, accountability is one of these catch-all words that admits a number of interpretations. Elliott and Ebbutt distinguishes between schools 'giving an account of themselves' to external bodies and being 'called to account'.[22] Articles framing the work of governing bodies make some version of the former mandatory, but it was our experience that teachers accepted that in at least some respect, the governing body should 'call them to account'. Governors were seen to have a legitimate interest in the educational product of the school. They could review its aims and objectives; they provided a valuable external perspective for testing what was being achieved; and, in the last resort, provided a safeguard against malpractice. It was worth meeting the demands of governing bodies in these areas because they could support the school with valued interests, such as the LEA or local employers. Significantly, the authority of the governing body in this process was never very clearly defined, either in role descriptions or in teachers' minds. Governors could expect to be given the information they required. It was also proper to engage in a process of consultation, to explain the reasons for actions and consider criticisms or alternatives. This might then lead to shared decision-making. It was doubted, however, if the governors could overrule professional decisions with their own interpretations. Conflicts of that kind would have to be passed to the LEA, who, in the normal course of events, would be expected to back the school. At root, educational decisions should remain the province of those who were most competent to make them – the education professions.

As far as the educational process was concerned, although teachers felt that governors needed to gain some understanding of how they worked, preferably by visiting the school during the day and seeing for themselves, they denied them the right or ability to modify the methods of teaching. This was seen as the core of professional work, and confirms Maddison's observation that professionals focus upon process rather than outcome,[23] and Sainsbury's argument that their interests lie in the skills of the job rather than in its purpose.[24]

### Teacher governors
However staff interests are also fragmented; that is, within the school,

as Becher and Kogan have argued,[25] individual teachers and groupings of teachers have their own values, objectives and beliefs and follow work processes that are different both one from another and from those of the headteacher who must represent the purposes of the total institution to the governors. Provisions for teacher membership of governing bodies and for the minutes of meetings to be available in the schools are ostensibly a reflection of these differences of interest. They recognise that headteachers cannot always be expected to speak for their staff, although this is the usual assumption, for staff do not always speak with the same voice and are certainly not necessarily of the same mind as their head. The research certainly provided examples of staff who presented different interpretations from those of the head and senior staff at governing body meetings, using these as an opportunity to influence school management. In one such instance, teacher governors presented staff criticisms of the scheme for the school to develop community schooling. However, there are strong tendencies that operate to reduce professional disagreement within schools. As Chapter 4 has shown, headteachers possess power to make their interpretations authoritative; for example, through their influence on teachers' career prospects or resource allocations. Yet although schools are hierarchical organisations, in many the degree of authoritarianism is small, and considerable use is made of collective working. School policies are thus less the decision of one man or woman and more the outcome of working parties, school conferences and staff meetings. This means that there may be greater understanding and possibly some agreement among the staff. It is in keeping with this wider staff participation in running schools that governors are urged to get to know the teachers and are provided with an alternative route to their opinions through the teacher governors. The theory appears attractive to governors. Our research suggested that they valued the opportunity to get to know the staff. Teachers, too, despite some scepticism about governors' knowledge and powers, appeared to believe that governors should know something about what they were doing and, even where they had a headteacher who deliberately canvassed and then expressed staff opinion at governors' meetings, valued the safeguard provided by the presence of teacher governors.

Teachers' motives for taking the position of teacher governor are various, as are the arrangements for selection and the way in which the role is performed. We found that in some cases the senior staff effectively nominated themselves or their own candidates. In other cases the union connection was important or the job was 'sold' as valuable career experience. Contested elections were, however, associated with size. In the smaller schools it was more a matter of finding someone who was willing to take the job. Many teachers seem to fit what Hoyle called 'restricted professionals',[26] concerned primarily with their own teaching, rather than with the wider organisational context of which it forms a part.

Once elected or selected most teacher governors appeared to work to the open-ended brief found by Bacon in his Sheffield study;[27] that is, they functioned as trustees of staff opinion. They certainly saw it as part of their role to explain the views of the staff, as far as they knew them, on particular agenda items and to raise issues of current concern. As governors, however, they would decide issues as individuals rather than as delegates from the staff. Indeed, given the fact that they were not elected on a specific programme, and in most cases had no regular means of canvassing the opinion of their constituents, this was the only option. However the use made of teacher governors by the school depended upon circumstances. Where the schools studied were under threat of change, such as closure, amalgamation or a significant alteration in character, the teacher governors were used by their colleagues as a lobby to put the staff viewpoint. Where the schools were in 'calmer waters', they were less likely to be used in this way.

Bacon has argued that the presence of teacher governors helps headteachers avoid confrontation with the staff.[28] However, at first sight their presence places headteachers in a potentially difficult position. The teacher, a subordinate of the head, becomes a member of the body which can exercise authority over him. An open disagreement between the head and a teacher governor thus threatens the former's competence as a manager, as well as exposing professional uncertainty to the gaze of the lay governors. Such disagreements do occur and some teacher governors saw themselves as incurring the headteacher's displeasure as a result. Teacher governors vary in their willingness to take up a radical role, and those who are politically active appeared to favour using other parts of the education system, such as the unions or the joint consultative council with the LEA, to promote their causes. However we encountered examples of headteachers seeking to pre-empt the possibility of conflict by holding a pre-meeting briefing, or perhaps an individual chat, at which they could outline their intentions for the meeting and check what issues teacher governors were likely to raise.

### Headteachers

Although most headteachers have attained their position through success as teachers, their interests with governors are different. It may well be that the differences have become less obvious, smoothed out by the development of collective policy-making within schools that was mentioned above. Heads, too, have retained their traditional power of securing likeminded individuals about them through their voice in the appointment and promotion processes as well as by their opportunities for exercising charismatic leadership. None the less, their work is different from that of teachers in that they are concerned with running a school, rather than teaching a class or a subject. This exposes them to totally different pressures.

As discussed in Chapter 4, the British educational system gives headteachers considerable freedom to shape what are seen as their schools in the way they see best, but as a corollary, they have to cope with the uncertainty which has beset education over the last decade and are the focus of demands from a number of different groups whose wishes often conflict.[29] Teachers, pupils, parents, education officers, advisers, councillors, local community groups, employers – they are all likely to come to the head with their demands which he must then weigh. He faces the representatives or members of some of these groups on the governing body and may see it as providing an appropriate forum for demonstrating professional competence and mediating various demands. However, headteachers' professional concerns are distinctive in that they are both comprehensive and managerial, concerned with the activity of the school as a whole and accountable for directing that activity.

This said, heads are individuals. They bring different experiences, assumptions and objectives to a role which affords great scope for personality if not for downright idiosyncracy. What is certain is that the way in which heads see their governing bodies and wish to use them is a major determinant of the latters' role for, notwithstanding the presence of the teacher governors, it is the head who provides the major link between the governors and the school that is governed. Heads in our sample explained how governing bodies had to be taught how to be useful. In practice they used their governors in different ways in different circumstances. Bacon's notion of the governors' presence providing the headteacher with protection in which to develop a seemingly more flexible form of management[30] was certainly valid, but so too was the notion of the governing body as a focus for accountability and a provider of resources for the school. None the less, despite the fact that a headteacher uses his governing body in different ways, at root he will have a view of its role – a partner, a necessity, a talking shop, an irrelevance – which becomes something of a self-fulfilling prophecy.

A second important variant originating with the headteacher is that of style. Given the importance of the head's role *vis à vis* the governors, he must spend a lot of meeting time 'on stage'. How does he act? Again it is impossible to generalise. Some heads are warm, friendly and informal, others appear as 'the educational expert' or perhaps as 'the business executive'. Yet others are withdrawn and seemingly preoccupied with weightier matters.

Although heads have to attend governing bodies willy-nilly, a third variant in the relationship comes from whether or not they take up membership. In our study we worked closely with ten heads; of these, seven were members of the governing body, whereas two preferred (and the head of the voluntary aided school was obliged) to be in attendance. The argument put for a head not becoming a governor throws light on the distribution of power between heads and governors; namely, that if a head were a member then his non-adherence to a majority decision would weaken the status of the governing body. As a non-member he can fight against, or disassociate himself from, decisions he does not like and is better placed to treat the governors as advisory.

The crucial point regarding the headteacher's relationship with his or her governing body is that it is more important in determining how the governors work than how the head operates. It will certainly be influential in determining how profitably professionals and non-professionals interact on the governing body. This will be discussed further in Chapter 6.

The general point made in this section is that although the professionals share common attitudes regarding the specialist nature of educational work, the governors cannot regard the interests of the headteacher as synonymous with those of the teaching staff, nor those of the school as synonymous with other educational institutions. The governors' relationship with professionals is thus complicated by cross-currents.

## Lay governors

It has already been indicated that a proportion of governors, the teacher governors and, if he has taken the option of becoming a governor, the headteacher, can be classified as the professional members. The remainder, the majority, can be classed as the laity in that they are not professionally involved with the school being governed. Not surprisingly, the interests of lay members of governing bodies are different from those of the professional members, but an examination of the laity further suggests that their interests are even less clearly focused and more fragmented.

All lay governors have their own reasons for serving. Research revealed a spectrum of motives ranging from self-interest or the interests of one's child, to public service or missionary fervour to promote some particular cause in education. While it was true that some individuals we interviewed became governors because they wished to make the school responsive to particular needs, these were a minority. Lay governors do not necessarily approach their job as agents of change and display a varying amount of enthusiasm and commitment.

It is hardly surprising therefore that we found that lay governors saw their role in different ways. While at a general level most broadly agreed with the professionals that they were there to 'help the school' or 'help the children', deeper probing revealed very different beliefs as to their role and authority. Some lay governors, for example, believed that their purpose was to hear the school give an account of itself and take an interest in its activities, while possibly providing a backstop if there should be serious professional malfunction. Others saw their role as stronger – calling the professionals to account. This involved scrutinising the work of the school in the light of lay common sense and experience and making the staff explain and possibly rethink their principles and objectives. The lay governors thus provided a source of advice: a second opinion. Others, a minority, extended their accountability further, in that they believed that governors possessed the authority to exercise a more decisive influence upon professional activity, and should attempt to ensure, for example, that the interests of ethnic communities were not ignored or that LEA policy was observed. Most lay governors agreed that they had the task of supporting their school, and should press its interests in collaboration with the professional staff.

Our researches suggest that most governors thus see their role as being primarily concerned with the school. Some, however, viewed the position of governor as a way of influencing wider areas of the education system or of advancing the objectives of political or interest groups.

Diversity also stems from personal abilities and background as well as from motivation. In 1888 the desirable attributes for governors were defined by the Cross Commission as breadth of view, business habits, administrative ability and the power of working harmoniously with others.[31] While our study suggests that broad vision, the capacity to understand administration and particularly the ability to articulate and debate ideas in a collective setting remain as relevant qualities, under present arrangements the sum of abilities of any governing body is largely a matter of chance. The school governing bodies studied conformed to the stereotype of public service in that the majority of governors were drawn from the middle class. This might be thought to bring certain advantages. Many middle-class governors can claim professional status in their own right, and are confident and articulate in dealing with the educationalists and in working collectively. In other words, the social distance between the professionals and the laity is reduced. However, this bias also means that in many cases the governing body is in no way typical of the catchment area of the school – a fact that prompted some governors and headteachers to seek to manipulate vacancies for parent or community governors to remedy deficiencies.[32]

It is debatable how far professional status is in fact a help to the lay governor. Certainly, it may allow him or her to relate to a particular area of the school's operation as an expert, yet the reactions we encountered from the education professionals and other lay governors to such individuals suggested that their presence was seen as a mixed blessing. The criticism was that they wasted time by taking meetings into detail that was best left to the education professionals to sort out with those who must actually do the work. Their individual contribution was too detailed for the collective task of oversight. A more interesting case arises when an educationalist is a governor – an ex-teacher perhaps, or a member of staff from a college in a neighbouring authority. Such members understand, or are thought by their colleagues to understand, the education world: they can 'take on the professionals at their own game'. In the course of the research governors identified knowledge of the education system as one of the prime requirements for serving on a governing body; some felt that the presence of an external educationalist strengthened their collective ability to make sense of what their own professionals were doing. However, others argued that the presence of an educationalist made the work of the governors too 'in house'. Professional solidarity suborns the educationalist into supporting the views of the school and his contribution also draws the governors into professional debates which they do not really understand and which are not germane to their oversight of the school.

It is often the case, then, that the lay professional experiences frustration as a governor. Initial expectations that his field of expertise gave him something to offer that was needed by the school prove unfounded as meetings go by.

Individual motivations and purposes are, of course, influenced by the constituency that the member represents. However, as will be shown later, the research suggested that the relationship of lay governors to their constituencies was frequently tenuous and was certainly less clear-cut than that of the professional governors. Most lay governors were left to do 'their own thing'. However, there were examples of stronger lay constituency links. Community governors who represented particular ethnic groups provided a case in point, as did those LEA representatives who were tied in with party political organisations, or parent governors who had a constituency base in a parent–teachers' association.

The weakness of lay governors' links with their constituencies, their predominantly middle-class background, and the fact that certain local interests may be unrepresented, all mean that the professionals may fairly claim that they are more familiar with the total range of needs and demands that impinge on the school than are the lay governors. The teachers in a school that is open in its dealings with the public are certainly likely to be in closer touch with parental opinion than the lay governors.

Another source of fragmentation among the lay governors is the different relationships they have with the professionals outside the governing body. Parent governors, for example, are at one and the same time clients of the school as well as members of a body that exercises authority over it. It could be argued that client status strengthens the ability to review what the professionals are doing, for the parents experience the results at first hand. Therefore, on those occasions, rare in our experience, when they can point to wide parental support for their viewpoint, parent governors represent a powerful lobby with the school. Yet viewed another way, their client status entails a degree of dependency which might act to mute criticism. Certainly, we found that parent governors emphasise the need to support the school and were generally among the more reticent members of governing bodies.

Governors other than parents may be appointed because of the relationship they have already established with the professionals. LEA appointments may in fact be suggested by the school, and coopted governors can provide another example of the same phenomenon. In such cases headteachers appeared to look for individuals who were fairly articulate and who, if they were parents, had already demonstrated that they were willing to support the school. Heads also sought those who typified an interest that was important to the school and absent from the governing body, such as employers or, in the case of a special school with a wide catchment area, an individual from a particular town.

The professionals appeared to see those LEA appointees who were councillors or tied into the party political system in a different light. Potentially, at least, they represented a controlling interest that needed to be 'won over'.

Taken in all, the sum of the various methods of lay representation on governing bodies is a curious amalgam of election and appointment. This may weaken the ability to contest professional definitions. Regan and Stewart express the argument concisely:

Professional knowledge and expertise are a source of legitimate power. They can only be challenged by an alternative source of legitimate power. An appointed member has a weak basis for challenge.[33]

However, this suggests that, because they are elected, parent governors enjoy a greater legitimation than other lay members and might therefore be expected to take the lead in challenging the professionals. This appeared to be far from the case.

## Promoting coherence
So far, the argument has shown the diversity that exists among lay members. But there are also elements that foster a degree of homogeneity. First, our research indicated that a number of governors knew

each other from contacts outside the governing body. These contacts may be social or concerned with other public activities. Shared external relationships help to 'oil the wheels' of collective working and strengthen the governors' sense that they are in a position to represent local community opinion to the professionals.

Second, governors may share party political affiliations. Party politics aggregate individual values into shared ideologies and thus give governors a framework for evaluating the work of professionals. As will have been gathered from Chapter 3, the deliberate use of political appointments varies from authority to authority. Some governing bodies studied had their quota of majority and minority party appointees; others appeared less concerned with the party label and more interested in getting councillors to serve as governors of their local schools. The interest shown by political parties in governing body matters is also variable. In three of the authorities the local Labour Party organised selection meetings and occasionally brought its nominees together to discuss educational policy. Generally, the links were weaker.

The preceding sections of this chapter have examined in some detail what comprises the two elements of professional and laity on governing bodies and exposed some of the factors that condition the behaviour of each. In addition to showing the different interests of professional and lay members, stress has been laid upon the way in which interests are fragmented. Neither professionals nor laity will necessarily be united in their objectives; thus their interaction, with all its own inherent potential for conflict, is further bedevilled by internal tensions and contradictions. It is time now to turn to this interaction within the governing body, and here again it is necessary to stress the diversity of practice. This reflects both the mix of individual abilities and capacities within any governing body and the issues that arise. It is possible, however, to isolate some of the general factors that affect the ability of professionals and laity to work together.

### Constraints

First, laity and professionals alike are constrained by the way in which meetings are conducted. Factors such as when the agenda is set and by whom, the detail in which minutes are recorded, and whether material for the meeting is circulated in advance so the governors have time to formulate a view and perhaps consult their constituents, are clearly relevant to their ability to participate effectively.

Admittedly, the governors have some discretion to shape a meeting to their own needs, but as Chapter 3 demonstrated, their room for manoeuvre is limited by the servicing cycle and its attendant proce-dures. These make it difficult for lay governors to raise their own concerns. One authority introduced a parent governors' item to all its agenda as a way of solving this problem. The professionals, from school or LEA, have rather more opportunity to raise their concerns as part of the standard agenda.

Second, it is significant that most meetings take place within the school. The governors may be welcomed with cake and wine, but this only underlines their status as outsiders, guests on the territory of the professional. The qualifications for their presence, unspoken but none the less powerful, is that they are there to help the school. The laity must demonstrate support and this tempers their criticism.

A third point concerns time. Most of the governing bodies studied met once a term, although if they faced major changes, or the agenda was packed out with items from the LEA, they would hold additional meetings. As a result, the lay members saw their role as essentially precessional and episodic – in contrast with the continuous responsibilities of the professional – and an interval of four months commonly elapsed before the governors learnt of the response to a particular initiative or the answer to a query. Despite receiving the minutes, governors would forget the arguments over such periods and their energies would wax and wane. What looked to be of crucial significance in May can be very small beer come October.

Finally there is attendance. Even termly meetings pose problems for some governors. It is only to be expected that there will be many calls upon the time of those members, such as councillors, who were active in public service. Our observations suggest that the professional members, the headteacher and teacher governors, are the most consistent attenders, which strengthens their influence in governing body work.

Chairmen occupy a key role in determining how the governing body will work. Under the terms of the 1980 Education Act, chairmanship is explicitly reserved for the laity, since employees of the LEA are debarred from serving. None the less, we found that chairmen are pulled towards cooperation with the professionals. As Chapter 6 will show, they work more closely with the schools than do most lay governors, and are, therefore, likely to bear in mind the necessity of maintaining good relationships with the professionals and will, anyway, be more familiar with professional viewpoints than are most lay governors.

**The work**
The critical area for professional and lay interaction is, of course, in the work that governing bodies perform. Our observations of governing bodies in action confirm Bacon's finding that more time is spent on school administration and management,[34] matters relating to the

organisation which enables education to occur, than upon the nature and constituents of the educational process itself.

In explaining this pattern of activities, it seems clear that there is resistance to governors becoming involved in what are felt to be professional concerns. As suggested above, teachers saw matters relating directly to their educational practice as far more of a professional concern than those relating to the ways in which it is organised and resourced. Furthermore, even when the school curriculum was discussed it was noticeable that the governors concentrated upon issues relating to the educational product – principles, aims, policies and results – rather than the process. This, however, still left the governors with the problem of how to assess the product. Their own experience of education is likely to be outdated or irrelevant, and the product is, in any case, dependent upon the processes applied. Although professional processes are rarely challenged it should not be assumed that it is always the professionals who are keeping the laity at arm's length. Many lay governors were reluctant to become too involved with running the schools, and felt that the professionals must be allowed to get on with the job for which they were employed. Indeed, it was often the teacher governors who initiated matters concerned with school practice and they then faced the accusation of promoting unionism or special pleading. Matters pertaining to the organisation and support of the school do not, it could be suggested, pose the same threat to the professionals. Indeed, as Bacon argued, it may make the headteacher's job easier if he can involve the governors in management.[35] Lay governors, too, may feel more comfortable with matters concerning school management. Their own experience is more germane to this area of activity, where they feel able to contribute, whereas they lack (or feel they lack) relevant knowledge of educational methodology.

There are, however, two areas of work where the lay governors do see themselves as exercising a decisive measure of authority regarding the professionals – staff appointments and suspension appeals. Governors saw appointments, and particularly the appointment of a headteacher, as a means of determining the nature of the school. In our research a number specifically identified this as the most important of their functions and interference from the professionals, whether from the school or the LEA, was resented. For their part, some professionals questioned the ability of lay governors to make an appropriate selection, feeling that they were unable to apply the necessary professional criteria. Appointment procedures may thus provide a forum where lay and professional interests and criteria are exposed and conflict.

Suspension appeals represent even more sharply an area of potential conflict between lay and professional members. The professional judgement of the headteacher in dealing with a particular child is specifically reviewed by lay governors. On occasion this judgement is found wanting, and the appeal allowed. Headteacher and teacher governors may not accept or be aware of the criteria applied, and feel that their own authority and professional judgement in running the school are being undermined by lack of support from the governors.

## Authority

On looking more widely at the governors' role, it is apparent that their area of authority regarding the professional is small. Many issues regarding conditions of service have to be taken as given because they are determined by national and local policy. At the time of our study this was particularly noticeable in respect of teacher redeployment – one of the most traumatic issues to affect the schools and one where the governors were virtually powerless. On matters where the governors do have a voice, their wishes are often effectively a recommendation, subject to confirmation elsewhere.

Exchange theory suggests that the relationship between professional, external and political interests reflects each group's command over resources:[36]

Only those groups and individuals who are seen to be useful, or have some sanctions they can impose or whose support may be necessary are given access to the policy-making process.[37]

The capacity of governing bodies to impose negative sanctions upon the professionals is small. They do have the powers of delay or obstruction, such as requesting further consideration but, except in voluntary aided schools, they have little control over the key resources – money, manpower or plant. If, however, they are to exercise any form of influence over professional activity, or mediate between the professional and other interests, information would represent a further relevant resource. How is this distributed?

## Information

Lay governors in a part-time capacity obviously have a problem in learning what a school is actually doing. One way of obtaining this information is by visiting. Handbooks of guidance to governors stress the importance of visiting the school during the working day and getting a sense of its everyday life. This was certainly echoed by many teachers and governors interviewed in the research. However, in practice, it proved to be a minority of governors who were anything like regular visitors to the school. Some anyway challenged the assumption that visiting is of any benefit beyond that of public relations. A visitor is a guest, not a colleague involved in a shared task and, it was suggested, guests did not gain an independent view of school life. None the less, governors' visits appeared to carry enormous importance for some teachers; visible evidence of a commitment to the school.

If, then, there are problems surrounding governors' ability to learn about the school from visits, perhaps they can learn from other sources: from their own children, from parents, or through local community networks. In the course of the research, governors drew attention to the value of such information. However, the overall impression was that such contacts were slight. When six parents contacted a parent governor regarding a particular aspect of school teaching, this was seen as quite exceptional. The majority of governors have low visibility in the community and, as has been suggested, weak links with their constituencies: most queries and demands would go straight to the school, not to the governors.

The professionals, then, can readily point to the piecemeal nature of governors' information and explain issues away as atypical. However, the case is different where governors are speaking for organised interests within the community, interests which, in Wirt's terms,[38] have 'grievances over the perceived gap between their needs and the resources that professionals provide to them'. The political governors who were linked to the party system or active community groups, and thus had their own information which is not so amenable to professional interpretation, were seen as the most influential. It could be suggested that their support is worth more to the professional than that of governors who only represent themselves.

Rather than learning about the schools from their own observations, most lay governors have to rely on what they are told in meetings, and our research indicated a number of different sources of information, the most important being the headteacher's report presented at each termly meeting. For most governors, this was their main opportunity to learn about the school. Although these reports all provided some information, their variety reflected the individuality of their authors. To overcome this, in one authority the education department had tried to improve the value of reports by laying down guidelines as to what they should cover.

Meetings may be used to dispense other information concerning the schools: one of the schools studied provided its governors with elaborate departmental reviews; it is common practice to provide tabulations of examination results; governors will also probably receive an annual statement of capitation and the school fund account; and they may regularly hear about the work of different sections or departments of the school from the staff concerned. It is still rare, though, for lay governors to table their own reports on aspects of the school's performance. There is no standard equivalent of the practice developed in the health service whereby members of health authorities report on their visits to particular institutions or departments, or consider the annual review of services made by the Community Health Council.

It was noticeable, however, that lay governors appeared to have greater influence over information concerning policy supplied by the LEA. An interpretation may be provided by the clerk and/or LEA officer present. But unless the officer has specifically attended to speak to the document, it is quite possible that he will be as much in the dark regarding its content as the governors. Indeed, where the latter include members of the education committee among their number, they may be on stronger ground *vis à vis* the professionals when discussing authority-wide matters than the affairs of the school. Discussion is more general, and the lay governors and school-based professionals can demonstrate their common ground in defending the interests of 'their' school. More general issues are likely to be of particular interest to some of the lay governors and a number will possess relevant information through their constituency or community links. However, unless the issues directly concern the school, as in the case of a closure or change of use, such items tend to come low down on the agenda and receive rather less attention than matters raised by the school-based professionals.

It appears reasonable that lay governors can provide information that is valued by the school. Interviews with staff and governors alike stressed that one of the major purposes of having a governing body was to open the somewhat cloistered world of the school to outside view-points. Undoubtedly this does happen. The professionals listen to what the governors say and, on occasion, act on their advice or take up their concerns for further consideration.

However the role of lay governors in mediating interests to the school is weakened because most issues emerge on the initiative of the professionals. Governors, as Howell has noted,[39] play a predominantly reactive role, their participation conditioned by what they hear. In addition, their ability to mediate is further weakened by their fragmented interests, lack of constituency links and the existence of the school's own channels of communication with external interests that by-pass governing bodies.

The same, of course, applies when governors mediate interests for the school, providing information about it – or more commonly about its needs – to other bodies and, in particular, to the LEA. The supportive role, it may be remembered, was what the school professionals looked for from their governing body and this was certainly seen by the lay governors as an important part of their role. Here, then, in their capacity to represent the school to valued interests, is one area where lay governors do have something to offer the professionals. Headteachers believed that the interests of their school could be furthered by a councillor governor having an informal word with the chairman of the education committee, or by the chairman of the governors following up a request from the school with a visit to an officer. Indeed LEA officers confirmed that approaches by governors did achieve results.

The supportive role, however, is more complicated than might first appear. The governors' action can range from no response, through passive support of the school as expressed in the minutes of meetings, active support in the form of letters, visits and lobbying, to unsolicited action taken on their own initiative, such as contacting a councillor or placing a letter in the local paper. Although generally initiated by the professionals, active support requires time and effort from the lay governors, some knowledge of the local government service, and political nous. Is it more productive, for example, to take a building problem to the Clerk of the Works or the property department? Does it achieve more to write to the Chairman of the Education Committee than the Director of Education, or is the local newspaper a better bet than either?

**Unequal power**

In working with professionals to govern a school, it must be concluded that lay governors encounter an unequal distribution of power in the professionals' favour. Governing bodies do not represent a significant location for exchange between professional and lay interests: professionals control the relevant information relating to school performance and prefer governors to focus on the organisation and management of education rather than upon the detail of its application. Further, their expert status gives the professionals authority in interpreting what information is made available and in defining what action should be taken as a result. The way in which meetings are organised, coupled with the diverse and fragmented interests of the laity, work to place the governors in the position of outsiders, largely reacting to professional initiatives. The governors may modify but are unlikely to overturn professional opinion. The relationship is asymmetric.

A minority of governors, both lay and professional, are aware of this, and have become disillusioned with their inability to effect educational change. But disillusion, it should be noted, is equally likely in respect of other aspects of their role, such as the inability to represent a constituency viewpoint adequately. The majority appear to have no wish to exercise a more directive role and are happy enough to be coopted and led by the school professionals. As Wilding explains, the laity defer to expertise and experience: 'In part it is genuine, in part it is the product of a realistic strategic appreciation of how the cards are stacked.'[40]

**Factors strengthening the role of lay governors**

It would be misleading to conclude with a totally bleak picture of the influence and effect of governing bodies as an institution of lay government. A number of factors foster the ability of lay governors to evaluate information and press their own interpretations and conceptions. Collectively, they represent a considerable diversity of experience with – always it seems – some members who are used to working in a group and to adapting professional viewpoints to their own purposes. Councillors, business executives, trade unionists and members of community interest groups come to mind. Many governors, too, obviously possess the capacity to extrapolate from what they have read or encountered elsewhere, including experience as a governor of other schools, to the business of their own governing body. Constituency contacts, particularly an association with groups that have definitive educational interests, provide governors with a perspective from which to test and broaden professional opinion. In this context it should be remembered that some authorities make a sizeable investment in attempting to improve the abilities of governors by running short courses and/or setting up resource centres, and that governing bodies may be given a role in LEA school evaluation schemes.

Some governors, too, appear to work more effectively with the professionals as individuals in private than as part of a corporate body. Their position as governor, however, provides them with the necessary entrée. We encountered an example of two parent governors who felt able to press the need for curriculum change on their headmistress at a private interview, yet felt it inappropriate to challenge her in public. Chairmen in particular are likely to be in this situation with their headteachers.

It is also the case that the professionals, themselves, are frequently trying hard to help the governors understand the issues and gain a sense of their response. We frequently observed heads and teacher governors raising educational issues and explaining details to their fellow members. Moreover, the governors do occupy a position of authority within the educational system, albeit a weak one, so they are able to help professionals attain their objectives with other parties. Further, they represent some of the major interests that impinge upon a school, and occupations in a mediative system such as education must increasingly anticipate, respond to or seek to control social pressures.[41] The very process of using the governors for professional mediation and management implies some degree of exchange and the professionals do, therefore, respond to and take up lay concerns.

Some professionals go much further and seek to involve the governors in shared tasks. Although it pre-dated the study, an example of this had occurred in one of the governing bodies observed, where teachers and governors had met together to formulate the aims of the school. Not all the governors had taken part in this exercise but some of those who had participated felt that it gave them a sense of purpose and cohesion.

Neither is it the case that all professionals speak with the same voice to governors. It has already been mentioned that teacher governors may vigorously advance opinions that run counter to those of the head-teacher and perhaps support the case of an interest being pressed by the lay governors. LEA officers present may provide comparisons from other settings within the authority that help the governors evaluate the performance of their own school.

Lay governors, then, are not inevitably passive and reactive to professional leadership, and governing bodies can be something more than a ritual that hardly obtrudes on professional concerns. We would conclude that the ability of the laity to influence the professionals appears to be largely conditioned by circumstance: the nature of the membership; the disposition of the professionals, and particularly of the headteacher, to work with the governing body; the expectations of the LEA, and the freedom it is prepared to allow its governing bodies; and the particular situations with which the professionals are confronted.

### Explaining the relationship

This chapter has examined the constitution of the professionals and laity on governing bodies and their respective interests and how they work together within the forum of the governing body. The purpose of this final section is to see if it is possible to apply the empirical material to generalise typologies that explain the state of professional and lay relationships in governing bodies.

The general conclusion must be that at present governing bodies are professionally-dominated institutions, in which power is unevenly distributed. The dependence of the lay members on the professionals far exceeds that of the professionals on the laity. However, as has been shown, this does scant justice to the diversity of motivation and practice that is revealed when governing bodies are subjected to detailed scrutiny.

At first sight, the model arrived at by Bacon in his study of school boards in Sheffield[42] appears apposite. Power is held by the educational establishment – the professionals and politicians who are concerned with managing the system. Governing bodies coopt the teachers, as one of the main subjects of school management, and the laity to render the task of management easier. Certainly, as was noted above, much of the work of governing bodies appears to be concerned with school organisation and management rather than with fundamental questions of educational principles or practice. Our evidence, however, leads us to question how far the educational establishment exists as a unified interest. Educational politicians, officers, advisers, headteachers and teachers frequently exhibit different managerial purposes. And head-teachers and teachers share a common focal point of interest in the school, which both encourages their unity and brings them into conflict with other professionals who have wider concerns within the educational system. It was also the case that in a number of governing bodies we observed, teacher governors and some of the lay members vigorously presented their own interests and interpretations and rejected attempts at managerial cooption.

Wirt has proposed a developmental model of professional and lay conflict which passes through five stages: quiescence, issue emergence, turbulence, resolution and closure.[43] The stage that conflict has reached determines the role played by political institutions. Governing bodies in England would, in total, appear to fall into the category of issue emergence. The Taylor Report and subsequent legislation articulated public demands for change in educational government and, at least temporarily, placed governing bodies firmly on the political agenda. On an individual basis there appears to be greater diversity, and governing bodies could be characterised as ranging from quiescence, with an acceptance of professional domination, to turbulence, with a degree of lay and professional conflict.

Although all the governing bodies studied were, to a greater or lesser extent, professionally dominated, there was a marked difference in lay reaction. On some governing bodies most lay governors expected and desired professional leadership, whereas in others it was seen as open to challenge.

In the former case the acceptance of professional expertise was seen as an act of reason, not of the blind faith that characterises Wirt's state of quiescence. The laity could not run the schools themselves, so had no option but to trust the professionals. Their trust however was dependent upon the explanations they received and their judgement of the school's performance. This approach is reminiscent of the neo-pluralist view of political institutions.[44] This suggests that political institutions – in this case governing bodies – cannot hope fully to understand and hence control all the activities for which they are responsible, and are therefore forced to rely upon the expertise of professionals. They expect, however, to hear what sort of job the professionals are making of running the school.

The professionals, for their part, recognise that the public has an interest in their activities so, if they wish to avoid conflict, they must be prepared to explain what they are doing and take note of reactions. This type of governing body, type A, would appear to be characterised by:

(i)   a concentration on the work of running a school;
(ii)  agreement that the professionals decide how the school is run;
(iii) professional definition and explanation of the issues;
(iv)  lay governors reacting to professional definitions as individuals; and

(v) professional determination of action as a result of lay reactions.

The alternative type suggested by the research would be more in keeping with the pluralist approach which sees political institutions as a forum for the mediation of interests. This approach assumes that different interests are legitimate and have their own strengths of organisation and the capacity to win support in the governing body. The greater the intensity of organised pressure, the stronger the impact because, to quote Archer: 'numbers, commitment and organisation are the stuff from which power is made.'[45] Professionals represent one, often fragmented, interest group but at any time they will be under challenge from other interests with their own demands. This type of governing body, type B, would thus be characterised by:

(i) a broader concern with the education system;
(ii) professional and lay conceptions of how the school should be run;
(iii) professional and lay definitions and explanations of the issues;
(iv) lay governors defining and reacting to issues as representatives of interest groups; and
(v) action determined by debate between professional and lay governors.

However, in connection with this type, it should be noted that the professional groups have might on their side. They still provide the majority of information and dominate the meetings. Many lay interests are unexpressed and those that do emerge are fragmented, intermittent and frequently unorganised. As Archer points out,[46] in a decentralised education system such as Britain, sub-élites will tend to push for their own specific institutional requirements. The results are small-scale and incremental change: for example, new classes in Gujarati, staff consideration of whether sufficient time is being devoted to science teaching. Governing bodies of this type can expect to experience longer and more contentious meetings than those in type A, so that, over time, they may progress to a state of professional and lay conflict. The current spasmodic articulation of lay interests is not evidence of their satisfaction. If sectional demands by the laity increase, coalesce and become continuous, the governing body will be unable to reach consensus.

These two types usefully encapsulate some of the major contrasts observed in the research. They are however very much the poles of a spectrum of professional and lay interaction.

**Notes and references**
1. Johnson, T., *Professions and Power*, Macmillan, 1972.
2. Ibid.
3. Kogan, M., *The Politics of Educational Change*, Fontana, 1978.

4. Robinson, T., *In Worlds Apart*, Bedford Square Press, 1978.
5. Macbeth, A., Mackenzie, M. and Breckenridge, J., *Scottish School Councils: Policy-making, Participation or Irrelevance?* HMSO, 1980.
6. Kogan, M., 'Institutional autonomy and public accountability', *British Educational Administration Society Journal*, Winter 1975.
7. *Royal Commission on the Revenue and Management of Certain Colleges and Schools and the Studies Pursued and Instruction Given Therein* (Clarendon Commission), Eyre & Spottiswoode for HMSO, 1864.
8. Baron, G. and Howell, D., *The Government and Management of Schools*, Athlone Press, 1974.
9. Etzioni, A., *The Semi-Professions and Their Organization*, Free Press, 1974.
10. Johnson, *op. cit.*
11. Parry, N. and Parry, J., 'Social work, professionalism and the state', in *Social Work, Welfare and the State*, Parry, N., Rustin, M. and Satyamurti, C. (eds), Edward Arnold, 1979.
12. Packwood, T., 'The school as a hierarchy', in *Approaches to School Management*, Bush, T., Glatter, R., Goodey, J. and Riches, C. (eds), Harper & Row, 1980.
13. Ibid.
14. Parry and Parry, *op. cit.*
15. Johnson, *op. cit.*
16. Kogan, 1978, *op. cit.*
17. Alford, R., *Health Care Politics*, University of Chicago Press, 1975.
18. Bush, T. and Kogan, M., *Directors of Education*, Allen & Unwin, 1982.
19. Becher, T., Eraut, M. and Knight, J., *Policies for Educational Accountability*, Heinemann, 1982.
20. Robinson, *op. cit.*
21. Elliott, J., Bridges, D., Ebbutt, D., Gibson, R. and Nias, J., *School Accountability*, Grant MacIntyre, 1981.
22. Ibid.
23. Maddison, D., 'Professionalism and community responsibility', *Social Science and Medicine*, vol.14A, 1980.
24. Sainsbury, E., *The Personal Social Services*, Pitman, 1977.
25. Becher, T. and Kogan, M., *Process and Structure in Higher Education*, Heinemann, 1980.
26. Hoyle, E., 'Leadership and decision-making in education', in Hughes, N. (ed.), *Administering Education*, Athlone Press, 1975.
27. Bacon, A.W., *Public Accountability and the Schooling System*, Harper & Row, 1978.
28. Ibid.
29. Kogan, 1978, *op. cit.*
30. Bacon, *op. cit.*
31. *Royal Commission on the Elementary Education Acts, England and Wales* (Cross Commission), HMSO, 1888.
32. Wragg and Partington suggest there is 'much to be said for parent governors being chosen from different parts of the school's catchment area'. Wragg, E. and Partington, J., *A Handbook for School Governors*, Methuen, 1981.
33. Regan, D. and Stewart, J., 'An essay in the government of health: the case for local authority control', *Social Policy and Administration*, vol.16, no.1, Spring 1982.

34. Bacon, *op. cit.*
35. Ibid.
36. Archer, M., 'Educational politics: a model for their analysis', in *Politics and Educational Change*, Broadfoot, P., Brook, C. and Tulasiewicz, W. (eds), Croom Helm, 1981.
37. Boaden, N., Goldsmith, M., Hampton, W. and Stringer, P., *Public Participation in Local Services*, Longman, 1982.
38. Wirt, F., 'Professionalism and political conflict: a model', *Journal of Public Policy*, vol.1, February 1981.
39. Howell, D., 'Problems of school government', in *Education in the Eighties*, Simon, B. and Taylor, W., (eds), Batsford, 1981.
40. Wilding, *op. cit.*
41. Johnson, *op. cit.*
42. Bacon, *op. cit.*
43. Wirt, *op. cit.*
44. Dunleavy, P., see *The Politics of Mass Housing in Britain*, ch. 5, Clarendon, 1981.
45. Archer, *op. cit.*
46. Ibid.

# 6 How governing bodies work

The 1980 Education Act left the door open for considerable continuing diversity in school government in both the structural composition of school governing bodies and the scope of their concerns. In this chapter the composition and work of the governing bodies studied during the research will be discussed. Attention will be paid to the ways in which the political, administrative and professional dimensions of school government are made manifest in the governing bodies concerned, and the extent to which the characteristics of the various schools impinge upon the style and work of their governing bodies. We shall draw more directly and explicitly on our empirical evidence than we have in previous chapters in an attempt to open up the 'black box' of governing body functioning.

## Composition of governing bodies

The 1980 Education Act envisages three categories of governor: representatives of the local education authority and of any relevant minor authority,[1] representatives of parents, and of teachers. Section 2(10) points out that the Act does not rule out the appointment of other types of governor, and local Instruments of Government, as amended by the early 1980s, do in fact provide for several additional categories of governor. Governors representing the non-teaching staff, the school's pupils and the community were encountered in one or more of the governing bodies studied during the research.

While categories of governor indicate the potential range of stakeholders or interested parties who may be represented on a school governing body, the balance of representation can only be appraised if the numbers eligible for appointment in each category are known. In practice, the standing of particular representatives, in terms of other public roles held, also influences the balance of composition. The balance of the sexes on a governing body at a particular time may also be relevant. Figure 6.1 shows the detail of balance of composition in the case study governing bodies.

The research provides evidence that categories of governor may be fairly evenly matched in number, or that governors representing the education authority may outnumber all other governors. But the political and the professional dimensions of governing body deliberations may be reinforced, or, conversely, attenuated, by overlap between governors' categories of interest. 'Politico-parents' (LEA representative

| School governing body structure | Lorrenshire | | Stapleton | | Robart | | Mead | |
|---|---|---|---|---|---|---|---|---|
| | Townmeadow Infants & Junior (joint governing body) | Daneshill (Special ESN(M) and (S) – Secondary) | Hendrick Junior Mixed & Infants (voluntary aided) | Parker Secondary | Carstairs First and Middle (joint governing body) | Sanders Secondary | Austen Secondary | Beckett Secondary |
| Local education authority | | | | | | | | |
| councillors | 4 | | | | 2 | 1 | 1 | 1 |
| non-councillors | | 5 | 2 | 12 | 2 | 3 | 5 | 5 |
| Minor authority | | | | | | | | |
| councillors | 2 | | | | | | | |
| non-councillors | | | 1 | | | | | |
| Diocesan board | | | | | | | | |
| clergy, *ex-officio* | | | 2 | | | | | |
| other | | | 4 | | | | | |
| 'Community' nominees | | | | | | | 3 | 3 |
| 'Higher education' nominees | | | | 2 | | | | |
| School | | | | | | | | |
| headteacher(s) | | 1 | | 1 | | 1 | 1 | |
| deputy head (*ex-officio*) | | | | | 2 | 1 | | 1 |
| teaching staff | 2 | 1 | | 2 | 2 | 2 | 3 | 3 |
| non-teaching staff | | | | 1 | | | 1 | 1 |
| pupil | | | | | | | 1 | 1 |
| Parents | 4 | 2 | | 3 | 4 | 4 | 4 | 4 |
| Coopted governors | | 2 | | 1 | | 2 | 2 | 2 |
| Total | 12 | 11 | 9 | 22 | 12 | 14 | 21 | 21 |
| % of women governors* | 41% | 18% | 40% | 27% | 66% | 12% | 43% | 38% |
| % of governors with children at the school | 42% | 18% | 11% | 36% | 42% | 28% | 19% | 28% |

* The question of the inclusion or otherwise of women in school government has until recently been an overt issue. The abolition of the School Boards in 1902 disenfranchised those women who had formerly served on them, as they were not eligible to vote or serve as local councillors. Note III to the Model Instrument of Government for County Secondary Schools, issued in 1945, suggests that 'adequate representation' should be given to women in the

governors who have children at the school) and parents or LEA governors who are also members of the teaching profession are not always ruled out by the Instrument of Government, and their presence on a governing body has an effect on the apparent balance or imbalance between categories in terms of numbers. The effect will not always be to strengthen the representation of a particular constituency. As we have seen, any propensity of the teaching staff constituency to dominate proceedings may in fact be offset by the presence of other teaching professionals on the governing body, familiar with the assumptions being made and tactics used. The politico-parent is, however, always likely to strengthen the parent governor contingent, in that the LEA representative governor who is also a parent may combine in his person both electoral legitimacy and stakeholder motivation.

## Manner of appointment
Unlike the members of a council who can all point to the ballot box as legitimising their entitlement to participate in local government, the legitimacy of governors derives from several different forms of appointment: nomination, election by their peers, or cooption by serving governors.

LEA governors, or minor authority representatives, are nominated not elected, but their nomination may derive from a number of different levels in the political system, and will in any case be subject to formal or informal structuring as between political parties. For example, in Robart, majority party nominations for school governing bodies were more or less *pro rata* to their party's representation on the council. But, in accordance with guidelines agreed between the parties, the 'major minority' party, who perhaps outnumbered the next most numerous minority group by only one councillor, might be able to nominate 20 per cent more governors than that adjacent party. In the various authorities, each of the principal political parties had different criteria and methods for compiling their list of governor nominations. But in Lorrenshire it was claimed that all LEA and minor authority nominations to governing bodies in the primary sector were totally apolitical, the political affiliation or activity of the persons appointed not being one of the criteria for their inclusion in the list of nominees.

Representatives of interest groups nominated as governors had usually passed through a process of what might be termed 'filtered' nomination, in that their sponsoring organisation had had to compete with other interest groups for the right to nominate. Success, in terms of achievement of the right to nominate, might depend on a rota system, education committee evaluation of relative strengths of interest groups, or some other form of selection. Where authorities provided for the nomination of governors to represent further and higher education (to serve exclusively on secondary school governing bodies) this appeared to be a full-blown and continuous eligibility to nominate. But where groups such as parent–teachers' federations, community relations councils or chambers of commerce vied with each other to nominate governors, it was usual for some variation of eligibility to be laid down at the outset of each four years of local administration.

In governing bodies which included parent, teacher or non-teaching staff governors it was customary for their appointment to be on the basis of election, the procedures for which might be more or less tightly decreed or monitored by the local authority. In the governing bodies studied, election practice varied from contested nomination, hustings and secret ballot to the election 'by default' of a sole nominee for these categories of governor who were required to be elected by their peers. In some cases the sole nominee had been singled out and persuaded into accepting nomination, perhaps by a headteacher who felt a responsibility for seeing that no vacancies existed in the governing body for parent or teacher governors, or by a retiring governor who wished to absolve himself of any feelings of guilt in declining to stand again by filling the gap with a consenting nominee. Of the fourteen opportunities to elect parent governors which occurred during our case studies, five were 'non-events', in that an uncontested nominee was appointed. This was also the case for nine out of fourteen opportunities to elect teacher governors.[2]

Formal elections of parent governors, where these occurred, were either conducted by pupil post, with an ensuing formal count by a teacher nominated as electoral officer, or else took place at school-based meetings of the parent body, which might be specially convened for the purpose or part of a regular programme of meetings in which parent governor elections were subsumed.

The cooption of governors to represent special interests was one of the few opportunities which governing bodies had to influence their own composition. The eligibility of individuals to be coopted was circumscribed by the Articles of Government and sometimes ruled out overlap with other categories of eligibility. For example, in Robart no parent might serve as a coopted governor. Nevertheless, serving governors could decide between themselves what types of interest they wished to see complementing their own, and which individuals or groups might be approached to fill a vacancy. This capacity was in considerable contrast to the impotence of serving governors in the face of changes in LEA representatives. In one of the case-study authorities, an electoral swing eliminated several long-serving LEA representative governors, including at least one chairman of a governing body.

**Statutory limitations on the role of parent and staff governors**
The standing of all categories of governor is nominally equal, but there are certain statutory limitations on parent and staff governors' scope of role in terms of their debarment from participating in certain business. Figure 6.2 shows the detail of these limitations.

Although these limitations might be interpreted as putting parent or staff governors at a disadvantage compared with community or LEA-nominated governors, other characteristics, such as the nature of their attachment to, and sources of knowledge of, the school (to be discussed in Chapter 7) tend to outweigh any such statutory disadvantage.

*Figure 6.2* Business regarding which governors are debarred from discussing or voting, and are required to withdraw unless the gb otherwise allows

| Parent governors | | Staff governors (i.e. any governor employed at the school) | |
|---|---|---|---|
| Admission of | the parent's child as a | Appointment, promotion, | of 'relevant employee' |
| Disciplinary action against | pupil of the school | transfer or retirement | |
| | | Similar, of other employee, leading to vacant post for which 'relevant employee' might be candidate | |
| (Para. 5, Schedule to SGB Regulations 1981) | | Conduct, continued employment, appointment of successor, of 'relevant employee' | |
| | | (Paras 3, 4 and 7, Schedule to SGB Regulations 1981) | |

Pupil governors are subject to the same limitations of role as staff governors. Their sources of knowledge about the school are in some ways unrivalled but, even more than other governors, they are hampered by the short-term nature of their governing body membership. Pupil governors with full rights, such as those permitted by the Instrument of Government used in Mead LEA, must be eighteen years of age, and thus are usually on the point of leaving school. No pupil governor observed during the research served for more than two school terms. These pupils' preoccupation with examinations, job-seeking or transfer to other educational institutions meant that it was not possible to interview any of them formally during the research period, but informal conversations and observation indicated that they seemed to interpret their own role as a low-status, 'pupil observer' position, despite their nominal equal rights with other governors.

Perhaps the most important limitation on the role of staff governors (and, indeed, pupil governors) is that they may not serve as chairman or vice-chairman of the governing body (Para. 8(5), Education (School Governing Bodies) Regulations 1981).

## Appointment of chairman and vice-chairman

The procedure for the appointment of chairman and vice-chairman was the same in all eight governing bodies. At the first governing body meeting of each school year, governors proposed and seconded individuals from among their number willing to serve as chairman, and decided the appointment by vote: the same procedure was then followed for the appointment of vice-chairman.

As we have seen in considering the professional dimension, the role of chairman was a key one, providing opportunities both for symbolic representation of the governing body between meetings, and for considerable influence over the style and emphasis of meeting activity. The importance of the appointment was undoubtedly appreciated in the case-study governing bodies, but custom or collusion appeared to rule out open competition for the Chair. Either a single nominee who had served as chairman before was proposed, seconded and appointed without discussion or delay, or if a change of chairman was necessary the first person willing to accept nomination (not always the first person asked to do so) was voted into the Chair. In no case was an election necessary. Yet manoeuvring to secure the role was undoubtedly taking place, and this became more overt when the new Regulations were issued (during the research period) and eligibility to take the Chair was widened from LEA representatives to other serving governors. However, although now eligible to be appointed to the Chair, many parent and other categories of governor proved reluctant to do so. Their principal reason for declining appeared to be that it would be more difficult for any category of governor other than an LEA representative to pursue governing body concerns with the local authority between meetings. A subsidiary reason put forward by parent governors was that being chairman would create role-conflict for the parent in their dealings with their child's headteacher – a conflict which they did not appear to find was generated by the ordinary parent governor role.

## The role of chairman

For those governors who are both eligible for and prepared to accept the position of chairman, the role has two aspects. The individual so elected by his or her fellow governors at the autumn meeting of the governing body must both chair the meetings of that body during the ensuing year, and also *hold the office* of chairman. This may entail representing the continuing life of the governing body between meetings in a number of ways, including the taking of urgent interim decisions. It may also mean giving leadership to the governing body in establishing its appropriate scope of concern with regard to the school and the LEA.

Not all chairmen place equal emphasis on the between meetings and at the meeting aspects of their role. Some, whether from lack of time or lack of inclination, find it difficult to make themselves available between meetings for anything more than the briefest of telephone conversations with school or LEA. Others make almost a full-time job of the role, making frequent visits to the school, keeping in close touch with the clerk and a network of contacts in the LEA, and devoting considerable thought to the development of governing body effectiveness.

From our research we can identify four ideal types of chairman, whom we shall designate the 'education committee member chairman', the 'consensual chairman', the 'radical chairman' and the 'single-handed chairman'. These labels indicate the 'heart of the role' for particular types of chairmen, and the resultant role interpretations have implications for the governing body as a whole.

The chairman for whom membership of the education committee is an important attribute views the governing body as an outpost of the political–administrative system, and takes care to keep fellow governors in touch with committee policy and local authority protocol. The governing body will have ready access to information which other governing bodies may seek out with difficulty and the chairman is in a position to play an enabling role on their behalf. Nevertheless, the school and governing body will not necessarily be advantaged in any request for resources by their chairman's connections. Such a person is likely to be at pains not to promote his or her governing body as any kind of special case in committee deliberations.

The 'consensual' chairman, who is concerned to work with the governing body as a collective, identifies a pattern for governing body work, and tries to involve all governors in this.

The 'radical' chairman is one for whom the most important aspect of being chairman is the opportunity to break the mould of governing body work as presently performed, and encourage fellow governors to explore their own potentialities as participators in the local education system, and also the potentialities of governing body influence and power.

The 'single-handed' chairman may be the product – or in some cases perhaps the cause of – a 'spasmodic' governing body, whose gubernatorial role would be moribund between meetings were it not for him. None of the governors get together *as* governors between meetings for any working or debating purpose, and they are not encouraged to do so by office, school or, perhaps, chairman. Such a chairman (who may have held the office for several years) finds it possible to handle everything that arises between meetings, by way of agreeing to pupil suspensions, participating in the occasional appointments panel, conferring with the clerk and following up the outstanding business of the governing body. Unlike the 'radical' chairman he or she does not look for extension or change in the governing body role. The chairman's relationship with the headteacher is likely to be a satisfactory one for both parties, whether this be at the level of regular meetings to discuss and clear problems, or of occasional correspondence.

As we noted earlier, governing bodies do not normally give open and frank consideration to the qualities and capacity desirable in a chairman. Nominations are either prearranged or, if reluctantly accepted on an impromptu basis, not contested by other nominations. Yet this appointment (which, once made, is frequently confirmed year after year out of courtesy to the 'sitting tenant' of the role) can make a considerable difference to the position of the governing body in the checks and balances created for it by the professional and political fields of force.

### The conduct of meetings

By definition, only one governor can be chairman. But for all governors the formal governing body meeting is the occasion when, if at no other time, they have an opportunity to make their contribution to the government of education. The way in which governing body meetings are conducted is therefore of considerable importance in any examination of how a governing body works.

All governing body meetings are to some extent formal occasions, but our research revealed considerable variation in their venue, timing and social style. It seems likely that a wider sample of case studies would have revealed even more variety in this matter. For example, all eight of the case-study governing bodies held their meetings on school premises, but in some authorities governing bodies meet in council offices, a circumstance which must have implications for the professional/political balance of influence. Parent governors, however, would remain 'visitors' in either setting.

Even on school premises, the exact location of, and physical arrangements for, the meeting reflect some of the characteristics of the school as an institution (as discussed in Chapter 4), and some assumptions (usually the headteacher's) about the nature of a governing body meeting. The notion of governors as visitors to whom hospitality is being extended seemed to prevail in all the meetings observed, although the scale of refreshment ranged from instant coffee and biscuits in one primary school, to pre-meeting drinks and fairly elaborate buffet-style suppers with wine at one comprehensive school.

In the latter case, the opportunity was being taken to display the skills of the home economics department, but the social style of the event seemed also to demonstrate the wish of the headteacher to coopt the governors into conviviality and accord. This governing body made the decision to open its meetings to the public, the only one of the eight governing bodies to do so during the research period. Once the public were entitled to be present, refreshments diminished to a token level, perhaps for fear that the sight of the governors partaking of supper would lessen their symbolic dignity as the representatives of those who came to observe.

As Figure 6.1 indicates, the governing bodies we studied varied considerably in size. Whether or not the governors sat round a table in formal committee fashion, or reclined in the shabby chairs of a well-used staffroom, was probably as much a function of the number of persons present and the availability of accommodation for them, as of the intention to conduct the meeting in a particular style. In Robart, where governing bodies were fairly small but each governor had armfuls of agenda papers to contend with, in the high school (Sanders) governors sat round a table in the school library, whereas in Carstairs First School they sat in a loose grouping of easy chairs, in the open-plan staffroom.

The timing of the meeting, perhaps even more than its venue and social style, embodied certain assumptions about the purpose and manner of school government. In cases where the local authority clerked the meeting, or sent officers or advisers to assist governors, the timing of the meeting no doubt chiefly reflected local authority assumptions about school government in the context of other educational responsibilities. (With the exception of the special school in Lorrenshire, all the governing bodies clerked by the local authority were held in the evening.) But where governors clerked their own meetings the timing of these events could reflect governors' own, sometimes strong, feelings about where the governing body stood in relation to the daily life of the school, and also in relation to governors' own life-style. In one governing body, governors found that a parent, elected to serve for two years, was unable to attend meetings at the time they were customarily held, in the morning. The governor resigned.

Whatever the social and physical setting of a meeting, it rests with the chairman to attempt to set the pace and style of the meeting itself. The eleven chairmen appointed to office in the eight governing bodies over the research period proved to have clear and sometimes idiosyncratic views about the appropriate length of a governing body meeting, views which they attempted to work to, whatever the number of items on the agenda. If the chairman's view was that the meeting should continue until each agenda item had been fully discussed, the meeting might last for four to five hours, or (as in one case) be held in two instalments of several hours each. If, however, the chairman's chief aim was to expedite and complete the business of the meeting, the agenda might be worked through, and the meeting brought to a close, in less than two hours. But governors, and in particular headteachers, had views of their own about the appropriate pace for their discussions, and although they could do little to speed up a leisurely chairman they could, and sometimes did, slow down a speedy one. One of the most flexible agenda items, so far as length of presentation and ensuing debate was concerned, was the headteacher's report. Figure 6.3 shows that in meetings of two governing bodies in Robart, with similar agenda, the time spent on the headteacher's report was the principal contributor to the differing lengths of the two meetings.

A study of the agenda of a governing body meeting can throw considerable light on the scope of governing body work, and we shall

*Figure 6.3* Comparison of time spent on agenda items at two governing body meetings in the same local authority, autumn term meeting, 1981

| Agenda item | Governing body of Sanders High School | Joint governing body of Carstairs First and Middle Schools |
|---|---|---|
| Election of chairman and vice-chairman | 2 mins | 6 mins |
| Minutes and matters arising | 6 mins | 8 mins |
| Clerk's report | 23 mins | 14 mins |
| Civic budget | 29 mins | 12 mins |
| Computing facilities in Robart schools | 20 mins | 11 mins |
| LEA proposal for trust fund for unofficial school fund | (inc. in HT's report) | 3 mins |
| Headteacher's report | 107 mins | First School 13, Middle School 14, 27 mins |
| Curriculum document (DES) | N/A* | 5 mins |
| Governor cooption | 12 mins | N/A |
| AOB | 1 min | 11 mins |
| | 3 hr 20 min | 1 hr 37 min |

* This document had been discussed by the governing body during the preceding term.

make further use of the agenda as a tool of analysis later in this chapter. But the life of a governing body cannot be adequately appraised on the basis of one meeting. Consideration must be given to the mode or modes of work which the governing body adopts.

## Modes of governing body work

Two main typifications of governing body mode of work – the continuous and the spasmodic – are suggested by our research experience. Differentiating features are not only the frequency or infrequency of meetings, but also the extent to which the governing body operates a division of labour.

The continuous governing body may be defined as one which meets regularly, as required by its Articles, once a term, but also shares a propensity to convene special, intervening full meetings to deal with particular matters, or discuss particular issues more fully. In addition, sub-groups of governors, nominated or elected by their peers for the purpose, meet in sub-committees or working parties to tackle particular tasks. For example a sub-committee of governors from Parker governing body worked on the validation of school-leavers' 'profiles', and two governors participated in a working party discussing a scheme to introduce worker-tutors to the school.

The visits which governors from a continuous governing body make to the school are not individual or *ad hoc* events, but part of a collective effort to keep the governing body informed about the school. A rota, or a transferable role of 'visiting governor', may be in operation, and the governing body receives a report on the visits made.

A spasmodic governing body, by contrast, comes to life only for the termly meeting. All the corporate work of the body is concentrated into that occasion, and in the four months which elapse between meetings governors may well forget that they are governors. Only the chairman is likely to have a sense of continuing role.

Figure 6.4 shows the number of full meetings each of the governing bodies held during the four school terms over which they were observed. The joint governing body of Carstairs First and Middle Schools during the research period exhibited a spasmodic mode of work. Many of its governors had no role between the termly meetings, and there was no intervening corporate activity. Parent governors kept in touch with headteachers, and occasionally debated issues with them in their capacity as governors, and the chairman made sporadic contact with headteachers and the LEA regarding the schools' many problems of repair and maintenance. But the other governors knew nothing of these activities unless and until they were reported at the termly governing body meeting. For the most part, parent governors' discussions with headteachers were *not* so reported.

*Figure 6.4*  Full meetings held by case-study governing bodies during a four-term period*

| | Town-meadow | Danes-hill | Hend-rick | Parker | San-ders | Car-stairs | Austen | Beck-ett |
|---|---|---|---|---|---|---|---|---|
| Number of meetings | 4 | 5 | 6 | 11 | 5 | 4 | 7 | 9 |

* Meetings reconvened on a second evening to complete outstanding business are counted as one meeting.

However, governing bodies, like schools themselves, pass through successive phases of institutional life. A new chairman, like a new headteacher, may seek to introduce a new mode of working. The institutionalised values of long-serving members may prove an obstacle to change, but if most of the governors are new to their task a hitherto spasmodic governing body may become a continuous one, or vice versa. In the case of Carstairs at the time of the research, members were in the process of adjusting to the departure of a long-serving, assiduous and expert chairman. The new chairman, and the mixture of 'new' and 'old' governors, had not yet established a mode of work which was satisfying for all parties.

Whether or not a governing body operates a division of labour might seem to be a direct function of the range of tasks which the Articles of Government require of the governors. If a governing body has wide responsibilities, one rational response is for groups of governors to specialise in particular tasks, such as staff appointments, reviewing cases of pupil non-attendance, and the like. But another response open to governing bodies is to delegate their responsibilities to the head-teacher. If the practice of delegation becomes institutionalised in a governing body with regard to particular tasks, new governors may not realise, unless they study the Articles with care, that the task is formally within the governing body's own remit. Several of the governing bodies we studied habitually delegated certain aspects of work to the head-teacher or chairman. Not infrequently, governors saw such delegation as essential, because meetings of their governing body were so widely spaced. The frequency of governing body meetings, whilst within the power of the governing body to change, is often linked to the clerking arrangements made by the local authority. We shall return to this point when discussing clerking later in the chapter, but before doing so, consideration must be given to the actual work with which governing bodies are faced.

**The substance of governing body work**

In continuing this chapter's attempt to open up the 'black box' of governing body functioning, we shall discuss the substance of governing body work under two main headings: tasks associated with the making of educational policy, and tasks concerned with various aspects of school management.

*Education policy-making*

Giving consideration to policy papers circulated by the LEA, or being consulted by the LEA in other ways, was an important part of the work of several governing bodies, sometimes taking up more governing body time than school-focused concerns. Yet the task of contributing to local education policy-making was not mentioned in any of the Articles of Government, nor is it referred to in the 1945 Model Articles, nor, indeed, in the Taylor Report. In some authorities the requirement to take and express a view on LEA policy and plans appears to have crept up on governing bodies, without making any official change to their longstanding terms of reference, which usually focus on the school. The Taylor Committee did in fact point out[3] that following the reorganisation of local government in 1974, developments in corporate management persuaded education departments that the existence of a wide constituency of citizens with special knowledge of the needs and interests of education would be no bad thing. It may be that LEAs which draw school governors into their consultative cycle concerning a wide range of educational policy issues are seeking to establish or conserve just such a constituency of potential supporters. If this is so, it can perhaps be assumed that authorities which do *not* ask school governors to comment upon policy matters do not feel the need of such a broadly-based group to support their interests, or do not see school governors as the basis for such a group. Certainly the shire county studied in the research did not seek governors' views on policy matters. By the range of tasks it required of governors, and the attitude it took regarding the resourcing of governing body work, this authority made it clear that Lorrenshire governing bodies were meant to be local and school-focused in their remit. They had no role to play in authority-wide educational concerns.

This requirement, or absence of requirement, to take a view on local education policy was perhaps the most fundamental difference we observed between governing bodies. Those governing bodies faced with the requirement in some cases found it a burden, reducing the energy and time available for school concerns. But some deprivation and frustration were undoubtedly experienced by governing bodies isolated from the policy-making process, and left to make what they could of their school-focused role, constrained by policy 'givens' which came out of the blue. Their view appeared to be that since so many of the parameters of school practice were subject to local and national decree, it was essential that governors should at least be made aware of, if not be enabled to discuss, the assumptions and objectives which underlay the more local of these constraints.

### School management

As a framework for analysis, three areas of school management can be identified: elaborating the objectives of the school; primary decisions which entail responsibility for such tasks of the school as the development of the curriculum and the distribution of resources; and secondary or support decisions concerning the day-to-day administration of the school such as timetabling, chasing up maintenance, keeping records, and the like. On the face of it the setting of objectives and the primary decisions are nearer the concerns of the governing body than are the secondary decisions. But when aspects of school management crop up on governing body agenda, in headteachers' reports or in governing body discussions, they are not neatly packaged as to area, with a reminder as to the parameters of governing body responsibility. In the course of a single meeting governors may raise, or respond to, issues which span these listed areas of concern, or where governing body responsibility is far from clear. The annotated agenda of two actual governing body meetings show the diversity of topic with which governing bodies were faced in practice (see Figures 6.5 and 6.6).

Figure 6.5 shows that the governing body of a high school, in the course of one meeting, switched repeatedly back and forth between *procedural concerns* (apologies for absence, welcome to a new governor, the accuracy of minutes, arrangements for ordinary and special meetings, opening meetings to the public); matters of *education policy*, both local and national (bilingualism, parents' access to pupil records, equal opportunities, an HMI survey, E2L teaching throughout the authority); *school objectives* (community school proposal and other future plans); *primary management concerns* involving the availability and distribution of resources (appointment of teachers, pupil roll, buildings and equipment, staff movement, staffing deficiencies); also the content of the curriculum (educational visits by pupils, report from the careers department); and *secondary management matters* concerning the day-to-day administration of the school (exclusions, burglaries, school lunches, visitors to the school). The governing body meeting in question lasted just under three hours.

For the joint governing body of adjacent infant and junior schools, Figure 6.6 shows a similar alternating focus of concern, but a narrower

*Figure 6.5* Annotated agenda for a meeting in March 1981, of the governing body of Beckett High School in Mead LEA

---

1. Apologies for absence
2. Welcome to new community governor
3. Report of joint committee for appointment of teachers
4. Minutes of the last meetings (ordinary meeting; special meeting)
5. Matters arising from the minutes (furniture; demolition of pavilion; bilingualism; unsatisfactory arrangement for special meeting)
6. Report of the headteacher
   (progress of proposal to offer community schooling; details of pupil roll; exclusions; staff movement and changes; buildings, furniture and fittings; burglaries; educational visits by pupils; visitors to the school; school lunches; report from the head of careers; future plans)
7. Reports from the Director of Education:
   (a) The advisability of opening children's records to their parents
   (b) Open government (opening governing body meetings to the public)
   (c) Equal opportunities for the sexes in the schools
   (d) 'Aspects of Secondary Education' (commentary on HMI survey)
8. English as a second language teaching
9. Time and date of next meeting
10. Other urgent business (teaching staff concern about staffing deficiencies; call for a special governing body meeting, to consider a report from a governors' working party)

---

range of subjects for consideration. Once again, there were *procedural concerns* (apologies for absence, the approval of minutes, their availability for parents, appointments of governors); *primary management concerns* (capitation, pupil rolls, staff movements, creation of a nursery class, special needs of the pupil population) and *matters of day-to-day administration* (school medicals, training courses, teaching practice, school events, visitors to the school, dogs in the playground, renovation work, progress of the governing bodies research). At this meeting, which lasted 2¼ hours, there was no reference to school objectives, but this governing body had discussed these on other occasions. The absence of any discussion of national or local education policy was, however, typical of all their meetings during the case-study period. As we have seen, Lorrenshire notified rather than consulted its governing bodies regarding policy changes (for example, the closure of a nursery school, which entered the scope of Townmeadow governing body's

*Figure 6.6*   Annotated agenda for a meeting in June 1981 of the joint governing body of Townmeadow Infant and Junior Schools, Lorrenshire

---

1. Apologies for absence
2. Minutes of the last meeting
3. Matters arising from minutes (capitation; dogs in playground; display of minutes on school notice boards)
4. Correspondence (all with the county council: two appointments of county council-nominated governors, refusal of funds for caretaker's telephone, addition of a nursery class to the infant school)
5. Report of the headteacher of the infant school
   (pupil roll and staff movement; school medicals; in-service training; governing bodies research; school building – renovation work; term events)
6. Matters arising from the report
7. Report of the headteacher of the junior school
   (school roll and staffing; status of school with regard to resource entitlement; student-teaching practice; parents' activities; school building and grounds; visits and courses; events; visitors; health; forthcoming events; representative governors)
8. Matters arising from the report
9. Nursery school
10. Any other business (Correspondence with the CEO regarding the status of the school (see 7 above). Report on the school governing bodies project)
11. Date and time of next meeting

---

concern only because it entailed the transfer of one of the nursery classes to the infant school), and the governors did not address themselves to educational issues beyond the sphere of their two schools.

Within the general sphere of school management, the two aspects[4] chiefly debated during the twentieth century regarding the role of county school governors have been the appointment of headteachers and other teaching staff, and the organisation and curriculum of the school.

## Appointment of headteachers

Since the 1944 Education Act there has been provision for some degree of governor involvement in the appointment of headteachers, but the question of balance between governing body and education authority opinion has remained open. The 1945 Model Articles suggested two possibilities: one gave advantage to the governors in the shortlisting procedure, and to the education authority in the final appointment process; the other was for a joint committee of (possibly equal numbers of) governors and representatives of the LEA, chaired by a nominee of the LEA, to shortlist, interview and recommend for appointment.

No indication was given in the 1945 Model Articles of what role if any was to be played by officers of the authority, as opposed to elected members. The Taylor Committee, however, in their consideration of procedures for headteacher appointments, clearly differentiated between the executive role of governors and the education authority in the persons of education committee members, and the professional advisory role of the director and his advisers.

The Taylor Committee recommended the equal representation of governors and representatives of the LEA on a small selection committee, to be chaired by a member of the education committee. The selection committee 'should make the greatest possible use of professional guidance and advice from the chief education officer and his staff', and would be helped by 'having available to it the experience and knowledge of the school acquired by the authority's advisers', and possibly also the advice of professionals outside the authority's service.[5] Taylor did not, however, stipulate the exact role to be played by the selection committee in the sequence of shortlisting and interviews.

In the four authorities studied, the procedures laid down in Articles of Government regarding the appointment of headteachers differed chiefly in the emphasis placed on the role of chairman of governors, and in whether or not teacher governors might participate in the processes of selection and appointment. The appointment of a new headteacher is an infrequent event in the life of any school, and only one such appointment was made during our case studies – this was to the headship of the voluntary aided primary school, and was of course an appointment into the employ of the governing body, rather than the LEA. Two governors (the chairman and an LEA representative, who also acted as clerk to the governing body) met with three advisers (two from Stapleton LEA and one from the Diocesan Board) to draw up a shortlist. Two candidates were selected for interview, at which all the governors and the three advisers were present. First the governors, and then the advisers, questioned the candidates. Throughout the whole process one candidate appeared to be favoured by the advisers. After some discussion governors unanimously supported and appointed this candidate. The overall impression was that the factor chiefly influencing the governors' decision was the view of the Diocesan Board adviser.

Morgan *et al.*, in their recent study of the processes of headteacher selection and appointment, suggest that at present headteacher selection is more of an exercise in group power relations than a systematic assessment procedure to which participant groups each bring their expertise.[6] Our own empirical experience is too slender for us to support or dispute this assertion, but the detailed wording of the various Articles of Government, on the subject of headteacher appointments, certainly conveys the impression that a balance of power between interested parties is at issue, rather than a selection process which identifies the needs of the particular institution, and the relevant qualities of the candidates.

Although headteacher appointments are infrequent, other staff appointments are less so, and a discussion of this aspect of a governing body's role in school management can be more adequately illustrated from our research experience.

### Appointment of other teaching staff

Where 'assistant masters' (as they were then designated) were concerned, the 1945 Model Articles envisaged that these appointments should be made by the governors in consultation with the headmaster. The Taylor Committee recommended that the selection of deputy heads and other teachers should rest with the governing body, who should determine their preferred selection procedure. Due weight was however to be given to the professional advice made available through the LEA. One suggested procedure was for the chairman, or his nominee, to interview with the headteacher and appropriate members of the teaching staff and the authority's professional advisers. But it was stressed that the governing body 'should retain the power to change these arrangements for delegation and play a more active role if at any time they had reason for disquiet about how the procedure was working.'[7]

A further view of the Taylor Committee was that it would be inappropriate for any member of staff (or, indeed, any headteacher) to be involved in the appointment of his or her successor. This point was of course apposite because of the Committee's recommendation that teachers and headteachers should be eligible to serve as governors, a possibility which the 1945 Model Instrument had explicitly ruled out.

Articles of Government in the authorities studied showed some variation in procedures, but did not always accurately describe what actually occurred with regard to the appointment of assistant teachers during the case-study period. Figure 6.7 gives the terms of the Articles. In practice (and by a decision of the education committee which had not

*Figure 6.7*  Appointment of assistant teachers

| Lorrenshire | Stapleton | Robart | Mead |
| --- | --- | --- | --- |
| LEA transmits the names of candidates to governors. Governors, in consultation with the headteacher, appoint teachers to the service of the LEA, subject to confirmation by the LEA. | For any posts above Scale 1, governors consider applications, and after consultation with the headteacher and the authority's inspectors, select one candidate for nomination to appointment. | Council transmits the names of candidates to governors. Governors recommend one candidate for appointment by the council. | Scale 4 and above (including deputy headteachers): Chairman of governors, with the Director of Education and the headteacher, draws up a short list. A joint committee of governors and representatives of the education committee, advised by officers, make appointments in the same way as for headteachers.<br><br>    Scale 3 and below: Teachers appointed by the Director of Education in consultation with the headteacher, acting under delegated powers from the education committee. Appointments reported, for information, to appropriate governing bodies. |

yet been incorporated into revised Articles), governors in Robart were only involved in the appointment of deputy headteachers (in which appointment procedures they were represented by the chairman of governors). All other assistant teacher appointments were notified to them *post hoc* in the headteacher's next report to the governing body. In Lorrenshire too, so far as the schools studied were concerned, responsibilities with regard to teacher appointments were customarily delegated to the headteacher, or jointly to the headteacher, chairman and one or two others.

In Mead the joint committee procedure for the appointment of 'Scale 4 and above' teachers was however in regular use, and in Stapleton all categories of governor from Parker governing body participated in the interviewing of candidates for posts above Scale 1 and decided appointments, votes being taken in some cases. At this school, a disjunction was experienced between the pre-interview procedures, when candidates visited the school, met teaching staff and discussed the educational philosophy of the school, and the actual appointment by governors, including lay governors, who had not always been made aware of the impressions the candidates had made on the headteacher and staff at the preliminary meeting.

Since 1945 some caveats on governors' rights to appoint assistant teachers have always been included in Articles of Government. The right of the authority to appoint from a pool of new entrants, or to redeploy assistant teachers already in the service of the authority, has always been preserved. More recently (for example in Articles of Government for Mead and Stapleton drawn up in 1974 and 1982, respectively) these caveats have been extended to the appointment of headteachers. These Articles stipulate that in special circumstances governors may be required to agree to the appointment of a headteacher returning to the service of the LEA after secondment, or being redeployed due to reorganisation or closure of a school, or be required to nominate a headteacher from a list of such headteachers. In fact, during a period of contraction in the education service (due to falling rolls and government policies) such as coincided with the case-study period, the potential role of governors in teacher appointments was in fact necessarily diminished by the lack of teacher movement and the diminution of available posts.

In summary, this discussion has shown that the responsibilities of governors with regard to the appointment of headteachers and other teaching staff have never been authoritatively determined on a nationwide basis. Governors in one authority's county schools may be regularly drawn into the onerous and responsible task of staff selection and appointment, whereas in another authority only the chairman of governors will have any part to play, and this only in the rare circumstance of the appointment of a head or deputy head. Variation of this kind, in a potentially important area of governing body work, does nothing to clarify a generalisable definition of governing body functions.

We turn now to the other area of governors' responsibility in important aspects of school management which has remained in a state of uncertainty over many years – the governors' role in the organisation and curriculum of the school.

## Governors and the curriculum

Even more than in the area of staff appointments governors' understanding of their intended role with regard to the curriculum of the school has been obfuscated by vague and imprecise phrases in official documents. The 1945 Model Articles attributed to the governors the 'general direction of the conduct and curriculum of the school' and stipulated that 'all proposals and reports affecting the conduct and curriculum of the school shall be submitted formally to the governors.'

More recently the term 'oversight' has tended to replace 'general direction' of the conduct and curriculum, in Articles of Government. The Taylor Committee made a sustained attempt to operationalise these vague responsibilities in terms of identifiable tasks for governors, and administrative procedures to be undertaken by education authorities, which included the strengthening and training of an adequate advisory service, including general advisers who would 'be available for consultation with, and report to, the governing body on request'.[8] Governors, the Taylor Committee recommended, should have responsibility for setting the aims of the school, and in doing so should give consideration to constructive suggestions made by any individuals or organisations with a concern for the school's welfare. Subsequent recommendations by the Committee (about the headteacher's formulation of plans for pursuing the aims adopted, the governors' delineation of guidelines, rules and sanctions regarding behaviour in school, governors' visits to classes at work, and their guidance to the headteacher regarding the aspects of school life on which information is required, and the form in which they require it) were all similarly hedged about with qualifications regarding the policy of the LEA and the need to negotiate and consult with teachers at every stage. The evidence submitted to the Taylor Committee had, it is clear, impressed them with the 'minefield' nature of governor exploration of the curriculum. Nevertheless, the recommendations conclude with two unequivocal proposals: every governing body should produce a first general appraisal of the school's progress, however incomplete, within four years of its formation. These appraisals should henceforward be made periodically, short reports on them being sent to the LEA by the governing body of every school.[9]

Bacon, in his account of school board democracy in Sheffield,[10] makes much of teacher reluctance to open up the 'secret garden' of the curriculum, and even suggests the headteachers were disturbed by the requirement that 'there shall be full consultation at all times between the headteacher and the chairman of governors', although this requirement dated from the 1945 Model Articles. Our own research suggests that some of the ideas discussed by Taylor have found their way into school and governing body practice, but that for each governing body the balance of governor involvement in, and knowledge of, the curriculum is negotiated anew between each new headteacher, group of governors or chairman, and can thus be a function of the phase of institutional life of the school or of the governing body itself. In particular the 'information system for governors', envisaged by Taylor, has taken the form of headteacher reports to the governing body which are dramatically different in different schools. Before turning to the discussion of these reports, however, some indication will be given of the extent to which the governing bodies we studied attempted to concern themselves with curriculum matters.

For all the governing bodies there seemed to be some problem in finding an accepted and effective way for the curriculum to be discussed between professionals and the lay governors. At two of the schools, some members of the joint governing body had in the past taken part with teachers in establishing the schools' aims, including the aims of the curriculum, but more recent governing body meetings rarely tackled curricular issues. In another governing body, the requirement to formulate a booklet of information for parents was being used by governors as a way into the discussion of organisation and curriculum with the headteacher. At the special school, the curriculum was treated as a matter for the professionals. Nevertheless, governors expressed a wish to understand, and possibly influence, the underlying objectives of the school, and linked this with a request to the headteacher to give them a systematic account of the school's organisation and curriculum. In four other schools (two of which had a joint governing body) governors seemed content to delegate all their responsibilities in this area to the headteacher, and leave it to him or her to inform them of such developments as might seem of interest. Nevertheless, *outside* the governing body meetings individual governors from some of these schools sometimes tackled the headteacher on particular curricular issues, and it can be inferred that some of the unease which governors seemed to feel about the sensitivity of the curriculum as a subject for discussion was linked with the committee nature of the governing body meeting, and the difficulty of raising issues or asking questions in a way which did not put the headteacher at a disadvantage in the presence of colleagues and a mixed group of laity.

At Carstairs, it was of interest that the only curricular aspects which governors jointly discussed at any length were fringe items provided in recognition of ethnic minorities in the pupil population (e.g. optional Gujerati). None of the governors was from an ethnic minority group, and this may have absolved them from the feeling that they were trying in any way to interfere in or influence their own children's education and progress when they discussed the more culturally specialised aspects of the curriculum. Alternatively, these topics may have seemed of more intrinsic interest than the more familiar and traditional subjects.

At two of the governing bodies the curriculum was not a 'no-go area'. At Beckett, where the possibility of giving offence was not seen as an inhibiting factor, turbulent discussion of organisational aspects of the curriculum took place. In this case it seemed to be the open expression of differences of professional opinion (between head and teaching staff) which encouraged the participation of lay governors in the discussion.

Parker was the governing body which appeared to approximate most closely to the ideals of those who favour new voices in the curriculum debate. Politico-parent governors in particular exhibited considerable interest in the curriculum, and governors made systematic visits to various subject departments in the school, reporting back to the governing body on these. These lay initiatives were counterbalanced by the regular and copious supply to the governing body of high-quality papers prepared by the teaching professionals, detailing the organisation and teaching of the school.

An issue which can be seen as a test case of the balance of influence between lay and professional opinion on a curricular matter was when the school discontinued preparation and entry for English literature 'O' level. Governors were not consulted about this decision. When they learned of it one LEA governor, whose children attended the school, proposed that this 'O' level option be reintroduced. However, debate on the matter concluded with a narrow majority vote supporting the judgement of the teaching professionals. It had already been made clear by the clerk that governors only had oversight of the curriculum, that the headteacher exercised control, and that even if the governors' vote went in favour of the 'O' level option it would not automatically be reintroduced, although the head would convey governors' feelings to staff.

Whether or not governors aspired positively to influence the curricular principles or practice of the school, all the case-study governing bodies were regularly informed by the headteacher about diverse aspects of school life, and for the most part these reports went beyond the legal minimum required of them.

Following the 1944 Act, the 1945 Model Articles did not require any regular rendering of account to the governing body by the head of the

normal running of the school. Only proposals and reports *affecting**
the conduct and curriculum of the school were required to be submitted
formally to governors. Examples of Articles revised in the 1970s
diminish this requirement, stipulating only that all *major** changes
affecting the school shall be reported to the governors, but additionally
state that 'the governors shall receive annually, and at such times as may
be deemed necessary, the report of the headteacher on the organisation,
curriculum and estimates of expenditure of his school.'[11]

Whether or not the Articles require it, it does now seem to be general
practice for headteachers to make a report to governors at each termly
meeting of the governing body. As in many other fields of governing
body activity, case-study experience revealed a wide range of interpretations of this practice. Several of the headteachers appeared to be
aiming for factual reports, dealing with factors conditioning the work of
the school, such as staff and pupil numbers, and the state of the school
premises. School events, mainly of a public nature, such as concerts,
were frequently listed. The chief differentiating features of this type of
report were usually the length of the account, and the style in which it
was couched. One head favoured a marked informality, even intimacy
of style, in his account of teacher and pupil activities. By contrast
another headteacher's reports, within the same factual genre, were in
the manner of a formal summarising review by a manager, acknowledg-
ing the contributory work of his supporting staff.

All these factual reports were, of course, selective in the items they
included, but other types of reports to governors were more obviously
adopting and promoting a particular point of view. One head, in
itemising many forms of professional activity with regard to all aspects
of school life, was obviously at pains to stress the professional nature of
school process, and to point out that within the school all policy-making
was the product of structured staff participation in decision-making
and evaluation exercises. At another school, the headteacher's reports
were openly polemical, taking a particular line and spelling out the
justification for it. These reports, unlike most others, seemed to be
addressed equally to the staff and lay governors.

Together with the other agenda papers, the mere reading of the more
lengthy headteachers' reports constituted a sizeable task for some
governors. But, as we saw in Figure 6.3, the oral presentation of the
report at a meeting was sometimes a lengthy event in itself. Alternatively,
a head might say that he or she had nothing to add to the written report,
and leave it to the governors to pursue or pass over the items it
contained. In the governing body where brief written reports had only

* our emphasis.

just begun to be supplied by the new headteacher, earlier oral reports had themselves been brief.

Despite the variation *between* governing bodies with regard to the style, content and presentation of the headteacher's report, considerable consistency was experienced *within* each governing body over the period of research observation. Governing bodies knew what to expect from their own headteacher, by way of a report, and the space which the chairman would give to its presentation and discussion could usually also be confidently predicted. But, like the wide variation in the part played by governing bodies in teacher appointments, the extreme variation in the type and apparent purpose of the information formally provided to the governing body makes any generalisation about governing bodies' knowledge of their schools impossible. Two of the case-study LEAs made no attempt to encourage any standardisation or similarity of coverage as between headteachers' reports in the authority, but one LEA had sent a letter to all headteachers, a copy of which was distributed to all governors, asking them to cover a particular range of items. Yet, of the two sets of reports in that authority studied in the research, one was polemical and the other factual, facing the two governing bodies with completely different assessment tasks. In this, as in many other areas of governing body activity, it was evident that headteachers were able to exercise a considerable degree of discretion, and the governing body had to negotiate a responsive role within the circumstances with which they were faced.

In 1977 the Taylor Committee, as we noted earlier, had envisaged periodic formal appraisals of schools by their governing bodies. This idea does not appear to have found favour either at central government or local authority level, but a number of authorities had begun to promote regular *self*-evaluation schemes by the schools by the beginning of the 1980s. Lorrenshire and Mead had introduced such schemes, but the 'turn' of the case-study schools in these authorities to evaluate themselves did not come round during the research period, so the role of governors in such a procedure was not observed in practice. Robart did not have an evaluatory scheme in operation, but Stapleton required its county schools to carry out a self-audit. Parker, in this authority, had an elaborate and stringently pursued procedure for evaluating each of its departments in turn. Governors had no role in the preparation of these review reports, but the reports themselves, which explored the strengths and weaknesses of each department in some detail, were made available to them. However, these reports never became the basis for sustained governing body discussion, although individual governors used them as information sources before any subsequent visit to the department in question.

Although the controversial issues of staff appointments and curriculum did not prove to be central items of concern for most of the case-study governing bodies, one other primary area of school management came to governing body attention in two of the schools during the research period. This was the question of operating as a community school. Whatever the sphere of responsibility of governors defined by particular Articles, it remains the right of the LEA to determine the place of the school in the education system. But two of the schools, in two different authorities, were making a bid to get the LEA to agree to a change of role which would enable education to be offered to a wider population over extended hours. The differing way in which this initiative had been handled by the two headteachers would make a case study in itself, but from the point of view of both governing bodies it was evident that the issue was one in which teaching staff attitudes, and the availability of resources, were fundamental to any decision. The governing body could do little more than test the strength of professional convictions about proposals, and then give these their support. In one case, professional opinion was divided. The governing body did not attempt to adjudicate, but referred the matter back for further staff discussion, and was eventually by-passed in further debate, the matter being directly resolved by negotiation between the school and the LEA.

In this, as in the other primary areas of school management already discussed, it can be seen that governing body participation was strongly influenced by the professional dimension, as discussed in Chapter 5.

Despite the fact that governors seemed to find only a minimal part to play in primary aspects of school management, the majority of case-study governing body meetings were clearly school-focused, and it was with the secondary aspects of school management – day-to-day administration, the maintenance of school premises, and the like – that these governing bodies spent time.

That governors spent time on these issues does not necessarily mean that their role was any more executive than for primary management matters. One governing body, throughout the research period, was dominated by concern about defects in the maintenance, repair and caretaking of the school premises. The governing body in question was a joint one, and the adjoining premises of both schools were in a similar state of disrepair. Governors shared a mutual concern about building deterioration, but for most of them their role was confined to 'witnessing' the exchanges between headteachers, chairman and clerk. This role, although not active, was nevertheless valuable as it put these exchanges on an official footing and ensured that they became a matter of public record through their inclusion in the minutes. Meanwhile, actual activity concerning the problems, in the form of correspondence, chairman's visits to the office, school site inspections, and disciplinary enquiries by the LEA, all went on outside the meeting.

This was also the case for other aspects of school administration, such as the closure of a school kitchen, the presence of dogs in the playground, etc. which came to the attention of some of the governing bodies, and it may be that an infrequently convened committee can do little more than receive an account of how such matters have been pursued on their behalf by some of their members since the last meeting. If this is so, it is important to note whether all or only some governors have an active role to play between meetings. Where school administration matters required a response from the LEA in the form of resources or a change of decision, in spasmodic governing bodies these were solicited by the chairman and/or the headteacher; but in a continuous governing body were more likely to involve a deputation of governors.

In this discussion of the substance of governing body work we have paid only slight attention to the role of the governing body in mediating between the interests of the school, community and LEA, although we have indicated that in these exchange relationships the teaching professionals usually held a position of strength. What it meant for governors to represent one of these categories of interest will be discussed in more detail in Chapter 7. Meanwhile, we turn to the question of what record is made of a governing body's work.

## How governing body views are determined and recorded

In their discussion of 'procedural arrangements for the new governing bodies', the Taylor Committee imply that there will be a procedural outcome from governing body meetings, possibly in the form of 'resolutions or recommendations which require specific consideration by the authority'.[12] However, they do not formally recommend that this shall be the case, nor suggest by what means the governing body should determine what *is* its corporate view on any matter. The question of whether or not votes should be taken, for example, is not touched on. The Education (School Governing Bodies) Regulations 1981, do however appear to imply that taking a vote will be the normal method for a governing body to decide any question coming before it (para. 11(2) and (3)(c) ).

As in many other matters, the governing bodies exhibited a wide variety of practice on the question of how views were determined and recorded. Nevertheless, their practice showed internal consistency over a range of topics in that if a governing body did not regularly clarify the strength of various points of view by the taking of a vote they almost *never* did so, however controversial the topics, whereas in other governing bodies taking a vote was the customary way of concluding one item and moving on to the next.

Similarly, while some governing bodies seemed to feel unable to move on to next business until a suitably worded resolution had been framed or at least adumbrated for subsequent wording by the clerk and/or chairman, other governing bodies made no use of this form of words. The 'resolution', as a procedural outcome, does of course seem to emphasise a governing body's link with the LEA, to whom its resolutions are invariably addressed. (No governing body ever framed a resolution which seemed to require specific consideration by, for example, the teaching staff of the school.) It was perhaps not surprising that a governing body like Townmeadow, which was not clerked by the LEA and had little contact with the authority, did not record its views in the form of resolutions, but rather noted what action, if any, the governing body proposed to take on its own behalf.

It is a requirement of the 1981 Regulations (para. 11(5)) that all meetings of the governing body of a school shall be formally minuted. All the governing bodies complied with this requirement whatever their clerking arrangements, and these minutes were one tangible product of the meeting's activity. From August 1981 it was required by statute that such minutes should be readily available for inspection by teachers or other employees of the school, parents of pupils or pupils themselves (School Governing Bodies Regulations 1981, para. 12(1)). The type of account given by minutes varied considerably, however. In minutes prepared by one of the governors, evaluatory comments about 'nebulous' letters from the CEO, or education officers 'passing the buck' might be found, whereas minutes prepared by clerks from the LEA were dispassionately worded, unless a formal resolution incorporated an expression of governing body judgement: 'Governors deplored . . .' etc.

### Resources available to the governing body by way of clerking, advice and information

Our discussion of some of the procedural detail of governing body operation has already indicated that governing bodies were differentially resourced by authorities; and within the authorities, resources in some cases varied according to the type of school. Voluntary aided schools in any authority have to clerk their own governing bodies, but in Lorrenshire, county primary schools also had to do so, whereas secondary and special schools were clerked by the LEA. The Taylor Committee had, as in many other matters, been divided in their views as to whether LEA clerks for school governing bodies were desirable, but on balance considered that 'the force of the arguments for central clerking[were] . . . outweighed by the advantages of a local appointment' (of the school secretary, one of the governors, or someone living locally) to clerk the governing body.[13] One of the suggested advantages of 'local' clerking was the greater independence of the governing body and we have seen that minutes prepared by governors themselves were sometimes more freely worded than those drafted by local authority clerks. But research observation of self-clerked governing bodies revealed many disadvantages inherent in the practice, not least the distancing from the LEA which might ensue. Especially in large rural counties, it seems that local authority policy not to clerk its school governing bodies is likely to be accompanied by a propensity to by-pass governing bodies when communicating or consulting with the schools. In a large authority with many schools, LEA representative governors are less likely to be elected members of council, and the self-clerked governing body may find itself out of touch with both the education committee and the education department.

One of the chief arguments against LEA clerking of school governing bodies is its cost. Although the Taylor Committee appeared to envisage that 'local' clerks would be paid, those governors who acted as clerks to case-study governing bodies (of Townmeadow and Hendrick Schools) did so without financial reward. But one of the case-study authorities (Robart) appeared to have come to the conclusion that money spent on its governing bodies was money well spent. Not only did they provide a minutes clerk for all governing bodies, but also an officer of the education department to attend the meeting, give a clerk's report from the LEA, and advise the governing body on matters of policy and procedure. This authority was also unstinting in its supply of relevant documentation to governors, another aspect of governing body resourcing which varied considerably between authorities. One of the principal differences in this respect was whether the headteacher's report to the governors was circulated with the agenda papers so that it could be studied in advance of the meeting, or whether it was cyclostyled in the school and tabled at the meeting.*

Clerking and resourcing of governing body meetings cannot be adequately discussed without having regard to the frequency with which the governing body meets. The 1945 Model Articles specified that governors should hold a meeting once in every school term, but a majority of the Taylor Committee recommended that governing body meetings should be held at least twice in every term.[14] Several members of the Committee disagreed with this recommendation, however, taking the view that any increase in governing body activity could well be through the work of sub-committees, specialist panels or working parties, and that the frequency of full governing body meetings should be determined by local circumstances and needs. This view appears to

* In justice, it must be stated that in some cases this may have been a function of headteacher preparedness and preference, rather than of LEA policy.

have prevailed when the 1981 School Governing Bodies Regulations were drawn up, para. 10(1) requiring that 'the governing body of a school shall hold a meeting at least once in every term'.

Some local authorities (including Robart) link their resourcing of governing bodies to what they see as the once a term meeting norm. Clerking and resourcing for any additional meetings convened by the governors have to be negotiated on an *ad hoc* basis. Other authorities (including Mead) take the view that if the business of a meeting is not completed in one evening, the reconvened regular meeting will be clerked, but if governors call special additional meetings they must clerk these themselves. Both statutory requirements and local authority policy therefore may tend to reinforce the notion that governing bodies can adequately fulfil their role by meeting three times a year. Unless governing bodies resist this assumption, either by convening additional meetings or by maintaining the continuous life of the body through working parties or sub-committees, the opportunities for governors to build up a sense of meaningful corporate activity are slender indeed.

**How the 'product' of governing body meetings is processed and organised**
As already noted, one obligatory product of a governing body meeting is a set of minutes. But resolutions and requests recorded in the minutes may call for a response, usually from the LEA. It is therefore vital to the understanding of how a governing body works to know how the outcome of its deliberations is administratively handled by the LEA. Can governors have confidence that they are not beating the air?

As we saw in Chapter 3, much depends on whether the department has a clerking section within it, with employees whose full-time role it is to clerk a number of governing bodies. If so, and if clerks are allocated to the regular service of particular governing bodies, it is likely that governing body correspondence, both internal and external to the department, will be handled by that clerk, who will also bring the governing body's wishes and enquiries to the attention of relevant officers. Such a clerk can be a point of reference for all governors between meetings, and can to some extent mitigate the spasmodic nature of some governing bodies' existence.

But whether or not the specific requests or enquiries of governing bodies are pursued by an identifiable employee of the LEA, the destination of the minutes as a whole is a matter of import. Authorities have varying policies as to whether governing body minutes are sent to education committee members, schools sub-committee members and/or senior officers of the authority. Figure 6.8 shows how governing body work was resourced and processed in the four authorities studied.

*Figure 6.8* The processing and promotion of governing body matters in the case-study LEAs

| | Lorrenshire | Stapleton | Robart | Mead |
|---|---|---|---|---|
| **Minute clerk for governing body meetings:** | | | | |
| primary | x | √ | √ | √ |
| secondary | √ | √ | √ | √ |
| Officer presence at governing body meetings | x (except for governing bodies of special schools) | x | √ | x |
| Adviser present at governing body meetings | x | x | x | x |
| Clerking section, with full-time governing body clerks | x | √ | √ | √ |
| Senior education officers see governing body minutes | variable | √ | √ | √ |
| Education Committee see governing body minutes | x | x | √ | √ |
| Parents' consultative committee convened by LEA | x | √ | x | x |
| Meetings of governing body chairmen convened by LEA | x | √ | x | √ |
| Standing committee on school governing bodies (elected members and teacher representatives) | x | x | √ | x |

Whilst most of the processing of governing body products, if it occurs at all, is a matter for the administrative arm of the LEA, some authorities also take steps to encourage continuing interest by elected members in the role of governing bodies. One such form might be a working party on school governing bodies, formally constituted each year from members of the education committee, and convened when developments require it. A more regular form of elected member involvement might be the chairing of a parents' consultative committee, or a joint meeting of chairmen of governors. Such gatherings, as their names imply, bring together particular categories of governors, on an authority-wide basis, in the presence of senior members of the education committee. The apparent purpose of all such LEA practices is to ensure that governing body interests and potential are not lost sight of as the work of the education committee proceeds, and that some governors have an opportunity both to contact their peers in other governing bodies and also to be kept in touch with local issues of education policy in a more direct way than through the receipt of policy documents. A by-product of these practices may also be to enlarge and strengthen the education lobby within the local authorities as a whole.

Discussion in this chapter, exemplified from our own research and from the slender recent literature on school governing bodies, has shown that these bodies are far from uniform. Central and local government requirements provide some marker-posts for their composition, scope of concern and procedures, but within the boundaries delimited by Acts of Parliament, Regulations, and Instruments and Articles of Government, school governing bodies continue to demonstrate widely differing forms. The purposes they appear or attempt to serve for LEA, school or local community are diverse. In Chapter 7 we examine the range of purposes which school governors envisaged for their work, and discuss the potential and actual contribution of the several categories of governor to the means and ends of school government.

### Notes and references

1. The Taylor Committee had suggested that if some governors were specifically chosen to represent local community interests, there would no longer be a need for 'minor authority' representatives serving a similar purpose. DES, *A New Partnership for our Schools* (Taylor Report), HMSO, 1977, para. 4.10. However, the 1980 Education Act did not, in the event, require the appointment of community representatives, but did require the inclusion of at least one 'minor authority' governor on the governing bodies of relevant primary schools.
2. In his account of Sheffield governing bodies, Bacon states that the majority of parent governor appointments were uncontested, and vacancies frequently persisted. Bacon, A.W., *Public Accountability and the Schooling System*, Harper & Row, 1978.
3. Taylor Report, para. 2.15.
4. A third aspect about which there has recently been some debate concerns an enlargement of governing bodies' role with regard to school finance. This debate was not a live issue in any of the authorities studied in the research. In one of the four authorities (Robart) governors were asked to comment on the education budget as a whole, but none of the authorities was experimenting with the decentralisation of decisions about individual budgets to headteacher and governing body. In the governing bodies studied, no discussion about capitation was included in headteachers' reports or other material supplied to governors. At most, governors were given retrospective information on the allocation of capitation to different departments in the school. In the voluntary aided school, where governors had responsibility for certain aspects of school expenditure, this was seen as a formal function of approval.

5. Taylor Report, para. 8.11.
6. Morgan, C., Hall, V. and Mackay, H., *The Selection of Secondary Head Teachers*, Open University Press, 1983.
7. Taylor Report, para. 8.13.
8. Ibid., para. 6.42a.
9. These, and other recommendations of the Taylor Committee, are listed in Appendix III.
10. Bacon, *op. cit.*
11. Articles of Government in Mead local authority, 1970s and 1980s revision.
12. Taylor Report, para. 11.10.
13. Ibid., para. 11.17.
14. Ibid., para. 11.6.

# 7 The governors

Governing schools is a corporate activity. The authority of the governing body resides in its group identity.[1] Nevertheless, the individual governors who together make up a governing body bring to it a variety of attitudes and attributes, which in combination, give each governing body its particular character and quality of corporate life. In this chapter we therefore shift our focus from the school governing body to the school governor.

## Governors' expectations and experience of governing body membership

In attempting to elucidate what it may mean to individuals to be a school governor it is necessary first to establish what they impute to the governing body by way of standing and purpose.

One of the fundamental points on which governors did not appear to have arrived at a collective view was whether the governing body was external to and separate from the school, peripherally attached to it, or integral to it. The assumption most frequently made was that the governing body, whilst at the periphery of the school, was nevertheless a part of it, but this assumption was not consistently held, in that some of the things which governors thought the governing body ought to be able to do entailed a different relationship with the school.

Among the functions which governors severally identified as appropriate for the governing body were those of: influencing education; supporting the school; calling the school to account; calling the LEA to account; being a channel for communication between community and school, community and LEA, or school and LEA; and mediating between interests. So far as governors' personal purposes in undertaking the role of school governor were concerned, these might be coterminous with one or more of these corporate functions. For example, a governor might individually aspire to have a say in education, or to support the school, as well as seeing these as appropriate functions for the governing body as a whole. But, in some instances, governors took part in school government for purposes separate from those which the body as a whole might fulfil. They sought to promote, or at least protect, the interests of a particular constituency, or they undertook the role of school governor as a civic duty, perhaps one among many. Alternatively, they might see the role as an opportunity to learn more about education, or even about local government in general.

Some of the activities in which governors took part outside the governing body meeting, either in support of their personal interpretation of the role or to further the corporate functions of the governing body, are discussed later in this chapter. But first the question must be asked: Where did all these ideas about school government come from?

When accepting nomination, a new governor might be guided chiefly by personal values, and these would continue to colour his or her interpretation of, and perseverance in, the governor role. But we have already seen that local authorities and schools have ways of promoting particular images of school government. At least by the time the first meeting was attended some indication of the local authority's view of school government would have been conveyed by the tone of the letter of appointment, the terms of the Instrument and Articles of Government, and the interpretation placed on these by the authority's handbook of guidelines for governors, if any. From these, the perceptive governor might already have become aware of some of the unresolved conflicts in the authority's approach to school government. For example, in a welcoming letter to new governors, the chief officer of Stapleton stressed that 'what matters above all else [in school government] is the good of the school', but by page 8 of the governors' handbook, the governor was being urged to see schools as partners in an education service for the whole community. Authority policy was spelled out, to the effect that individual schools and other educational establishments were not perceived as separate and self-contained institutions, but as part of a wider education service: 'initiatives designed to achieve this purpose are encouraged and supported'.

Formal training was another way in which governors' expectations might be influenced by the authority. But although some form of training was intermittently available in all the case-study authorities, the voluntary nature of attendance, coupled with the episodic programming of provision, made training a hit-or-miss affair: very few of the governors interviewed had attended any kind of training event, and none had completed a systematic course.

As noted in Chapter 6, the principal ways in which the schools', or at least the headteachers' views of school government were conveyed to governors, were through the coverage and style of the headteachers' reports, and the ways in which governors were invited to, and received at, the school.

But it was the governing body meeting itself which had the greatest potential for corporate socialisation of the new governor, a socialisation into the unspoken rules of the game for that particular governing body. Custom and practice, by way of delegation of particular tasks by the governing body to the headteacher, might have altered the functions of the governing body out of all recognition from those outlined in the Articles of Government. Or the new governor, approaching the role with the intention of 'keeping her head down' for a meeting or two, might encounter a style of chairmanship which expected and exacted instant participation from all members of the body.

Notions both of corporate and individual purpose might, then, be gradually or rapidly amended by the various stages of induction to the governor role. The role interpretations of individual governors in the various governing bodies bore some family resemblance to those of their fellow governors, whatever their category of nomination. Nevertheless, in surveying the activities in which governors took part, some forms of participation were more commonly found among particular categories of governor.

**Governors' activities outside the meeting of the corporate body**
The principal activities to be discussed here are the symbolic representation of the governing body by governors attending school functions, and governors' visits to the school.

*Attendance at functions*
The concept of symbolic representation has already been mentioned in Chapter 2. Since governing bodies are not distinguished by flags or regalia, the most overt symbol of their participation in school life is perhaps the reservation of seats for them at school functions. Members of the case-study governing bodies were regularly – and in most cases formally – invited to a variety of school functions. Teacher governors tended to see themselves as tacit exceptions to these general invitations, and no teacher governor was observed to sit with other governors at a school function, although at least one non-teaching staff governor did. At one school, parent governors felt the designation of special seats to be undesirably élitist, and hence excused themselves from the only symbolic representation of their membership available to them, but most governors accepted their VIP treatment without comment, despite the fact that they had no role to play in the proceedings. The practice seemed to be a hangover from the earlier tradition of governors' prizegivings, long superseded in all the schools (except the voluntary aided school, where the final prizegiving took place during our research, before being phased out).

This somewhat trivial point of seat reservation has seemed worth enlarging upon because of its symbolic quality. For the most part, the role of a school governor in the early 1980s was either a working or a ritual one, but it did not confer glory. Only those candidates in local elections who included in their election material mention of being 'governor of such and such a school' saw their role as in any sense a badge of office, and even these individuals were probably more concerned to claim familiarity with educational issues than to vaunt their status.

*Governors' visits to the school*
The invitation to visit the school tends to be extended to governors by headteachers with the same regularity, if not the same specificity, as invitations to attend school functions. Governors' handbooks and training sessions stress the visit as an important means of acquiring knowledge, and the Open University course on governing schools[2] gives detailed advice on how a governor can get the most out of a visit. In practice, governors' visits took one of four forms and served four purposes. None of these was symbolic, although the visit did have some potential overtones of 'being seen to be visiting': however, these do not seem to have been exploited by governors.

The chairman's termly or twice-termly visit to the school to confer with the headteacher was one form of visit. At this meeting, chairman and headteacher might update one another on progress with outstanding business from the last governing body meeting, and mutually prepare for the next meeting. The purpose of such an encounter can be defined as consolidation of a relationship, and mutual exchange of information.

A second form of visit was the unheralded, almost *sub rosa*, visit of a chairman to the school, to view some aspect of the school's work or amenities without giving advance notice of the intention to do so. One chairman made such a visit, guided by the non-teaching staff governor but without the knowledge of the headteacher, to the latter's subsequent annoyance. Such visits no doubt serve the purpose of acquiring information on behalf of the governing body which might not otherwise be forthcoming. However, such visits break all the unwritten rules of governing body solidarity, and are probably in breach of those Articles which enjoin 'full consultation between the chairman of governors and the headteacher at all times'.

A third form was the headteacher-sponsored tour of the school by a new governor, or by serving governors on an irregular basis. Almost all LEA and community governors interviewed had made such a visit at some time, and in many cases seemed to feel that this had absolved them from any obligation to make further visits. Many, but not all of such familiarisation tours were conducted by the headteacher, other guides being a senior pupil or a member of the teaching staff. Although most governors appeared to approach such visits in a spirit of learning how things were done, some flavoured this with a spirit of critical enquiry into how and why some things were done, or not done.

The fourth form (for which only Parker, of the case-study schools, provided examples), was the focused visit of enquiry into a particular teaching department or aspect of school life, such as pastoral care. The purpose of such a visit was to acquire and relay to the governing body in-depth knowledge about aspects of school provision. Only a division of labour among governors about visiting can make this comprehensively possible. In the case of Parker, governors prepared for such visits, often by reading the self-evaluatory review reports prepared by the department in question, spent a morning or an afternoon in the department, discussed the available resources and the methods of working with the teaching staff, and provided written or verbal reports to the next governing body meeting. Considerable unease was expressed by the headteacher about these visits and their likely effect on teaching staff, but the extent to which these visits avoided 'rocking the boat' seemed to depend more on the tact with which governors handled their approach to teachers than on whether their enquiries were penetrating or superficial.

Governors usually acted on their own when involved in activities outside the governing body meeting. For those governors who were members of a continuous governing body, their solo activities could be understood as a planned and needed extension of the life of the corporate group, part of the way in which the governing body as a whole kept itself informed. But for those whose governing body only came to life once a term, interim activities were more a matter of individual choice, and personal priorities chiefly influenced the decision to accept or decline invitations.

Whether or not governors found themselves attached to spasmodic or continuous governing bodies, each individual knew him or herself to come within a particular *category* of governor – LEA representative, parent, teacher or community representative, or some other. Each had to face the question of what, if anything, he or she should attempt to make of this representative function.

**Representing a constituency of interest on the governing body**
For those categories of governor who are required to be elected by their peers, there is clearly an intention in the national or local statutes recording their eligibility that these governors should represent their fellows. The categories of governor in question are parent and teacher governors (required for new governing bodies by the 1980 Education

Act), ancillary staff governors and pupil governors (envisaged in the 1981 School Governing Bodies Regulations, and provided for by some local Instruments of Government).

The form of representation envisaged by democratic election can be seen as 'descriptive' in Pitkin's terms (see Chapter 2), if the task of the representative is to embody the characteristics of the represented, and/or give accurate information about the represented. The majority of case-study parent governors felt this was exactly the form of representation they should provide, but one for which they were singularly ill-equipped.

Their first problem was one of identifying the 'represented'. Theoretically, this should be the entire parent body, but typically only a small proportion of parents had actually voted in the election. In several cases there had, in fact, been no election, as the sole nominees for the parent governor role had been unopposed. Parent governors had to assume that the majority of parents were barely aware that they *were* represented on the school's governing body.

So far as 'embodying the characteristics of the represented' was concerned, not infrequently parent governors felt themselves to be positively *un*typical of other parents. This belief was based on subjective impressions of fellow members of the parent body seen at school events or known to reside in the school's neighbourhood, particularly on council estates. These subjective impressions could not however be checked against firm data, since schools do not keep systematic, collated records of the demographic and social characteristics of pupils' families, and even teachers' and headteachers' statements about the type of families using the school tend to be based on undocumented stereotypes and generalisations.[3] One characteristic of the parent body about which governors and teachers of the case study schools seemed to feel fairly confident was the ethnic balance of the pupil population. In several of the governing bodies parent governors considered that the ethnic composition of the parent governor group, and indeed of the whole governing body, did not mirror the ethnic composition of the pupil population. One parent governor commented: 'We are [all four] white, articulate, middle-class.' In the headteacher's assessment, one-third of the pupil population at that school were from ethnic minority groups.

The other main requirement of descriptive representation is to 'give accurate information about the represented'.[4] The non-availability of such information in any systematic form has already been touched on, but several parent governors considered they should try to obtain such information by keeping in touch with parents during their period of office. Case-study documents show that this had been attempted in a variety of ways – by attending PTA meetings, being present at parents' evenings wearing a 'parent governor' label, and by canvassing parents at the school gate. The last form of contact was the only one which was rated a success, but it was only feasible for parent governors in primary schools who themselves went regularly to the school to deliver or collect their children, and they met only those other parents who followed a similar practice.

The difficulties of descriptive representation by parent governors have been fully discussed because this was the form of representation many such governors felt they were expected to provide. In practice they found they had to operate as trustees, putting forward their own views in the hope that these would be in the best interests of all parents.

The other categories of elected governor seemed to refine less on the concept of representation, and to accept the role of trustee more readily. But teacher governors in particular were conscious that although they might not be typical of the whole teaching staff, nor be in regular touch with all their colleagues about their views on governing body concerns, their constituency was an available and quantifiable one. Soundings could rapidly be taken, or meetings called, if a matter arose on which a teacher governor felt the need to canvass the views of his colleagues. One of the governing bodies was faced with a chairman with new and to some extent unwelcome ideas about an appropriate relationship between the governing body and the education committee. A teacher governor, who as a rule seemed more of an observer than a governor, lost no time in calling a meeting of teaching staff and establishing their views about the place of politics in school government. Parent governors were equally uneasy about developments, but at a loss to know how to inform all parents of their disquiet. This incident demonstrated the greater flexibility of the representative capacity of teacher governors, compared with parents.

Categories of governor who were nominated or coopted, rather than elected, were also aware that representation was part of their role, but the views they expressed on this varied within as much as between categories. Community governors who had been appointed by the LEA through a process of filtered nomination had perhaps a greater propensity to pursue the interests of the group they represented. A community governor nominated by the Community Relations Council saw himself as taking part in governing body work primarily as a delegate to represent the point of view of ethnic minorities. But a community governor coopted from the senior management of a local industrial concern interpreted the governor role as dictated by the 'social responsibility' which was part of company policy, and saw himself as a contributor to the general level of education and experience of the governing body as a group, rather than the representative of a sector of the local economy.

Coopted community governors had, it seemed, in effect surrendered their interest by joining the governing body, and were concerned only to use their affiliations and experience to support or advise the other governors and the school. The local policeman, coopted to one of the governing bodies, was however disappointed to find that his experience of wayward juveniles was not consulted. This question of frustrated governor expertise will be returned to later in the chapter.

Among LEA-nominated governors, those who were councillors could look to the ballot box as their licence to represent local people. But in many cases councillors saw governing body work as an extension of a general civic duty, rather than as an explicitly representative role. Most LEA-nominated governors were of course not councillors. Those who had been nominated because of their active work in party groups shared some propensity to advance party views in governing body discussion, but not all felt the need to speak on behalf of their party nor to report back to a party caucus. As the discussion in Chapter 3 has shown, the political culture of the authority is an important factor influencing the attitude taken by LEA governors on the place of party politics in school government. In the case of politically inactive individuals nominated as LEA governors, they were sometimes at a loss to understand the criteria used in their nomination. They had no choice but to operate as individuals rather than representatives of particular sectors of viewpoint or experience.

Of the eight governing bodies studied, the seven governing bodies of county schools were already in line with the 1980 Education Act by their inclusion of parent and teacher governors (see Figure 6.1). Only the voluntary aided school had no governors of either sort, although one foundation governor who had a child at the school saw himself to some extent as a parent 'representative'. For most of the governing bodies, however, it could be expected that the mediation of parent or teacher interests with school or LEA would be an occasional or regular task for the governing body as a corporate group.

The interest of *individual* parents or teachers were in fact rarely brought before any full meeting of the governing bodies,[5] although interview work revealed that in a very few cases the interests of particular parents had been discussed with a headteacher by a parent governor outside the governing body meeting. But the interests of *groups* of parents (never the whole parent body), of groups of teachers, and also of the whole teaching staff, were on various occasions laid before a governing body, sometimes in the form of a letter to the chairman, but more often as items of 'Any other business'. One such representation, through which certain members of staff voiced an objection to the acting headteacher's having 'covered' certain staff duties during a period of industrial action, placed the governing body in a quandary as to how to mediate this interest, which they merely noted. In other cases, as when a parent governor registered a complaint from certain parents that children were being pressurised to arrange sponsored activity on behalf of a particular charity, the headteacher debated her viewpoint in the matter with all the governors. Both the parents' and the headteacher's view on the matter were duly recorded in the minutes. It was of interest that the head partly justified her position by the fact that she had not received any complaints directly from parents. She seemed to suggest that the parent governor's representation of certain parents' views was somehow less valid than a direct approach – an example of legitimation being denied to a group of governors, perhaps because of their self-confessed 'untypicality'. Nevertheless, the raising of this issue at a governing body meeting, and the ten minutes or so of edgy debate which ensued, did serve a mediatory purpose for the interests of the parents concerned in that the competitive work for the charity was not repeated.

These parent governors were drawing on information about school activities brought home by children. As we saw in Chapter 4, the structure and process of schools as institutions are complex, and not readily permeable by outsiders. Some of the principal differentiating characteristics between categories of governor are the relationship between their eligibility to govern and the nature of their attachment to the school, if any, and the sources of information on which they can draw for an understanding of the structure and process of the school. We now turn to examine the characteristics of the various categories of school governor in these terms, and discuss their implications for the work of the governing body as a corporate group.

## Homogeneity or differentiation in school governing bodies

Conceptually, it is possible clearly to differentiate between the main sectors of governor (LEA, parent, teacher, community) under the headings of basis of eligibility to govern, degree of attachment to the school, and access to information about the school.

As we have seen, the various categories of governor may or may not feel adequately able to represent a particular constituency of interest, but their basis of eligibility to govern is clearly distinct. For teachers and ancillary staff of the school governed (and for headteachers or deputy headteachers whose place on the governing body is *ex officio*), it is their employment which entitles them to serve. For parents, it is the particular phase of parenthood through which they are passing, during which they have a child attending the school. For both teacher and parent governors, their connection with the school is direct and personal, although for parents of secondary school pupils the relationship between home and school may be less direct, and more adequately mediated by the pupil, than it is for the parents of primary school pupils.[6]

The eligibility to govern of nominated community governors is less likely to link them directly with the school than the eligibility of those who have been coopted to the governing body. Nominated governors are likely to have been put forward by an interest group, perhaps one with a general interest in education (see Chapter 3). Their eligibility to govern is contingent upon their affiliation to that group, but need have nothing to do with the particular institution they are appointed to govern. Community governors coopted by governors already serving on the governing body, however, may well have been drawn in because of some established connection with the school. The local health visitor may, for example, be coopted onto the school governing body. Such individuals may already be 'licensed visitors' to the school, by virtue of their occupation.

The basis of eligibility to govern of LEA-nominated governors, however, rarely involves any previous or present connection with the school, except possibly the somewhat tenuous link of local residence. As we have seen in earlier chapters, the LEA governor's eligibility may reside in the ballot box through which he or she has acquired councillor status, or may be an outcome of past or present political activity or acquaintance.[7]

The nature of governors' connections with the school in turn has implications for their access to differing sources of knowledge about the school.

We have seen that in their reports to governing bodies, headteachers put forward their own implicit or explicit analysis of the constraints which exist and the choices which are available in the operation of the school. They provide all governors with selective and edited information about what is going on in the school. Those governors unconnected with the school except by their governorship, may be readily persuaded by the headteacher's view of the world. Staff governors, however, may be aware of competing analyses put forward by other groups within the school, even though these analyses are unlikely to be laid before the governing body so long as some process of inter-staff negotiation remains viable within the school. Parent governors, from their own contacts with the school and their vicarious knowledge of its processes acquired through their children, can form their own impressions of how adequate the headteacher's analysis of constraints and choices is. Coopted governors linked with the school by their occupational role may also know something of the school's inside story, but most nominated community governors and LEA governors would be unlikely to do so. Exceptions might be those few LEA governors who are not only elected members of the local authority, but also members of the education committee. But even membership of the education committee does not of necessity give access to inside knowledge about a particular school. Rather, it may equip the governor to evaluate the school 'not as a separate and self-contained unit, but as part of a wider education service', on the lines favoured in Stapleton.

It can be seen that a governing body constituted on the lines recommended by the Taylor Report and partly endorsed by the 1980 Education Act and 1981 Regulations, is made up of categories of governor who differ from each other in a number of ways. Yet despite the differing bases of governors' eligibility to govern, and the differing sources of their knowledge of an attachment to the school, in several of the governing bodies studied the sectoral affiliations of particular governors were not readily apparent to observers nor, indeed, to new governors.

The reasons for this apparent homogeneity were not always the same. In some cases governors seemed to have found a common purpose in the corporate activity of the group for which their sectoral affiliations were irrelevant. In others, governors had overlapping social connections which blurred the distinctions between, for example, parent and community governors. In the governing body of a special school, governors were conscious of the wide spread of personal circumstances and geographical area from which they were drawn, and there was an apprehension that if sectoral interests were too strongly emphasised this might fragment the governing body.

Although the proceedings of these undifferentiated or homogeneous governing bodies seemed more consensual than those of more loosely aggregated governing bodies, in which sectoral views were frequently articulated, some governors were not satisfied with what was being achieved. Where the governing body had established a common denominator of an agreed, if limited, purpose – as, for example, one governing body which operated as an educational forum debating LEA policy, but leaving the school to operate undisturbed on long-established lines – governors found their meetings agreeable and enjoyable, but in several cases concluded that being a governor was not a worthwhile, continuing use of their time. In other cases it transpired that governors' values were not all as socially homogeneous as they appeared, and that some governors were simply keeping quiet about their differing views on education or social need because they felt isolated by the prevailing weight of opinion.

In several of the governing bodies, the distribution of governors' participation in the meeting could be conceptualised as three concentric circles, with an inner-ring consisting of chairman, headteacher and one or two long-serving governors, an adjacent ring of governors who made a comment from time to time, and an outer-ring of governors whose participation took the form of nods of agreement. In interview, a considerable number of governors seemed to place themselves in this fringe category, declaring that they did not know enough about what was under discussion to take a meaningful part. Their sense of inadequacy must be contrasted with the different but equal frustrations of those governors, probably located in the middle ring, who played an occasional part in governing body deliberations, but not at the level at which they had hoped. These governors felt they did have specialised knowledge which was relevant for school or LEA concerns, but this knowledge was not being called upon. For example, some of the governors of the special school had considerable experience of dealing with mental handicap, but the work of the governing body did not seem to require this expertise.

If the governor role was unsatisfactory for so many governors, why did they continue to serve? One answer is that in many cases they did not. A 'cooling-out' of their original enthusiasms took place, and they did not stand for re-election at the end of what was, for many, in any case only a two-year period of service. Others took an even earlier opportunity to resign for 'personal reasons'. Some governors, however, persevered in the role, and some perceived it as having developmental or career characteristics. A governor could acquire experience and confidence, and through long service hope to penetrate to the inner-ring. Or a parent might have the opportunity to gain experience as a governor in a number of educational institutions as children in the family passed through the various phases of schooling. With such experience, it would become possible to appraise the institutions which one was currently governing in the context of the whole local education system. Several of the governors recognised a dynamic in the role, and perceived that it might be more worthwhile being a governor at one time than another, and that in particular the representative aspect of their role might be more crucial and more viable under certain circumstances.

It was this sense of the pressure of possibly changing circumstances which convinced the majority of governors that, whether or not they found it personally worthwhile to continue to serve, there ought to be a continuing governing body for the school. Almost every participant in the research drew attention to the possible 'last-ditch' or residual role of a school governing body if 'something went wrong' – if a headteacher made a serious error of judgement, or part of the school building fell down, or pupil numbers were decimated, or national circumstances forced a change in educational provision. Whether realistically or not, governors seemed confident that under such circumstances, when neither the professional nor the political elements of the education system would be adequate to cope, the school governing body would suddenly find its true *raison d'être*. But our research gives us cause to doubt whether a hitherto acquiescent governing body could in fact provide a more coherent lead than any promoted by the strong interests of administrators or professionals. It seems to us that a more feasible way forward for a governing body whose members are dissatisfied with their role would be to identify the primary purpose of the governing body under present circumstances, and make what adjustments are needed by way of structure and process to enable that purpose to be fulfilled. In the next chapter we discuss a number of potential models for school governing bodies.

### Notes and references

1. *Report of the William Tyndale Junior and Infant Schools Public Inquiry* (The Auld Report), ILEA, 1976. Criticisms were made of a governor who took action without the knowledge and backing of the full governing body.
2. *Governing Schools*, Open University, Course No.P.970.
3. Johnson, D. and Ransom, E., *Family and School*, Croom Helm, 1983.
4. Pitkin, H., *Representation*, University of California Press, 1967.
5. The individual interests of particular families were, however, discussed when governors joined a panel hearing an appeal against the suspension of a pupil.
6. See Johnson and Ransom, *op. cit.*, Chapter 5, for a full discussion of the changing role of parents in relation to the school, as pupils pass through adolescence.

     Pupil governors might seem an appropriate substitute for parent governors in the later secondary school years. However, the legal requirement that pupil governors must be eighteen years of age puts a serious limitation on their continuity of service as school governors. They may have been part of the school for over six years, but they are unlikely to be part of the governing body for more than a term or two. In the governing bodies we studied, pupil governors did not seem to have resolved the conflicts inherent in status passage to electoral maturity, while remaining a dependent client of the institution they were now eligible to govern.
7. An exception to this general statement would be the politico-parent who, in an authority whose Instrument of Government permits this, is eligible to serve as an LEA-nominated governor of the school his or her children attend.

# 8   Models of governing bodies

With the revival of interest in governing bodies in the 1970s, and their subsequent increase in numbers, governors became suitable subjects for instruction. Some local authorities provided training courses and interpreted their Articles and Instruments of Government in hand-books of guidance. Governors who wanted to find out more for them-selves were increasingly able to turn to a variety of references,[1] including, eventually, a course of training from the Open University.[2] Yet despite the attention that their role has received in recent years, our research with governing bodies confirmed the findings of Bacon[3] in presenting a picture of considerable uncertainty. Governors were un-sure what they should be doing and consequently doubtful if they were spending their time on the right things and, in particular, whether they were being as effective as they might be.

Much of this uncertainty stems from the structural position that governing bodies occupy within the local educational system. They are placed at the intersection, and under the shadow, of two strong insti-tutions, the school and the local authority, both of which have a continuous and visible role in the system.

Further, as Baron and Howell indicated,[4] they also stand at a point in the system where different forms of authority – professional, administrative and political – meet. Thus governing bodies are sur-rounded by a constellation of values and purposes from which they must select a role of their own.

As we saw in Chapter 3, the institutions and forms of authority that surround governing bodies are themselves structurally interrelated and seek to influence one another. Some of these influences are transmitted through, and mediated by, governing bodies. A considerable portion of their time, for example, is spent in making approaches to the LEA on behalf of their schools. By their nature such relationships contain a large element of uncertainty and their quality cannot be determined in advance. Rather, they develop from practice. Governing bodies forge their own patterns of relationship and the result is likely to be quite distinctive; a product of past experience, the issues that have to be handled and the skills of individual governors. Here then, in the reliance of governing bodies on relationships with other bodies, lies a further cause of uncertainty.

A second implication of the position occupied by governing bodies in the local educational system is that unless they make strenuous efforts to the contrary, they spend much of their time in reacting to the concerns of others. Their business is fashioned by the traffic which surrounding institutions, schools and LEAs or groups in the community, send their way. As a result their work has an unpredictable character. It is outside the governors' control; ebbing and flowing according to the needs of others.

Uncertainties about relationships and work are exacerbated by the absence of any common view as to what governing bodies are about. The institutions and forms of authority that surround them are likely to hold very different expectations of what governing bodies can be expected to do. Not only is there variation between institutions, as when schools see governing bodies as a way of promoting school interests and LEAs see them as a way of enforcing authority policy, but also within institutions. Local councillors, for example, may see governing bodies as an extension of the political system, determining that professionals follow the wishes of the public. Officers of the same local authority, however, may hold the view that the governors' role is essentially advisory and serves to link the school to local interests.

To summarise the argument so far, governing bodies experience uncertainty because they face different expectations and demands and need to create different relationships with the surrounding institutions and interests in the local education system. However, because of their own differentiated composition with members who are appointed by the very institutions and interests concerned, these differences become sucked in to the governing bodies themselves. This is shown diagrammatically in Figure 8.1.

In these circumstances it is hardly surprising that members of a governing body differ widely in the way they see their role and are uncertain whether they are concentrating on the right things.

As we have seen, Articles of Government indicate the areas of concern for governing bodies but cannot determine how they work. Governing bodies have to shape their own role, or have it shaped for them, through their interaction with surrounding institutions and interests. Much, then, depends on what is seen as important at any one time, who sees it as important, and the strength of particular interests within the governing body.

Looked at in context, the uncertainties and variety are a realistic response to what governing bodies face. This makes it meaningless to suggest any single description of a governing body as a model for general application. Obviously there is value in comparing and categorising governing bodies in a number of key dimensions, as in earlier chapters of this book. The results may explain the variety, but they do

*Figure 8.1* How different viewpoints are drawn into governing bodies

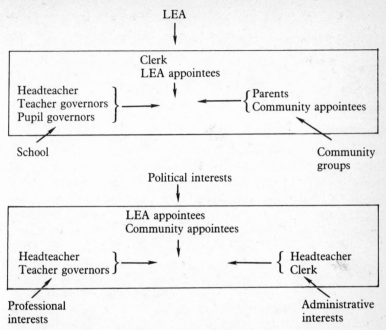

not define what is or is not a governing body. Any such model could only be based upon its author's normative conception of what governing bodies should do. The governing body that would have emerged if the recommendations of the Taylor Report[5] had been fully implemented would be only one such normative model. If, however, it is accepted that it is legitimate for governing bodies to serve a number of purposes, any interpretation of their role similarly requires a number of models.

Our study of governing bodies enables us to suggest different models, each based upon a different conception of what a governing body has as its purpose. Further, we can draw upon the knowledge of the factors which condition the work of governing bodies, which were discussed in earlier chapters of the book, to suggest desirable properties for each model.

The governing bodies depicted in these models contain elements which do not accord with current practice. The models are presented to show the implications of pursuing different purposes, not as an account of reality or as a prescription for the future.

Four such models are presented in the following pages: (1) The accountable governing body, (2) The advisory governing body, (3) The supportive governing body, and (4) The mediating governing body. The purpose of each is described and then its associated properties are suggested under the headings of: authority, representation, resources, public relations, style of work, and demands of the work. The first three (authority, representation, resources) concern inputs that are necessary for the governing body to achieve its purpose, while the latter three (PR, style and demands of work) specify aspects of its process of working. A final section for each model considers how it is related to ideas of government, to models of governing bodies suggested by other commentators, and to current practice as experienced in our research. The chart on pp. 162–3 summarises the main features of each model, and thus provides for easy comparisons.

## The accountable governing body

This type of governing body centres its efforts on its school. Its purpose is to ensure that the school is working satisfactorily within the policies and prescriptions of appointing authorities, normally LEAs but in the case of voluntary aided schools religious foundations. Where the appointing authority is willing to delegate decisions and tolerate variety, the governing body is able to concentrate upon the school's ability to meet the needs of the community it serves. For this role to be effective its properties would be as follows.

### Authority

The range and scope of authority exercised by this form of governing body depends upon the discretion allowed to the governors.

With minimum delegation of authority the governing body would function as a sub-committee of the LEA or foundation, enforcing the decisions of the appointing authority. It provides a safeguard for the authority in checking that its policies and requirements for the school are being observed and alerting it to any deviations or special needs.

With maximum delegation of authority the governing body, while still ensuring that prescribed policies are followed, is delegated some authority to shape the school on behalf of the various interests with a stake in its work – the LEA or foundation, parents, teachers, community groups. This could mean that it is involved in determining the objectives of the school and in taking primary decisions, such as the selection of staff, the nature of the curriculum and the allocation of money. The extent of the governing body's authority is a matter for negotiation, between the appointing authority and the governing body, on the one hand, and the governing body and headteacher on the other. The governors cannot realistically expect to manage the day-to-day work of the school.

At a minimum, then, the governing body would require the authority to ensure that the LEA or foundation provided it with the relevant information to monitor the school's activities. The school, for its part, must accept the authority of the governing body in the restricted version of accountability developed by Elliott *et al.*, to 'call it to account'[6] in dimensions of its work specified by the appointing authority and must abide by the rulings it receives.

If, however, discretion is extensive, the authority of the governing body is wider. Taking the LEA or foundation first, the governing body would be likely to see it as accountable for providing the school with adequate resources. The governors could naturally expect to be provided with information on policy guidelines for the school and, since the governors express community needs, that the LEA or foundation would consult with them regarding the substance of policies. The school could be 'called to account' in respect of any aspect of its activities; anything involving the school might potentially involve the governors. This would mean providing the governing body with such information as it might require, taking part in consultation regarding past, present and future activities and implementing the decisions that are made. Naturally, if the governing body felt that its authority was being disregarded by the school it would have the sanction of referring the matter to the LEA or foundation as the responsible authority.

The governing body could, itself, be called to account for the way in which the school was performing. With the minimal delegation this would only be likely if there was a crisis, or the school was persistently failing to meet the specified criteria laid down by the appointing authority. Where greater discretion is allowed it could be argued that the appointing authority needs to be familiar with the way in which the governing body applies its delegated authority. There would thus be a case for the governing body to present an annual report, or for its chairman, together with the headteacher, to meet with the chairman of the education committee and senior officers for a review of school performance along the lines of regional and district reviews in the NHS.[7] Groups within the local community might also regard the governing body as accountable for ensuring that the school was serving community needs. There might thus be a case for the governing body holding an annual public meeting to give an account of its stewardship to interested parties.

*Representation*

Clearly, the governors must be aware of both the values of the appointing authority and of the policies it has laid down. In voluntary aided schools this knowledge is provided through the requirement that the majority of governors are appointed by the foundation that established the school. In LEA-maintained schools the requirements of the 1980 Education Act do not prohibit the LEA-appointed governors providing a majority of the membership, although the Secretary of State hoped that this category would also be used to appoint members from the local community or from industry and commerce.[8] In any event, it would seem appropriate that the LEA appointments should include members who can speak to, and interpret, authority policies. This means appointments from the ruling political party, with some councillors and ideally a councillor from the education committee or one of its sub-committees. If the governing body has little delegated authority other sources of membership are largely irrelevant. However, if it is expected to exercise local discretion, additional members must be provided who can express the values of all those other interests with a stake in the satisfactory operation of the school – teachers, older pupils, parents and local community groups. If the governing body is to represent these interests in running the school, members should serve as delegates, mandated to follow particular lines of action, or at the least as trustees, with the capacity to accurately reflect the general opinion of their particular constituency.

### Resources

These depend upon the authority exercised by the governing body. At a minimum the governing body requires information from the LEA or foundation, in order to be aware of the requirements which the school must follow. From the school, the governing body will require information, which may well be standardised in report form, regarding those aspects of school management which are considered important by the appointing authority. Where the governing body is delegated wider authority it requires all this, together with advice from the LEA or foundation on the pros and cons of alternative courses of action and their implications. The presence of a clerk and perhaps a senior officer from the appointing authority would seem essential. Demands will be heavy on the school, since the governing body requires information on any aspects of school management and is likely to be particularly concerned with ways of evaluating what is being achieved.

### Public relations

The need for the governing body to be visible to the public depends upon its authority. If it is the expectation that it does no more than check that prescribed policy is being followed and pass demands to the appointing authority, public relations are relatively unimportant: the governing body can remain anonymous. If, on the other hand, it is expected that the governing body has some freedom to shape the school, public relations take on an enormous importance. The governing body requires to be known, and recognised as such, by the appointing authority, in the school and in the local community.

*Style of working*
The accountable governing body would be led by the lay governors. If it is a sub-committee of the appointing authority, leadership would come from the politicians, or members of the foundation, who would require a report from the headteacher and use the meeting to acquaint him with, or stress, relevant requirements. Much of the meeting time would probably be taken up by hearing what the school needed in the way of resources from the appointing authority. If the governing body has delegated authority the leadership is more open. The governors would require a wide range of inputs, from the headteacher, from other staff of the school, and from their own number. Since the authority of the governing body gives it the power to benefit some interests and disappoint others, meetings would be likely to prove contentious and party politics would probably play a more prominent role than is currently experienced in many governing bodies. The chairman would have a particularly crucial role in securing consensus and in coordinating and progressing the breadth of work involved. There is obviously a suspicion that he or she would become the *de facto* chief executive of the school, and the development of a close and trusting relationship with the headteacher would be essential.

*Demands of the work*
If the governors have little discretion, their role is primarily symbolic of the LEA or foundation. The governing body becomes a route for communication between the school and the appointing authority, with decisions being taken at each end by the school and authority, respectively.

Were governing bodies to be delegated greater authority, there would be considerable demands, although without doubt the governing body would need to delegate a good deal of authority to its headteacher and guard against becoming drawn into the day-to-day running of the school. The demands of the work would exceed the current norm and this might well prove a constraint in attracting members, particularly members who were already engaged in other public activities. The governing body would require a deeper and more continuous oversight of the school and its affairs than is possible through termly meetings and would need to work through sub-committees and working parties. The relationship with the teaching staff would be highly sensitive, so governors would need to know, and become known in, the school. They would need to feed back information to their particular constituencies and arm themselves with constituency opinion. They would need to be familiar with the policies that impacted upon their school and be aware of their implications.

### Basis of the model

This model, with either limited or extensive discretion, is based upon the premise that the governing body exists to control the activities of the school. At a minimum this is according to the prescriptions of the appointing authority. With greater delegation of authority it could include the views of the interests represented on the governing body, within a framework defined by the appointing authority. The former, then, is explained by traditional democratic theory, in which authorities represent the public, or sectional, interest in determining the activities of the institutions they provide.[9] The latter contains elements of this in its delineation of a clear line of accountability from school to governing body and from governing body to LEA or foundation, but also owes something to the ideas of pluralism (discussed in Chapter 2) in so far as authority is delegated to local interests to shape their school as they see fit.

Accountability with minimum delegation was common, as Baron and Howell illustrated,[10] with the education committee or its subcommittees putting on different 'hats' and becoming the governing body for all their schools. Dissatisfaction with this practice and the narrow role that it allotted to both governors and professionals, was one of the forces leading to change that culminated in the Taylor Inquiry and the 1980 Education Act. The Taylor Committee, itself, advocated the accountable governing body with greater authority, recommending that there should be a clear line of delegated responsibility from the LEA through the governing body to the school, and that the governors should be responsible for the life and work of the school as a whole.[11]

From our experience, the accountable model is not found widely in current practice, although a few LEAs are deliberately delegating more authority to their governing bodies. However, our research certainly provided examples of governing bodies, or groups of governors within them, seeking to exercise accountability for their schools. This was apparent in such activities as deciding on pupil suspensions, or appointing teaching staff, but also included attempts to formulate objectives and monitor performance. Nevertheless, such efforts were intermittent, and were liable to be treated as recommendations rather than decisions. The research indicated just how formidable are the obstacles to governors exercising full accountability for their schools: domination of professional interests; reluctance of LEAs to allow or afford governing bodies a stronger role; resistance of many governors to greater involvement; and doubts as to whether the local educational system has the space for strong governing bodies.

## The advisory governing body

This type of governing body also centres its efforts on the school. Its purpose is to provide a forum in which school activities are reported to the laity and tested against their ideas of what the school should be doing. It thus provides some safeguard against professional malfunction.

For this role to be effective it is necessary to satisfy the following conditions.

### Authority

With this model the governors possess the authority to 'call the school to account'.[12] The school, through the headteacher, is obliged to inform the governing body of its actions, explain the reasons behind them, and consider the governors' viewpoint. The authority of the governing body is advisory, but this is more substantial than common usage of the word implies. The governors must be told what is happening and provided with reasoned explanations. Their suggestions or responses must also be given due consideration. In other words, there must be a degree of give-and-take, for an advisory relationship rapidly becomes meaningless if the advice is never taken. As a last resort, if the governing body feels that it is never being given the true picture, or that its suggestions or criticisms are consistently disregarded to the detriment of the children's education, it has the sanction, as borne out by the Tyndale Inquiry,[13] of pressing the issue with the LEA, as the higher authority responsible for the school. This could also serve to make the issue public and the power of public criticism can be potent.

### Representation

This type of governing body benefits from broad membership, with members who can speak as trustees for local interests that have a concern with the school's work. Appointees are in a position to know the values of the various interests, and what they want from the school, through their own contacts; they do not come to the governing body as delegates committed to promote particular policies. In making its appointments, then, the LEA is less concerned with nominating councillors or ensuring that the membership reflects party political strength, but is more interested in matching its appointments to the particular needs of the school. If, for example, appointments are to be made to the governing body of a special school, it could be helpful to select one or two individuals with experience of working with handicapped children.

All governing bodies of this type might benefit from the presence of one or two members with educational knowledge, who can help their colleagues make sense of what they are told and provide a source of comparison to the school. A LEA that wished to work to this model might usefully frame its Instruments of Government to allow a sizeable proportion of appointments to be coopted. The governing body could then consider its own membership in the light of the needs of the school and deliberately seek out individuals with desirable attributes. It might, for example, approach someone living in a part of the school's catchment area that was unrepresented, or someone who had always shown an interest in the school, or seek a member from the main source of local employment.

### Resources

Such a governing body would require little from the LEA. It might even be unnecessary for the authority to provide an official clerk, for governors could provide one of their own number to service their meetings and, providing he is briefed by the authority, the headteacher could keep the other governors informed of policy developments. An officer presence would, however, provide the LEA with an early warning of any dissatisfaction and, where a major change in authority policy was envisaged, it would naturally help the governors if an officer or adviser attended to explain the issues.

Far more would be required from the school. If the governing body is to act as an advisory forum for the school, the governors need to be familiar with all aspects of school management – the objectives of the school, the primary decisions such as staffing and curriculum that give effect to the objectives, and the secondary activities that make up the school's day-to-day life. If, moreover, the governors' advice is to influence school objectives, the governing body must be drawn into discussions at an early stage, when ideas are fluid, not presented with a *fait accompli*. The governors are also likely to be concerned with how objectives can be measured and evaluated. If the governors are to influence the primary decisions of the school, they must have a presence at the appropriate events. Governors should thus have a voice, although not the decisive voice, in staff selection. They should similarly be able to comment upon curriculum proposals and financial allocations. Governors must also hear of the daily life of the school: its triumphs and its failures. In this context it may be helpful for them to receive regular reports on the activity of particular aspects of the work, such as the arrangements for pastoral care, careers work or transfer of children to the secondary school, from the responsible staff, or individually to associate themselves with particular departments or sections of the school.

If the governing body does its job well, it will generate its own demands for information. This imposes additional demands upon the school, but should be regarded as potentially useful in providing fresh insights and generating wider support.

### Public relations
The prime requirement is that the governing body is known to all directly concerned with the school. Teachers and parents, in particular, need to recognise it as an interested party in the educational process and accept that it has a contribution to make in respect of school activities. The governors need to meet the staff, collectively and individually, see them at work and generally demonstrate their interest in the life of the school.

### Style of work
This type of governing body is professionally led. It provides a public witness and sounding-board for professional activity. The model assumes a rational world, in which people do listen to reasoned argument and may alter their behaviour as a result, and that it is possible for the laity and professionals to reach agreement on the appropriate course of action. The governor working to this model thus requires the abilities to listen and consider the arguments of others and of articulating his or her own. The governing body functions through debate and discussion, and the member who cannot present ideas, or finds argument threatening, is unlikely to make much of a contribution.

The chairman needs considerable skills. In meetings he or she must ensure that adequate professional explanations are forthcoming and can be understood, encourage a wide range of lay contributions and formulate an agreed view to present to the school. In meetings and without, the chairman must work to sustain a climate of trust between the lay governors and the professionals.

### Demands of the work
Being a governor under this model is moderately demanding. Governors need to know their school, and be known in it. Their work is done better if they keep in touch with local interests or gain some knowledge of the education system as a means of assessing the performance of their school.

*Basis of the model*

For the lay governors this model is based upon the necessity, or some would argue the sound sense, of trusting the professional. Lay governors lack the expertise and time to run the school, hence they must leave the job to the specialists. However, their trust is not unconditional but depends upon the achievement of satisfactory results. This means the laity must be able to learn what the professionals are doing.

For the professional, the model is based upon the recognition that professional authority requires public support. Indeed professional activities will be strengthened from knowing the feelings and demands of the consumers.

The model thus fits with the neo-pluralist conception of government (discussed in Chapter 2). Governments today have no choice but to delegate a considerable amount of freedom to professionals, but they, for their part, have the responsibility of listening and responding to the public interest.

In evidence to the Taylor Committee, Glatter suggested that governing bodies could perform a role more suited to their capabilities if they were placed, like Community Health Councils, outside the executive structure.[14] Their function would thus be advisory, representing views to those who have the authority to take decisions.

Aspects of this model can be widely found in current practice. Our research suggests that governing bodies do focus a lot of attention upon their schools, are commonly professionally led in their work, as evidenced by the central importance of headteachers' reports, and provide a witness and second opinion for professional performance and intentions. They are predominantly reactive bodies, and therefore, provide schools with feedback on their activities as advocated by Howell.[15] Further, it was also apparent that governors introduce their own viewpoints and concerns for consideration; suggesting, for example, a different means of achieving an objective, or questioning the resources allocated to a particular activity. However, it was also our impression that professional acceptance of the right of governing bodies to hear about any or all aspects of school performance and of their own obligation to consider and respond to lay inputs, was not so common. Lay advice on issues concerned with school management, such as the maintenance of the estate, was legitimate. Concern with educational practice, such as with the curriculum, teaching methods or class control, proved more contentious.

**The supportive governing body**

Although this type of governing body also centres its activities on the school, it is looking outwards to influence the activities of other bodies, rather than inwards on the activities of the school. Its purpose is to provide support for the school in its relationship with other institutions and interests in the local educational system. For this role to be effective the essential properties are as follows.

*Authority*

With this model, the school gives an account of its activities to the governors rather than being called to account, selecting those items that it feels are relevant for them to know.[16] These mainly concern matters where it is thought that the governors can provide some help. Thus governors are more likely to become involved in the area of primary decisions which determine the resources that are available to the school, or with problems of management, than with the objectives of the school, which will be seen as a professional matter. Indeed, unless there is a crisis, the attention of the governing body is focused on resource inputs and the management of educational processes, rather than the nature of the processes themselves, or the ends they serve.

The needs of the school will usually be presented to the governors by the headteacher. However, while headteachers are leading professionals, they are primarily concerned with school management and may seek to use their governors to confirm their own managerial role. But if the school is under threat, the governors may be drawn into its defence in any area of activity. The requirement by the LEA that a school undertakes a process of evaluation may thus cause the headteacher to discuss objectives with the governors as a defence against possible criticism from the authority.

The LEA may well be seen by this type of governing body as accountable for providing the school with the resources it needs. Becher and his colleagues noted how some governing bodies are used by the professionals to hold the LEA to account in this way.[17]

*Representation*

Since the LEA is an important source of authority and resources for the school, it is important that the LEA appointments to the governing body should provide some councillors, including members of the ruling party. Such appointments provide the school with a route for transmitting its demands directly to the centres of power and influencing key decision-makers. Other appointments could usefully be made by co-option, or after consultation with the headteacher, in order that they provide a link with those interests that can help the school. Active parents, local employers or prominent local residents serve as examples.

With this model the value of representation lies in the members themselves and what they can contribute to the school through their own contacts. Members are required to take on the values of the school. They thus serve on the governing body as individuals, speaking for themselves, rather than as trustees or delegates for particular interests.

### Resources

The supportive role will be strengthened if the LEA keeps the governing body informed of decisions relevant to the school. Since much of the supportive role is inevitably going to concern the LEA, it will help the governing body if the authority provides a clerk and/or senior officer to attend their meetings to process their concerns and report on progress. From the school, the governors require information on needs and some guidance as to how they can help in their promotion.

### Public relations

The governing body needs to be visible to the LEA and other interests valued by the school. Thus the LEA must recognise that governing bodies will act as a pressure-group on behalf of their particular schools. Similarly, the governing body should be known as representing the school in relationships with interests in the local community, such as parents or employers. The governors' supportive role is made that much harder if their existence is unknown.

### Style of work

This form of governing body is led by the professionals from the school or, and the concerns may be different, by school management. The governing body exists to help the school and needs to be shown what to do. The chairman must ensure that the skills of individual members are drawn upon as appropriate and can have a time-consuming job in progressing and coordinating any action taken by the governing body.

### Demands of the work

For most governors the work is undemanding, their presence is largely symbolic and where they do provide support this is frequently passive, expressed in the form of resolutions supporting the action taken by the headteacher. However the chairman and other key members are likely to be more actively involved and this can involve considerable time and effort. It also presents the governors with a dilemma in calculating the appropriate strategy to adopt. This is particularly the case in seeking to influence the LEA. Is it, for example, more productive for governors to leave it to their clerk to express their opinions, or to take personal action? If the latter, how do they proceed: by letter or by personal visit? By trying to influence officers, or councillors, or both? By keeping issues within the educational system, or publicising their dissatisfaction in the local paper? The difficulty in receiving any response, let alone satisfaction, from the authority is a frequent grumble of governing bodies. It helps, therefore, to have governors who are familiar with the local government environment.

*Basis of the model*
This model is based upon the premise that the governing body exists to help the school, whose professionals are to be trusted and supported. It thus fits the élitist conception of government (discussed in Chapter 2). According to this argument school government is dominated by professional interests and governors are coopted in their defence. However, there is probably more substance in the view of educational government as dominated by a managerial élite, comprising headteachers, education officers and advisers, and educational politicians and which thus extends across the local educational system from the school to the LEA. Members of this élite serve on and service governing bodies, the latter being coopted to serve the interests of the managers. This was the role of governing bodies defined by Bacon in his Sheffield study.[18]

Again, aspects of this model are widely found in current practice. Most governors we interviewed suggested that one of their reasons for joining a governing body was to help their school; many mentioned the importance of backing the headteacher. LEAs, too, appeared to expect that governing bodies would act as a lobby for their particular school. The supportive role is primarily deployed *vis à vis* the LEA as the major resource provider for the school, but the research identified many other examples, as where parent governors were given fund-raising responsibilities, or governors made contacts with the press or with employers on the school's behalf. It appeared to be a characteristic of their supportive role that the governing body supplemented what was already being done, albeit along a different route, by the school. Indeed, much supportive activity was stimulated by head-teachers presenting problems or requesting help, although governors also volunteered their efforts spontaneously. The supportive role provides governors with something definitive to do but, as we frequently observed, can prove time-consuming, complicated and frustrating.

The supportive purpose is frequently combined with other functions, but the largely unquestioning support and external promotional forms which characterise this model do not sit easily with the more critical scrutiny of the school, which is a characteristic of other purposes.

### The mediating governing body

This type of governing body is concerned with the local educational system. Its purpose is to express the interests of the various parties and promote a consensus that can be taken up in action by those concerned. It thus provides some safeguard against things going seriously wrong in any part of the system – the LEA, the school or in the negotiation of particular interests with the school. For this role to be effective the following properties are required.

*Authority*

The governing body requires the authority to be informed and consulted by all the major interests in the local educational system regarding matters affecting the school. Thus the LEA may be called to account[19] for the effect of its policies upon the school and/or the local community, as well as for its provision of resources to the school. The school may similarly be called to account, and the governors could require information on any aspect of school performance, and expect the professionals to consult and indeed allow the governing body a voice in the determination of objectives and primary decisions for the school. If the governing body is dissatisfied with the response to its authority, it has the sanction of publicising its lack of effect to the interests it represents.

However, the precise delineation of authority is not the essential feature of this model. The governing body is concerned with creating and maintaining relationships between different parts of the local educational system. At a minimum it provides a channel for communication. However, it is successful if its advice leads the various parties becoming aware of wider viewpoints and altering their actions as a result. The governing body serves as an 'early warning system' for discontent and new demands, while at the same time attempting to filter such inputs to secure an outcome that is productive.

*Representation*

It is obviously important that the governors are able to express the values of and speak for the various constituencies they represent, or their mediating role becomes impossible. This suggests that governors serve as delegates for particular interests, with the means of contacting their constituents and learning their opinions. Parent governors, for example, should be linked to a parental organisation, such as the PTA. LEA appointments would need to include some councillors, and some of these should include members of the ruling party and the education committee, or its sub-committees, who could be expected to speak for the authority. If they cannot be provided any other way, LEA appointments must allow for representatives from relevant community interest groups – ethnic or residents' associations, or the local churches, for example.

Not all interests, however, will be formally recognised or incorporated into the local educational system. Working to this model, governors must be prepared to take up worries and demands from all sections of the community.

### Resources

From the LEA, the governing body requires information regarding relevant policy and its implications for both the school and the local area. It is important, then, that the LEA provides a clerk and/or senior officer or adviser to attend meetings.

From the school, the governing body requires information regarding its objectives and the primary decisions that have to be satisfied if these are to be achieved.

From the community, the governing body requires information on the impact of both LEA policies and school activities and of the needs and demands of the various interests in respect of education.

### Public relations

This form of governing body needs to be visible within the local educational system: to the LEA, to the school and the local community. The governors might hold an annual meeting with all of the school staff, a similar meeting where they could meet parents, and be prepared to hold *ad hoc* meetings with other interested parties as seems desirable. Chairmen of such governing bodies, at the least, might meet regularly with the Director of Education and Chairman of the Education Committee.

### Style of work

Leadership of the governing body is shared by the professionals and the laity, changing with the issues under discussion. Indeed, governing bodies adopting this model can expect to cover a wide area of work; at one point in their meeting concerned with the effects of the lack of nursery provision on the community and in the next breath with the state of the floor in the school hall. Since this type of governing body expects to hear and test different viewpoints, it is important that its members have the confidence to articulate their concerns. The governing body also expects to be able to reach a consensus and present an agreed viewpoint to the body concerned, so it is important that members are prepared to accept the conventions of collective working.

The chairman needs the skill both to ensure that different viewpoints are aired and that some agreed position, even if it is that the governors find it impossible to reach a decision, emerges from the discussion. He or she will probably have to devote considerable time to developing and maintaining relationships across the educational system.

### Demands of the work

Working to this model is demanding. Governors need to gather the viewpoints of their own particular constituencies regarding the outputs of the local educational system and also assimilate the impact of LEA and school performance. Naturally, the amount of work is dependent upon the issues that arise, but termly meetings will probably prove insufficient, and governors will need to meet more frequently and/or make use of sub-committees.

### Basis of the model

This model is based on the premise that a number of different interests have a stake in education and that they should have a voice in how it is provided – the members of the authority, the officers and advisers who work for it, the professionals in the schools, parents, and community interests. Governing bodies provide a forum in which the various interests can be expressed and negotiated. The model thus fits with the pluralist conception of government (discussed in Chapter 2). Educational policy emerges from a process of negotiation between organised interests.

Aspects of this model are widely promulgated. The Taylor Committee recommended that the governing body should devote attention to developing good relationships between the various constituencies represented by its members, although they saw governors as trustees for particular interests rather than delegates as advocated here.[20] LEA handbooks of guidance to governors regularly stress the importance of the governing body in bringing community interests to the attention of the school. Howell suggests that governors' links with other parts of the local educational system reinforce their ability to provide their schools with feedback and that they can act, as suggested in this model, as demand regulators to protect schools from stress.[21]

Aspects of this model were apparent in our research, where groups of governors were able to articulate the views of ethnic minorities and the reservations of the teaching staff regarding a proposal to become a community school, or were able to speak with some confidence for the parents. However, it was clear in the contexts we studied that the various bodies and interests in the local educational system develop their own relationships and do not have to relate through the governing body. LEA officers and advisers will, for example, develop close and influential links with schools that never reach the governors. Parents, too, may similarly enjoy a close relationship with the school, both individually and collectively through friends' organisations or the PTA, which remain completely divorced from the governing body. From our experience, governing bodies do not, as might have been expected from their remit and membership, act as a focus for issues circulating on the community grapevine.[22] Indeed, community interests may make their own links with the LEA through the party political system and never seek to use governing bodies for transmitting their demands. This 'underemployment' may be attributed to invisibility in the system, to the weakness of governors' links to any constituency, or reflect judgements of relative power. However, in practice, it means that the governing body is by-passed. The relationships it provides are 'B roads' with the important issues passing direct between the parties concerned.

Problems are also associated with the purpose of mediation. It could be argued that promoting consensus between different interests rules out any but minor adjustments to the *status quo*. For example, could such a governing body sustain a major challenge to the way in which the professionals were running the school? What sanctions could it bring to bear if it was at odds with the LEA? In the final analysis, the power of this type of governing body depends entirely on the willingness of the interests represented first, to make use of it and, second, act upon its mediation.

## Models and reality

Attempting to model human interaction is one thing: reality quite another. As has been suggested, our research found that in their current operation governing bodies and even more so groupings within them, exhibited characteristics from all of the models presented in the preceding pages. Indeed, the models themselves represent a spectrum of activity ranging along the two dimensions of focus of attention and type of authority. The position on this spectrum occupied by any governing body at any one time is a product of what is brought to its attention and the power it is allowed to exercise by the school, the LEA and other interests. It is also a product of past traditions and of the preferred ways of working of the headteacher, the chairman and the governors themselves.

Although none of the governing bodies we studied corresponded precisely with what are ideal types, it is possible to generalise. Over the fifteen-months study period the majority (five of eight) of our governing bodies approximated closest to the advisory model. These governing bodies spanned all four LEAs and we concluded that local factors such as professionalism and the respect it is accorded by governors,

*Figure 8.1* Models of governing bodies

| | Accountable | Advisory | Supportive | Mediating |
|---|---|---|---|---|
| **Focus** | School | School | School in the local education system | Local education system |
| **Purpose** | Ensure that school is operating satisfactorily within prescribed policies. *Minimum* Reflects interests of local stake-holders. *Maximum* | Legitimate and test professional activities. Safeguard against professional malfunction. | Support the school with other interests. | Bring together and negotiate different interests in education. Safeguard against malfunction in any part of the system. |
| **Authority** | Ensure that prescriptions of the appointing authority are followed. Decide how to shape the school within prescriptions of the appointing authority. | Learn what the school is doing and have governing body views considered by the school. | Decide how to promote school interests. | Learn how the system is working and have governing body views considered by other parties. |
| **Values** | Appointing authority. Interests in the local education system. | Interests concerned with the school. | School. | Interests in the local educational system. |
| **Representation** | Representation of the appointing authority. Delegates or trustees from major interests concerned with the school. | Trustees for major interests concerned with the school. | Individuals connected with major interests valued by the school. | Delegates from major interests concerned with the school. |

| | | | | | |
|---|---|---|---|---|---|
| Resources | Information regarding limits to be observed by schools and whether these are being adhered to. Information on needs of the school. | Information regarding policies affecting schools and on all aspects of school management. Require clerk/officer presence. | Information on all aspects of school management. | Information on needs of the school. Clerk/officer presence helpful. | Information regarding policies affecting schools and community, on school policies and needs, on community needs. Require clerk/officer presence. |
| Public relations | Unimportant. | Governing body known in school and by the appointing authority. | Governing body known to school. | Governing body known to valued interests. | Governing body known in local education system. |
| Style of working | Political or foundation leadership. Professional report. | Lay leadership. Importance of articulating different viewpoints and achieving agreement. | Professional leadership. Importance of rational argument. | Professional or managerial leadership. Importance of individual contribution. | Professional or lay leadership. Importance of articulating different viewpoints and achieving agreement. |
| Demands of work upon the governors | Undemanding. | Demanding. | Moderately demanding. | Undemanding, except in crisis or for key members. | Demanding. |
| View of educational government | Classical, democratic. | Pluralist. | Neo-pluralist. | Élitist. | Pluralist. |

the absence of dissatisfaction with the schools, and the weakness of governors' links with any constituency were relevant in explaining the dominance of this model.

One governing body could be characterised as occupying the mediating model. This was made possible by the LEA seeking to involve governing bodies in consultation on educational matters, and by the presence of governors with strong links with external institutions and interests.

The other two governing bodies we characterised as predominantly supportive in their approach. In both cases it was significant that the schools had recently experienced a change in headteacher. The former incumbents had not encouraged external interference and both governing bodies were in the process of renegotiating their role with the new heads. In one case, too, serious problems with school buildings, which necessitated support from the governors, dominated the agenda.

None of the governing bodies in our case studies could be characterised as occupying the accountable model. They were not seen in this way by appointing authorities, by schools, or indeed by the majority of their own membership, and lacked the authority, resources and, for the most part, inclination for such a role.

However, in their practice governing bodies resist tidy categorisation. Their various purposes are not clearly differentiated and they swing between them according to the situations and demands that present themselves. The variation in the work of governing bodies that was discussed at the beginning of this chapter is thus also due to pursuing multiple purposes, even although, as the preceding analysis should have shown, these require different approaches and relationships to succeed. Indeed, in the light of the discussion of theories of government in Chapter 2, it is plausible to suggest that different ideas of purpose reflect quite distinct conceptions of the role of lay authorities in educational government. Howell wondered whether governors 'will manage to meet and reconcile all the diverse and possibly conflicting demands being presented for them'.[23]

No doubt flexibility is a great virtue, but it is expecting a lot of the members of any institution that they should operate as rulers, advisers, mediators and assistants at one and the same time, and doubly difficult when they belong to an institution as spasmodic in its operation as a governing body. In these circumstances the 'woolly' definition of the governing body's role lends itself to manipulation by those interests that happen to be the most powerful – school or LEA, professional or political.

It is suggested, then, that the promotion of a number of potentially conflicting purposes combines with the structural position of governing bodies in the local education system to cause uncertainty in their work. The models of purpose represent ideal types and would no doubt require major changes in practice if any were to be implemented as set out. The emphasis on the contribution of local authority members, for example, reflects both the increasing importance of the LEA in defining the activities of schools and the increasing importance of party politics within local government.[24] Clearly, however, it is difficult to provide a councillor presence when each school has its own governing body. Such involvement might only be possible by such means as returning to grouping schools; providing one governing body to each secondary school and its feeder primaries or making governing bodies responsible for all schools in a given locality, as is the case with school boards in the United States.

Similarly, some of the models would require LEAs to devote considerable resources to governing bodies in terms of attendance of officers, provision of information, and time spent in negotiating decisions. This runs counter to current feelings in a number of authorities that withdrawal from governing body work is one of the least harmful ways of securing educational economies.

Such difficulties aside, the crux of our argument is that governing bodies have a number of possible roles open to them. Identification of a range of models may aid governors and those associated with their work in deciding what they really wish to do and what resources they require to apply their efforts effectively.

## Notes and references

1. See Bullivant, B., *The New Governors Guide*, Home and School Council Publications, 1974; Burgess, T. and Sofer, A., *The School Governor and Managers Handbook and Training Guide*, Kogan Page, 1978; Sallis, J., *The Effective School Governor*, Advisory Centre for Education, 1980; Wragg E. and Partington, J., *A Handbook for School Governors*, Methuen, 1980; Brooksbank, K. and Revell, J., *School Governors*, Councils and Education Press, 1981; National Union of Teachers, *Teacher Governors*, 1982; Socialist Educational Association, *Handbook for Labour Governors*, 1982.
2. Open University Governing Schools Course Team, *Governing Schools: Training Manual*, Open University, 1981.
3. Bacon, A., *Public Accountability and the Schooling System*, Harper & Row, 1978.
4. Baron G. and Howell, D., *The Government and Management of Schools*, Athlone, 1974.
5. Taylor Report *A New Partnership for our Schools*, HMSO, 1977.
6. Elliott, J. Bridges, D., Ebbutt, D., Gibson, R. and Nias, J., *School Accountability*, Grant McIntyre, 1981.
7. DHSS, *Health Care and its Costs*, HMSO, 1983.

8. DES, *Circular 4/81. Education Act 1980: School Government*, June 1981.
9. Kogan, M., *The Politics of Educational Change*, Fontana, 1978.
10. Baron and Howell, *op. cit.*
11. Taylor Report, *op. cit.*
12. Elliott *et al.*, *op. cit.*
13. *Report of the William Tyndale Junior and Infant Schools Public Inquiry* (The Auld Report), ILEA, 1976.
14. Glatter, R., 'Reforming school management: some structural issues', *Educational Administration* vol. 5, no. 1, Autumn 1976.
15. Howell, D., 'Problems of school government', in Simon, B. and Taylor, W. (eds), *Education in the Eighties*, Batsford, 1981.
16. Elliott *et al.*, *op. cit.*
17. Becher, T., Eraut, M. and Knight, J., *Policies for Educational Accountability*, Heinemann, 1981.
18. Bacon, *op. cit.*
19. Elliott *et al.*, *op. cit.*
20. Taylor Report, *op. cit.*
21. Howell, *op. cit.*
22. Becher *et al.*, *op. cit.*
23. Howell, *op. cit.*
24. Alexander, A., *Local Government in Britain Since Reorganisation*, Allen & Unwin, 1982.

# 9 Policies for school government

Some years have now elapsed since the publication of the Taylor Report on the future of school governing bodies, and the passing of legislation about them which might have been expected to lead to more uniformity. Yet our study provides evidence of the extent to which they vary. At the same time, however, there are important regularities of governing body performance and behaviour which give indications for future policy.

There remains a wide degree of choice among the kind of governing bodies that may be sponsored. In Chapter 8 we provided four main models which respond differently to such purposes as ensuring accountability, or advisory, supporting or mediating functions. As we read recent literature, however, including the Auld[1] and Taylor Reports,[2] the 1980 Act and the DES *Circular 4/81*,[3] the generally endorsed pattern is towards that of a governing body that will be accountable for the work of its school and which will, in effect, have authority to mediate between the professional decision-making of the teachers and the demands of parents and other client and community groups. This trend is consistent with the increased exposure of schools, and with the increased mandatory publication of information about them, including HMI reports. As researchers, we are clear that whichever model has been adopted by a particular authority the consequences have not been worked through. Instead, governing bodies have been left to negotiate and accommodate their role with other involved institutions. In Chapter 8 we summarised the reasons for governing bodies' uncertainty: they face a wide range of expectations and demands, and have to create different relationships with the surrounding institutions and forms of authority in the local educational system.

In considering the issues to which policy-makers and politicians should address themselves, we are saying no more than that the 'good' governing body is one which is clear about its purposes, whatever they are. Once this is achieved, it can then be endowed with the authority and other characteristics needed for it to fulfil those purposes, whether these are concerned with accountability or mediating purposes.

**Lack of autonomy**
Our first main group of conclusions concerns the degree to which governing bodies display sufficient autonomy to make any worthwhile

impact on either the setting of objectives and reviewing the performance of the school, or on policy creation in the wider political system.
Our evidence is clear that the local authority political–administrative
system provides a framework within which governing body powers and
behaviour are construed and constrained. No matter how free-stand-
ing, the governing body will be strongly affected by the political and
administrative systems which surround it, but these do not alone
account for the marked variations between their powers and tasks,
behaviour and performance. These result, too, from the variations in
formal degrees of delegation made to them, as well as in resources made
available.

Variation in the power delegated to governing bodies may corres-
pond to characteristics of local authorities. Governing body discretion
follows local authority views of what role the governing body should
occupy and with what resources. Although it is not always so, where the
ruling political party insists on strong party control, governing bodies
may have correspondingly lower degrees of discretion even if in some
areas weak political control also accompanies weak governor discretion.
At any rate, it does not follow that politicians who might be expected to
believe in 'more politics' are necessarily prepared to give more freedom
of action to those bodies formerly subordinate to them.

Issues for policy then arise. The first is whether such serious variation between the powers of governing bodies is tolerable in a society
where there might be assumed to exist common norms about democratic behaviour and institutions for its achievement. The general
public view, if informed on the matter, would be that such variation is
not tolerable; the governing bodies are 'Sleeping Beauties' whose time
for awakening is now. As a minimum, even if the strongest of the
models depicted in Chapter 8 is not deemed acceptable, the choice of
models made should at least be explicit, and a moral contract struck
with those entitled to be represented through governing bodies about
the extent of their powers.

There will then be important corollaries. Our sense is that, for
example, governing bodies whose chairman is a member of the education committee benefit from that fact, although the evidence about
commitment to the school rather than to political colleagues is ambivalent. Given a clearer role, however, a governing body could rightly
expect that the chairman becomes their representative rather than the
spokesman for the education committee whilst acting as chairman.
That much is expected of many key roles in public institutions which
are at the boundaries of institutions, or which are required to act as
brokers between one sub-system and another.

The same issue arises in the role of the clerk. He is usually a member of local authority staff and some belong to a division of the education department devoted to governing body matters. A governing body can hardly fail to benefit from the expertise and contacts of someone who is fully conversant with the working of the education department. The advantages derive partly from the ability of a practical administrator to work better at the mechanics of clerking; but administrators are also the repository of precedent and administrative practice and of the developing norms of those with whom they work. The feelings and knowledge of governors better enter the administrative and professional bloodstreams if members of local authority staff are committed to attending governing bodies and, during that time, empathising with governors' aims by working for them: the benefits should be two-way. It follows that, whilst clerking, the clerk must be unequivocally the servant of the governors and not of the education department. Public institutions abound with analogous cases of officers working at different levels of committees, and no committee would expect other than that the clerk should be entirely loyal to them in pursuing their concerns.

**Extension of role**
If in both structure and behaviour the governing bodies are weak, so are the expectations of local authorities and of governors themselves of the governing body role. In Chapter 6 we showed how the attitudes towards the governing body partly hinge on the extent to which it is regarded as part of the local authority's policy-making and consultative system and how far it is regarded as a way of introducing lay and local opinion into school decision-making.

Governors can develop corporately and individually if they are given the right information, argued with as equals, and expected to occupy roles well beyond those of symbolic representation (see Chapter 7). They can be empowered to view the school's self-evaluation critically and fully, and take seriously quasi-judicial functions such as suspension cases or, indeed, disciplinary cases affecting teachers.

The role of governors in the appointment of heads and assistant teachers is variable. It has never been determined authoritatively on a nationwide basis, and we find this surprising. The professionals may claim that the selection of other professionals is a matter for expertise: so it is. It is also a matter, however, of more general judgement in which laymen have been shown elsewhere to be capable of performing a useful function. And lay governors might include those expert in selection. In all, it does seem that the DES must decide how far governing bodies are the creatures of local authorities, or are to be in a weak position in relationship to the professionals, and how far they will be able to develop personality and powers of their own.

If all of these are regarded as serious tasks in which governors require help and education, it surely rests with the heads, and to some extent as well advisers and administrators, to educate governors to the full potential, although that would include the ability to criticise the school. It is not clear from the studies how far advisers regard governing bodies to be part of the educational system which they should advise. Expertise in the working of governing bodies may not be part of their already crowded requirements and, certainly, the political science of school government is hardly a leading component of the expertise they are expected to profess. There is a range of relationships between lay and professional in the work of the governing body. The lay element is fragmented and its place in setting objectives and reviewing performance correspondingly uncertain.

There are great variations in the governing body role in the oversight of the curriculum. For the most part governors are diffident, and leave it to the teachers or other professionals on the governing bodies. What the Taylor Report called 'an effective but unobtrusive information system for the governing body' has never been systematically thought through. Advisers' reports about a school are not a regular source of information for governors. Not all local authorities are committed to developing school self-evaluation in which data are used for the self-development of teachers and the school at large. Authorities and schools, then, vary in whether data are made available to the governors as a basis for their evaluation and interaction with the professionals. All heads, it is true, make reports to governing bodies. These have the merit of being consistent in the way they are made to each governing body, but there is extremely wide variation in the kind and status of the information which the governing bodies receive from this source.

## Governing body–school relations

The larger political administrative framework described above is in many ways easier to comprehend than what actually happens in practice. The most difficult issues inevitably concern the contacts between the governing body and the school. The picture we gave in Chapters 4, 5, 6 and 7 is one of governing bodies finding it difficult to establish a corporate personality of the kind assumed by the Taylor and Auld Reports.[4] It is difficult for governors or the governing body to develop contacts and relationships with the school. Because of multiple sources of membership, the infrequency of meetings, and other causes of collective or individual diffidence, governors are unable to develop a corporate viewpoint of the school. In their relationship, the full-time professionals are certain to become dominant. The governors do not feel able to evaluate performance, and depend on the different professionals we have described – the teachers, administrators and advisers, or the teacher governors – for leadership.

In Chapter 4, too, we depicted how the values of the school are institutionalised to the point where it is difficult for patterns of decision-making to be modified by gubernatorial action. At the same time, we produced examples of how the governors' role need not be simply that of acquiescent dummies. The way in which the chairman conducts meetings, and the extent to which the head gives a lead in helping governors find their feet, can help or hinder the new governors' ability to work in the governing body.

The interaction of governors with both the school and with each other may be constrained by such factors as the way that meetings are set up. The very fact that they take place within the school, so strongly boundaried and identified as an institution, underlines the status of the layman as an outsider, a guest on the territory of the professional. Meetings are episodic, with intervals of four months between meetings the norm. No wonder it is the professional members, in particular the teacher governors, who are the regular attenders. Our evidence too, is, that chairmen are pulled towards managerial interests and cooperation with the professionals.

**Teacher governors**
Among the professionals there is the special position of teacher governors. Our view is that the case for teacher governors is an open one. Teacher membership of the governing body (as opposed to active attendance, or observation) is a mixed blessing given the governors' task of ensuring accountability. Teacher governors may be directly committed to the work of the school and able to bring both general expertise and particular knowledge to bear on matters of concern for the governors. But they may feel that they are there primarily to defend and support the position of their colleagues on the teaching staff. And if governing bodies are to gain strength in evaluating the school such actions become more difficult if the potential subjects of critique, or those who represent them, are present on an equal footing.

**The head and governors**
Among the educational professionals, the head's attitude is a major determinant of governors' performance, powers and development. This would always be so under any conceivable structure for governing bodies, and our suggestions for improving governing body performance closely involve the heads' behaviour. Governing bodies can be viewed narrowly in terms of power relationships between different stakeholders in education. They might indeed be a key point at which

accountability is reviewed and discharged. Equally, however, they have a strong *expressive* potential. They can embody a sense of community concern for the well-being of the school and a breaking-down of barriers between professional providers and lay recipients of educational services. If heads are concerned, as many must be, with what can be called the second-order tasks of the school – the education of the public, including parents, whose attitudes towards schooling and the particular school can make so much difference to its progress and well-being – they will regard the enabling of governors to act strongly to be part of their educational task.

### Governors and the community

The lay governors have difficulties not only relating to the professionals – and the difficulties, we emphasise, are those of role and expectation, as well as those that might arise from the behaviour of the professionals we have observed – but also in relating to the community. The laity among governors is fragmented inasmuch as its own mandate is variable. Not all have any sense of a constituency, and not all have strong constituency links. The contrast with members of the education committee is marked; they feel fully mandated to act. And, increasingly, councillors regard it as an essential condition of their political survival that they keep these links strong. This may point to the need to increase the elective composition of governing bodies' membership. But for people to want to become governors more power would have to be allocated to them.

We find, too, that local community networks are not a good source of information for the governors, and are not used in a systematic way. Parents tend to go directly to the school rather than to the governors. Even if visits to the school are made, governors do not have a grip on the information necessary for them the evaluate the school and/or to play any accountable role for it. We do not think it unnatural that parents should complain, or make other representations, or offer views directly to the professionals. That is appropriate behaviour. It is surprising, however, that no other and secondary feedback occurs through governors. The general conclusion is, indeed, that governing bodies do not represent a significant location for exchange between professional and lay interests, though some occur through personal contacts. Professionals may help to educate governors in their roles. There can be sharing of tasks; but in general there is not. In Chapter 5 we displayed two types (A and B) of interaction. In type A the governors essentially leave it to the professionals; in type B, it is a shared role. We do not find, and would not propose, a role in which governors are dominant and managerial in their relationship with professionals.

## Models for action

But that brings us full circle to the question of objectives. At a time when it is no longer acceptable for public institutions to lack mechanisms whereby those affected by their work participate, within a broad span of definitions of that term, or are part of the consultative process, a residual and trustee fire-fighting role seems hardly adequate. This point can be argued from abstract principles of representative democracy and from the point of view, too, of what makes a 'good' school and 'good' education. The influences of the non-educational environment of the peer group, of the media, of the political and social temper of the times, press hard upon young people and those who seek to educate them alike. The school needs direct and continuous information about what its clients express, or fail to express, as their educational needs, and how those needs can be placed in the setting of the wider social, employment and political environment. In other words, the school cannot do without the information that a strong governing body could provide. Teachers can be expected to be responsible for the interpretation of social values and their acknowledgement, in the curriculum and in the behaviour of the school. That is why the stronger governing body role is appropriate.

Simply to provide training for governors will not meet the case. Training of governors – or anybody else – depends upon a secure grasp of what might be the objectives of training. We may ask why governors bother to sustain membership. The answer is that many do not. Many 'cool out'. Where governors remain as long-standing members it is because they have an effective role to play. Others stay on because they believe that there is an important residual trustee role in case things go wrong and the school manifestly falls down on its obligations to its pupils. But so residual a role fails to exploit major resources for the schools.

The strong and accountable model of the governing body conveys with it considerable optimism about the ability of the schools to attract devoted service from people who are prepared to learn enough about the school and to be active in helping to fashion its policies and practice. It could be argued that if the governors become more powerful the problems just described may become less obvious. Yet all of the problems of representation then remain. Councillors keep in touch with their networks because they have to stand for election and are compelled to make themselves known to their constituents for that purpose. They also possess real power by virtue of their membership of committees or access to those who make decisions on local authority committees. Similar inducements are unlikely to be available to school governors since the first point of access will always be the teacher if parents or others are troubled about their children's education or merely want to know more about the school.

These doubts therefore raise issues of a more general kind. A major conceptual problem is whether the governing body is, or is to be regarded as, part of the school or as an institution occupying a position between the school and the local authority and the community. The more it is part of the school the more it is bound to occupy a supportive and an advisory role. Only if it feels itself to be, to some degree at least, external to the school would it be able to take on the accountability purpose. Again, it is unclear whether the governing body is or should be not only concerned with governing or supporting the school but also acting as one of many other institutions in society which contribute towards the agenda-forming of the larger political system. We get no sense of the governing bodies as being part of the wider network, although they are surely affected by the attitudes and degrees of delegation created by the political–administrative system. Alternatively, one could take a more optimistic, pluralistic view which assumes that the more powerful political entities, such as local authorities, would see the benefit of conferred power to smaller groups such as governing bodies on the grounds that bureaucrats and politicians need opposition.[5] If issues can be tested and argued on the site of their potential impacts, it might be said, the political system will be sure of its ground before it goes on to formulate policies of wider application. Or again, it could be held that because education depends so strongly on client–practitioner development, powerful entities such as local authorities must delegate to lower levels.

But it is not clear whether governing bodies are expected to support and advise, or whether they are expected to govern the school. And it is not clear whether they have freedom within the larger political system to strike up their own identity, or whether the larger political system expects them to pick up and help collate the changing norms in society. Because of these uncertainties of purpose governing bodies have a peculiar lack of identity and sponsorship. The people they are supposed to serve do not feel them to be an active component in the development of their children's education. The local authorities have a legal sponsorship role in that it is upon their drafting of Articles that governing bodies are created and it is local authorities who determine which resources and powers governors will possess.

For these reasons we feel that the DES decision to fund our research was timely. This is a period when local politics and decision-making are going through radical reappraisal, and when decentralisation is on the agenda of many local authorities. It should be all the easier to recognise that if strong governing bodies seem to have little to offer in exchange for more power they can at least legitimise education by enhancing local commitment to it. The case for strong governing bodies has been cogently urgent for nearly 25 years by a succession of interest groups: CASE, ACE and NAGM. But it is essentially for the DES to take the lead in determining the balance that should be struck between the powers of local authorities and of governing bodies which are closer to the schools which both serve. At present governing bodies lack political sponsorship.

In Chapter 2 we set out some of the theories and concepts against which our empirical analysis might be set. Our research has led us to endorse none of them to the exclusion of others; all have something to contribute to our understanding of particular cases as we observe them.

We hope our analysis and description will contribute towards the process of clarifying and strengthening governing bodies' position.

**Notes and references**
1. *Report of the William Tyndale Junior and Infant Schools Public Inquiry* (The Auld Report), ILEA, 1976.
2. *A New Partnership for our Schools* (Taylor Report), DES and Welsh Office, HMSO, 1977.
3. *DES Circular 4/81. Education Act 1980: School Government*, June 1981.
4. Auld and Taylor Reports, *op. cit.*
5. Peters, B. Guy, 'Insiders and outsiders: the politics of pressure group influence and bureaucracy', *Administration and Society*, vol.9, no.2, Sage Publications, 1977.

# Afterword: The Government's Green Paper: Parental Influence at School. A New Framework for School Government in England and Wales

Shortly after our book was prepared for publication a Green Paper was presented to Parliament (Cmnd 9242, HMSO, May 1984). Green Papers are important documents which may play a part in the formulation and subsequent enactment of legislation. Following consultation, however, the new legislation about school governing bodies may, in the event, bear little resemblance to the proposals of the Green Paper. Nevertheless, its publication so directly touches on the concerns followed in this book that we cannot forbear to comment on it in this Afterword to our research.

*Parental Influences at School* is a courageous document which proposes a decisive break with the past. Whereas school government both before and since the 1980 Education Act has been primarily a local authority activity in which other groups such as parents and teachers have been allowed to take part, the Green Paper envisages governing bodies which act as independent forces to focus on and improve the work of the schools, and in which parents will have the leading voice.

The new proposals have two main objectives: to give parents the right to form the majority of the governing body of each school (Para 3(1)); and to enable the more effective working of school governing bodies through a clearer definition of their range of functions (Para 3(2)). We shall comment briefly on each objective in the light of our research.

### Parent governors as a majority
The composition of the governing body is an obvious focus for examination by those who seek change. The 1980 Education Act tackled the question of who should govern before it dealt with grouped or individual governing bodies. Similarly, the Green Paper lays great emphasis on the numbers in and balance between particular categories of governors, with the aim of ensuring that the collective parental voice is potentially the loudest on the governing body.

It was not however our experience that the composition of a governing body gave the key to its internal balance of power. Regular attendance, eligibility to continue in office for several years, a sense of competence to address the issues under discussion, and of legitimacy to represent the views of others, all contributed to governors' propensity to influence their fellows, and parent governors did not score highly where these qualities were concerned.

However, the broad proposal of the Green Paper for a parental majority may be intended as a positive spur to the parents as a group, helping to counteract the weakness of their position relative to the politicians and the professional teachers who are their fellow governors. And some of the more detailed proposals of the Green Paper will affect parents' capacity to govern. A standard three-year term of office is suggested for all categories of governor (Para 18) – but this will not fully meet the problem of high turnover of parent governors as they will still cease to hold office immediately they no longer have a child on the roll of the school. The parental group on the governing body may well be strengthened by the presence of what we dubbed 'politico parents' (see p. 97) – LEA nominated governors who have children at the school – as it is now proposed that 'no one should be eligible to become a governor by one route because he is also eligible to become a governor by another' (Para 14). Formerly, Articles of Government in certain LEAs explicitly ruled out such double eligibility.

In summary, we feel that the proposal to favour parent governors by legislating for a parental majority on school governing bodies does not directly address the problems with which parent governors have been faced, in attempting to work in partnership with professionals and politicians on the governing body. But, as an enlarged if not a majority group who seem to be being offered the accolade of 'sponsorship' by central government, parent governors may become more visible to the parent body as a whole, and the position of parent governor may be more prestigious and sought after than hitherto.

## The effective functioning of school governing bodies

Our research found that one of the major hindrances to effective work by governing bodies was their uncertainty of purpose. They faced a wide range of expectations and demands but had been left to negotiate and accommodate their role with other involved institutions. Any attempt to clarify the proper function of the bodies is therefore to be welcomed, although it will be likely to be interpreted in different ways in different local authorities.

The Green Paper is at pains to put forward proposals which touch on several of the areas where there is presently uncertainty. It provides, for example, much needed clarification of the role of governing bodies in appointing head teachers and assistant teachers. However, what the Green Paper has to say is not always beyond criticism in its own clarity, but it provides a solid and thought provoking basis for consultative discussion.

### The governing body and the school curriculum

There are two models of curricular development which enable some involvement by the laity. In one model, the professionals formulate and deliver the curriculum, but are subject to critique by the laity. A more radical model is that in which the laity (the whole governing body) create the school's curricular philosophy, which the professionals then 'deliver'. This second model is the one which the Green Paper appears to favour. Nevertheless the text of the paper is ambivalent in its treatment of the distribution of functions between governing body, the head and other teachers, where the curriculum is concerned.

The governing body would have a duty to determine the statement of the school's curricular aims and objectives, and to review that statement from time to time (Para 43(1)). In performing these tasks it would however also have a duty (a) to seek the advice of the head teacher; and (b) to consult the LEA. While boldly stating that the governing body should have scope to 'determine the range and pattern of the school's curriculum' (Para 45), the Green Paper recognises that no curricular statement is likely to be given practical effect in what the pupils are taught unless it is compatible with the curricular intentions of the LEA, the head and other teachers.

The rock bottom intention of the proposal, it seems, is to 'provide an opportunity for open debate on the school's curriculum in which parents and other interested parties could join' (Para 45). This, in our view, would be a desirable outcome, but it is not quite the purposeful grasping of the curricular nettle which the Green Paper seems at first to presage. In particular, the Green Paper is silent on the professionalism to be expected from the whole body of teachers in a school, and their rights to contribute and formulate the curriculum, and not merely join the head in 'advising' and 'delivery'.

### The clerking of governing bodies

Our research indicated that while governing bodies may in theory have an important part to play in the work of the school and the LEA, in practice their contribution can be made or marred by the administrative support at their disposal (pp. 124–128).

The Green Paper appropriately acknowledges the governing body's need for the services of a 'clerk with adequate knowledge and experience of the LEA's operations', and that this need would be all the greater if the Green Paper proposals for changes in governing body composition were adopted, causing some 'loss of expertise . . . and fairly frequent changes of membership' (Para 69). However, the paragraph also lays emphasis on the need to consult the governing body before appointing or dismissing a clerk. Our research suggests that the greatest need is not to avoid enforcing an unwelcome presence but rather to ensure that LEAs are willing to make a clerk or officer available. A theme of the Green Paper as a whole is that LEAs should treat governing bodies as a more important part of the system than hitherto, including giving them a higher priority in financial terms. Clerking is an area which should benefit from this.

The balance of loyalty of the clerk between the LEA and the governing body, identifed as a problem in some of our case studies, is not discussed in the Green Paper. Whilst scarcely a subject for legislation, some guidelines might prove helpful.

### The role of the chairman
The realities of power, in school governing bodies, circle at present around the headteacher and the chairman (who is frequently from the LEA-nominated group of governors). Our book has drawn attention to the importance of the chairman's role, and the ways in which chairman and headteacher may be constrained to work together (Chapter 6).

The Green Paper duly and repeatedly acknowledges the powers and responsibilities of the headteacher both in the school and in interation with the governing body. But, beyond a fleeting reference to election in Para 21, the role of the chairman receives no mention in the Green Paper's pages. This is an unfortunate omission. Whatever changes were made in governing body composition, who became chairman would remain an important consideration, as it is at present. The Green Paper proposals perhaps make it marginally more likely that a parent would become chairman. There would no longer be any competition from community governors, who were formerly eligible in areas where such governorships existed. However, LEA members might well make even more strenuous efforts than hitherto to assume the chairmanship role.

### The governing body, the school and the LEA
The Green Paper grapples conscientiously with the vexed question of the division of functions between these three bodies so far as particular aspects of education are concerned, but it begs some of the most fundamental questions about the role of the governing body in the education system which our research has attempted to address.

The Green Paper's very title – *Parental Influence at School* – embodies an assumption that the proposed new framework for school government will enable governing bodies to focus on and influence their particular schools. It does not say whether governing bodies should expect to play a consultative role in the formation of ecucation policy in the LEA as a whole. Nor does it refer to the possible role of the governing body in absorbing and collating changing norms in society. The Green Paper's proposals have been framed 'after consideration of the wide-ranging recommendations of the Taylor Committee', but some of the spirit of the Taylor Report which had filtered into school government in many areas would be negated by the proposals of this paper. Parents might gain an enhanced opportunity to influence the school (although, for reasons stated above, we doubt this). But other voices which were tentatively being raised, through the medium of school government, in the schools and the local education authorities would now be silenced. In the interests of limiting the size of the governing bodies, the Green Paper proposals do not leave scope for appointing additional categories of governor or for co-option (Para 16). In some authorities this would mean that representatives of particular groups in the community, local employers, representatives of higher education, pupils, non-teaching staff would all cease to be eligible for nomination or co-option.

Our research showed that these governors did not find it easy to advance their particular points of view in the governing body, nor to use the governing body as a way through to the LEA. But the channel for communication was there, and sensitive adjustment might have made it a more free flowing one. The Green Paper proposals would block the channel altogether, and place upon parents alone the task of bringing an alternative perspective to the deliberations of the teaching professionals and the politicians.

It remains questionable whether parents are indeed eager to advance their own point of view – levels of interest currently displayed in serving on governing bodies would suggest not – and whether these would be capable of translation into coherent programmes that were both acceptable to the teachers and possible within the policy and resource framework that must be maintained by the LEA.

Such doubts aside, the Green Paper is important in confirming that governing bodies matter. They are more than symbolic. They have a role to perform and this requires a more continuous relationship to their schools than is commonly the case today. The Green Paper recognises that this carries implications for support and training (Paras 92–95). From our experience we would add that it also carries considerable implications for key roles, such as the chairman, headteacher and clerk, and for the style and ethos by which governing bodies function. Service as a school governor is the most common opportunity of public service available to the citizens of this country. The Green Paper has asserted its importance (Para 91) and laid out a clearer and more demanding role. It remains to be seen whether this is attractive and viable.

# Appendix I

**Methods of the research**
The overall strategy of the research was one of naturalistic enquiry, in Denzin's terms.[1] There was no need to mark out artificial boundaries for an area of study, or to set up experimental situations. Governing bodies already existed in which we could explore, in microcosm, the nature of political systems, the exchanges and dependencies between them, the relationship between values and process, theories of representation and participation and the nature of accountability in education. Governing body meetings were the natural and primary focus for our research. Our methodological problems were to ensure that our observations of these and other events accurately, reliably and validly reflected the behaviours recorded, and to decide how, and how far, we should explore around and beyond the corporate life of the governing body to understand its meaning for participants and its political and institutional context. A further problem was the need to assemble, reflect and report on our research material in a way which would be helpful for practitioners and policy-makers in school government, as well as for political scientists.

*The case study mode*
Given the resources available for the study – a small team of researchers able to work full-time on the project over a period of three years – and the apparently episodic corporate life of the phenomena to be studied (governing bodies), the case study mode was an obvious choice. Case study work (rather than, for example, a survey method which might entail the employment of hired interviewers) would make good use of the resources of people and time already available for the research. Extended case study work enables the dynamic of institutional processes, and individual relationships, to be monitored and appraised over time. Moreover, case studies provide a data base for analytic description of components and processes and for model-building, and these were among the objectives of our research.

*Comparability of the case studies*
The case study method has as one of its strengths the ability to explore diversity of practice. Nevertheless, if several such studies are carried out as part of a single project, some comparable elements should form

part of each case examined. In the school governing bodies project the same range of techniques was employed in each study – observations, semi-structured interviews, and the study of documents. Coverage, in terms of interviews undertaken, was founded on two principles: the notion of reputational sampling (i.e. making contact with those who are seen to be important to other people) and the more systematic coverage of a range of incumbents of formal roles which, although not necessarily seen to be important reputationally, plainly had legitimacy and relevance in our study area.

The first stage in each case study was the general examination of current educational and political issues in the LEA, through the study of documents. Field work with the particular governing body usually began with the observation of a governing body meeting, together with the study of minutes of earlier meetings. Interviews then ensued with the chairman, all or most of the governors, the headteacher, and other staff at the school, using the 'reputational' and 'systematic' criteria described above. Where relevant, school meetings were observed and documents examined, to identify points of organisational change, development and/or stability, and to monitor the emergence of demands which might or might not impact on governing bodies, also the reactions of teachers to any governing body initiatives. All governing body meetings, whether regular or specially convened, were observed over a period of four school terms. During the same period, some parents were interviewed to explore the practice as well as the rhetoric of home/school relations. Beyond the immediate orbit of the school, local educational issues were monitored through a study of the local press and attendance at public meetings. Where appropriate, meetings of educational interest groups were attended and interviews undertaken. At the level of the local authorities, key councillors and officers were interviewed, some non-public working parties and sub-committees observed, and other regular meetings monitored through the study of documents. Repeated interviews were held with key governors (in particular the chairman and the headteacher or deputy headteacher) and any changes in governing body membership were followed up.

Particular educational or political issues which happened to become a focus of interest during the period of case study were followed through, in school and/or locality, and provided an opportunity to study interaction between school, governing body and community. Examples of these were the expansion of a school's sphere of operation to include community education, and a proposal to establish tertiary colleges in one of the authorities.

*Validity of the data base*

In this project, the problems of validity in the case study mode were tackled at a number of levels. Cross-checking took place through the use of differing research techniques (interview, observation, study of documents). Validity was also tested through team discussion, when the accumulated knowledge of the individual researcher about his research 'patch' was explored and criticised. At the end of each case study, a written account of acquired information was submitted for confirmation to the chairman of the governing body, the headteacher and senior figures in the local authority. Towards the end of the project reflective analysis was tested in seminar groups of research participants and practitioners in the field of study.

*Selection of LEAs and governing bodies for case study*

Consideration of the criteria to be applied in selecting local education authorities and governing bodies passed through several stages, some of them preceding the funded period of the research.

Eventually it was decided to make a judgement sample based chiefly on four criteria: type of local education authority, political culture of the local authority, type of school and governing body composition.

Once the criteria for selection are established it is relatively simple to identify suitable authorities and institutions. Research access can never be taken for granted, and must always be carefully negotiated, but it is equally important not to request access and then fail to follow through with research because of a change in criteria. No insoluble problems with regard to access were encountered in the authorities eventually approached. The sample of eight case studies chosen had the following features:

| | | |
|---|---|---|
| Type of local education authority: | 1 shire county | |
| | 1 large metropolitan | |
| | 2 outer urban | |
| Political culture of local authority: | 2 Labour, 2 Conservative (1980–2) | |
| | | age range |
| Type of school(s) governed: | Infants & Juniors | 5–11 |
| | J, M & I voluntary aided | 5–11 |
| | First & Middle | 5–12 |
| | High | 12–16 |
| | Secondary | 11–18 (n = 3) |
| | Special (ESN M&S) | 11–16 |

Governing body       6 individual governing bodies
composition:         2 joint governing bodies
(pattern and balance of membership was varied. See Figure 6.1, p. 98)

The selection of the actual schools and governing bodies to be approached was influenced by local authority suggestions and guidance, but in all cases research access was personally negotiated with the headteachers and chairmen of governors concerned.

## Local authorities and schools studied in the research
The schools are described as they were in January 1982. Staff and pupil numbers quoted are taken from statistics supplied to the DES at that time.

### Lorrenshire LEA
Lorrenshire was predominantly rural, although heavy industry was significant in the county town and in one or two centres elsewhere. The county town was also a centre for higher education. Tourism was an important activity. The southern part of the county had important scientific research establishments. Good road and rail communications enabled residents to commute to London and industrial centres in neighbouring counties as well as to the county town itself.

Throughout the study the authority was controlled by the Conservative Party. However, following the elections of May 1981, this party's overall majority was reduced to three.

### Townmeadow Infant and Junior Schools
The Townmeadow schools were situated in a suburb on the edge of Enton, in the south of Lorrenshire. Enton, with an old history as a market centre, had become something of a dormitory for the nearby county town with its considerable service and industrial employment. The suburb in which the schools stood was predominantly post-second world war development. The housing itself was a mixture of public and private estates, children attending the schools being drawn from both types.

The two schools shared a single site. The older of the two sets of buildings opened in 1972 as a first school, but became an infant school in 1977 when Townmeadow Junior School was opened on the same campus.

In 1982 the infant school had 108 children on roll (58 boys, 48 girls) aged from 5 to 7 plus. The staff comprised a headteacher and four assistant teachers, one of whom worked part-time. Classes combined children from two age cohorts – five and six-year-olds, and six and seven-year-olds. Classes were of standard size with a single teacher. Much of the teaching was based on groups.

The junior school, taking children from 7 plus to 11 plus, had 265 children (129 boys, 136 girls), on roll in 1982, with a staff of head-teacher and ten assistant teachers, one of whom worked part-time. The basic form of organisation was large, double-year classes – two for the eight and nine-year-olds, and two for the ten and eleven-year-olds – each class having two class teachers. There were groups for English work, different groups for number work, and different groups again for project work, although this was often organised on an individual basis.

The two schools had a joint governing body. The headteachers of the junior and infant schools respectively were husband and wife.

Daneshill Special School
Daneshill Special School opened in 1959. It catered for children of secondary school age (11–16), who under the regulations in force prior to the 1981 Education Act had been classified as ESN mild or severe, or as maladjusted.

In 1982 the school had 117 pupils on roll, boys outnumbering girls by a proportion of two to one. 57 of the pupils were classed as ESN(M), 25 as ESN(S), 13 as maladjusted, and 9 in other special categories. 13 children attended primary schools, and came to Daneshill on a part-time basis for help with their reading. The school was co-educational.

The school was staffed by a headteacher (appointed in 1978) and twelve assistant teachers, of whom one was part-time. The school also employed five full-time child care staff to assist the teachers in the classroom.

ESN(S) and (M) children were allocated to separate classes. There were five classes for (M) children organised on a year basis, and three classes for (S) children organised broadly on a two-yearly basis. The (S) classes contained 9–11 children, the (M) classes 14–17. Each of the three (S) classes had a child care assistant, in addition to a teacher, and there was one child care assistant to support the five (M) classes.

Daneshill school was situated in a suburb on the south side of Enton. Because it was a special school, Daneshill did not have an immediate local catchment area. Although some children lived in nearby streets, the school served the south of Lorrenshire and took children from villages and towns up to twelve miles away from Enton.

*Stapleton LEA*
Stapleton LEA was a single-purpose authority, responsible for the provision of education for the central part of a large conurbation, which

included both very affluent and deprived inner city areas. In terms of employment the whole area was a major commercial centre and the service sectors, both public and private, were major employers. Manufacturing industry had tended to move away in recent years. Because of the nature of employment people had a considerable distance to travel to work.

In parts of the area a high proportion of births was to mothers born in the New Commonwealth and Pakistan. The authority's own survey of school pupils showed that one in ten children spoke English as a second language and 125 different mother tongue languages were spoken in its schools. Parts of the area had a high population density and a correspondingly high level of social and housing deprivation. A large proportion of families in the whole area lived in rented accommodation, some of which was in a poor condition.

Politically, the authority had a Labour majority throughout the period of the research.

Parker School

In 1956 two schools were opened on the site now occupied by Parker School. One was a boys' grammar school, the other a boys' secondary modern school. In 1969 these were combined to form a single-sex comprehensive school. A new headteacher was appointed in 1972, and still held this post at the time of case study. In 1976 Parker School had begun a phased development towards becoming a mixed school by admitting girls to the first year.

The school stood in an affluent part of the metropolis, but nearby were areas with inner city characteristics. In 1982 there were 1068 pupils on roll (469 girls, 599 boys) in the 11–18 age range. Of these 116 were in the sixth form. The pupil population was from a broad social mix and multi-racial in character. A survey carried out by the school into mother tongue teaching revealed approximately 200 pupils speaking a first language other than English with a total of 36 languages spoken.

Full-time teaching staff comprised 75, with additional support from a number of part-time and specialist teachers. The school also had a large number of non-teaching staff, including technicians, library and resource staff, clerical staff and school keepers.

Parker was a Group 11 school, with a seven-form entry. Teaching departments were grouped into three faculties: arts, humanities, and maths, science and technology. The pastoral structure was based on a tutor system coordinated by a year head. In the main, the staff of one teaching department was responsible for the pastoral care of a single year group.

Hendrick Junior Mixed and Infants School
Hendrick School was a voluntary aided Church of England school. It was founded in 1834, and by 1982 had become a Group 4 combined junior and infant school taking children from the ages 4 to 11, with one form of entry.

In 1982 there were 148 children on roll (75 boys, 73 girls). The School was organised into six classes based upon mixed age groups with children moving between classes on two occasions each year.

The former headteacher had retired because of ill-health in 1981. At the beginning of the case study the deputy headteacher was serving as acting head until the appointment of a new headteacher in January 1982. In addition to the headteacher there were six full-time members of staff and one part-time teacher. The school also had three helpers, a resident schoolkeeper and a school secretary.

The majority of pupils lived within a mile of the school. Teachers distinguished between the different parts of the catchment area. Most children came from a recently constructed estate of tower blocks which was felt to have a poor reputation locally. The next most sizeable group came from the blocks of flats nearer the school which were built in the 1950s and were seen to serve traditional working-class families. Finally, some children came from more affluent apartments nearer the centre of the city. Some of these were from overseas families currently working in the city.

The major characteristic of the pupil population was its wide ethnic mix. Just under half the school population were from ethnic minorities and at a recent count this included 29 different nationalities. The largest groups within this were Africans, Bangladeshi, Pakistanis and Chinese. This variation in ethnic background contributed to the social mix in the school.

*Mead LEA*
Mead lay between the suburban and inner city areas of a large metropolitan authority. It had been formed by the amalgamation of two former local authorities, and had a population of approximately 240,000. The area was important as a centre for railways and industry, with three large trading estates within its boundaries. The southern part of the authority had a high concentration of ethnic minorities, a mixed housing stock, and displayed some of the characteristics of an inner city area.

Mead was Labour controlled and had been since 1971. The May 1982 elections resulted in a hung council with the Labour group controlling the council only by the casting vote of the mayor.

## Austen High School

The building now used by Austen High School originally housed two single-sex grammar schools, opened in the late nineteenth century. Austen School was established as an all-through mixed comprehensive school using the split site in 1973. A new headteacher was appointed in 1976, and was still in post at the time of case study.

The school stood in a suburban area in the southern part of Mead, the two sets of buildings being divided by a busy road. In 1982, there were 877 pupils on roll (439 girls, 438 boys), in the 11–18 age range. Of these, 124 were in the sixth form. About one-third of the pupils were indigenous white, one-third West Indian and one-third of Asian extraction.

Teaching staff comprised 76, of whom two were part-time. A cultural liaison teacher and an education welfare officer were also based at the school, and worked closely with the pastoral staff.

Austen High School was a Group 11 school. Teaching departments were grouped in six faculties: technology, science, mathematics, modern languages, English and humanities. There were also three extra departments: drama, music and art.

Pupils were allocated a class and a particular room in their first year, and retained the same 'home-base', tutor, and head of year, throughout their time at the school. Heads of year oversaw both the pastoral and academic needs of their pupils.

## Beckett High School

Beckett School opened as a secondary modern school in 1956. In 1973 it became an all-through comprehensive school. A new headteacher was appointed in 1975, and was still in post at the time of case study.

In 1982 there were 899 pupils on roll (395 girls, 504 boys) in the 11–18 age range. Of these 143 were in the sixth form.

Beckett was a Group 11 school. Teaching staff comprised 85 of whom twelve were part-time. In addition there was a cultural liaison teacher and two education welfare officers based at the school. Teaching departments were grouped into six faculties: language and communication, maths and business studies, science, design, expressive arts, and social science and environmental studies.

Year heads and form tutors were responsible for the pastoral care of the pupils. Pupils had the same year head throughout their period in the school. The cultural liaison teacher, education welfare officers and school-based nurse all worked closely with the pastoral staff.

Beckett School stood in an affluent enclave of middle-class housing, but most of the pupils came from council estates and terraced housing a short distance from the school. About 85 per cent of pupils were from ethnic minority groups broadly made up of 70 per cent Afro-Caribbean and 15 per cent Asian, but including a number of other minority groups, At a recent count made by the school there were approximately 52 different nationalities in the pupil population.

## Robart LEA

Robart's boundaries, as a unit of local government, had remained unchanged since the nineteenth century. It lay in the border suburbs of a large metropolis, and had a population of approximately 200,000.

Local employment was for the most part confined to the retail trade and commerce, although there were a few long-established specialist factories and works. Robart could however be broadly characterised as a commuter area, housing many professional people.

Some parts of Robart had a well-established Jewish population. At the time of the research, the overall New Commonwealth and Pakistani population of Robart was estimated at 15 per cent. Although there was some clustering of minority groups in residential areas, the catchment areas of particular schools were not markedly socially or culturally diverse.

Robart had a long-standing and substantial Conservative majority. The council was consensus-seeking rather than conflictful in its mode of operation. The leading minority party, although slenderly based in comparison with the controlling party, was accorded official status and privileges and a disproportionate share of committee places. In May 1982 a slight electoral swing led to the outnumbering of Labour councillors by Alliance councillors, who became the leading minority party.

## Sanders High School

There had been a school on the site now used by Sanders since 1929. Following the 1944 Education Act the original elementary school became a co-educational secondary modern school. The headmaster appointed to this school in 1969 was still in post at the time of case study, but the school had been reorganised as a comprehensive high school in 1974.

Sanders was a Group 10C school. In 1982 there were 950 pupils on roll (442 girls, 508 boys), their ages ranging from 12 to 16. Pupils were organised in four year groups (Year 13, Year 14, Year 15, Year 16), each comprising eight forms. Over 60 per cent of pupils continued their education elsewhere after leaving the school at age 16. There were 59 members of teaching staff, of whom one was part-time.

The socioeconomic range of families from which pupils came was wide. The majority of pupils lived in middle-class housing, some of it extremely highly priced. The catchment area of the school at the time of case study also included two estates of local authority housing, where about 30 per cent of the pupils lived. One of these estates housed former residents of Inner London. There were very few pupils from ethnic minority groups, nearly all the families sending children to Sanders School being indigenous white.

Carstairs First and Middle Schools
Carstairs First and Middle Schools shared a campus. Their adjoining buildings were purpose-built in 1966, in a corner of Robart which was difficult of access.

In 1982 there were 340 pupils on the roll of the First School (172 girls, 168 boys). These included 52 half-time pupils in a nursery class (30 girls, 22 boys). Because of the term-by-term intake to the school, the organisation of classes was flexible, some children being grouped in classes spanning two age years, and others in classes of a single year group, at certain periods of the year. The preferred pattern was for all children to be taught in single-year group classes, and this was possible in some terms of the year.

In 1982 the First School was staffed by a headmistress (appointed in 1976) a deputy headmistress and eleven other full-time teachers, together with two part-time teachers. In addition, the nursery class was staffed by one full-time teacher and one nursery assistant, plus two students in training.

The Middle School catered for children aged 8–12. In 1982 there were 366 pupils on roll (179 girls, 187 boys). Middle school staff comprised a headmaster (appointed in 1980) a deputy headmistress and fourteen other full-time teachers, together with three part-time teachers. Four peripatetic music teachers also visited the school. Teaching staff worked chiefly in year teams.

The two schools shared a caretaker (and a governing body), but in all other respects their organisation was separate.

Most of the pupils lived within a mile of the schools. Their home backgrounds spanned a wide socioeconomic range. At the time of case study, about 50 children in both the first and middle schools were receiving free school meals.

The pupil population of both schools was ethnically heterogeneous, at least one-third of all pupils being the children of parents born outside the United Kingdom. This ethnically-mixed sector of pupils included Chinese, Malayan, Korean, West Indian and Asian children. Asians formed the most substantial ethnic minority.

About one-third of the children who joined Carstairs via the nursery class or the first school were not English-speaking. Of those who were bilingual, not all could name their mother-tongue. A few older children who came directly into the middle school did not speak English. The schools were used by a number of families from overseas diplomatic services.

*Scope and manner of the fieldwork*
In all, 369 interviews were carried out, and 51 full meetings of the case study governing bodies were observed; 52 other meetings or events were also observed. These included sub-committee meetings of governors, LEA working parties, parents' meetings and staff meetings in the schools, and various other school events, as well as training meetings for governors and meetings of local groups.

Governing body meetings and other observation sessions
Researchers received the same agenda papers as governors. They did not contribute to the meetings, unless asked to report on the progress of the research. Following each meeting, a typewritten analysis of what took place was circulated for internal discussion by the research team. These analyses were prepared from notes.

All other meetings observed, including staff appointments meetings, were similarly written up.

Interviews
These were recorded in note form by the researcher concerned, and typed up for team study. Interviews lasted from 40 minutes to 2½ hours. Most interviews were single events, but some key informants were seen 4 to 6 times.

A very flexible approach was taken to the task of interviewing governors. Interviews were arranged at whatever time and place was convenient for them. In a handful of cases, when it proved impossible for a governor or other respondent to see the researcher, telephone interviews were conducted. A few interviews of this kind were also carried out when exploring the ramifications of interest groups in the community. The particular problems of mapping community links with schools and governing bodies are further discussed below.

Before embarking on any of the field work, guidelines for the interviews with the main role-holders (headteachers, governing body chairman, education committee chairman, education officers) were jointly worked out by the research team. A checklist was also prepared of the items to be covered in the case study as a whole.

Study of documents
In each LEA a special study was made of local Instruments and Articles of Government, as amended over a period of 10–15 years, and of any Handbooks or Guideline Notes supplied to governors. Minutes of the

Education Committee and/or schools sub-committee spanning a three-year period were studied. Where appropriate, internal education department documents, joint consultative committee and Diocesan Board papers were also studied. Local newspapers were monitored throughout the research period for relevant issues in the local authority.

For each of the case-study governing bodies, the minutes of meetings over several years prior to the research were examined, together with headteachers' reports to the governing body over the period, where available. Papers submitted to the governing body by other members of staff were also studied, together with certain internal school documents such as staff bulletins and minutes of staff meetings. Where appropriate, PTA and PTFA documentation was examined, and information provided to parents by the school was monitored over the research period. This included brochures and material circulated by pupil post, including parent governor election papers. Papers relating to certain local groups were also studied.

### Exploring community links with education

This was the least cut-and-dried area of the field work, and a number of techniques were used to establish which sections of the community had special educational interests to promote, and what channels they attempted to use.

Depending on the character of the area, researchers severally:

made a broad scan of local interests by examining locally available lists of organisations and groups;

drew on previous research experience and used local knowledge to make contacts with particular networks of interest; identified key informants from the study of documents or by a 'snowballing' system of interviews;

followed up publicity material displayed in schools or local libraries, also news items in local papers;

interviewed individuals, in person or by telephone, entered into correspondence and/or attended meetings;

all with a view to ascertaining what interest groups existed, what aspects of education they were concerned to influence, if any, what knowledge they had of school governing bodies and whether in particular instances they made representations to governing body, school or LEA.

**Note**
Denzin, N.K., *The Research Act*, McGraw-Hill, 1978.

# Appendix II

**ELIZABETH II**

# Education Act 1980

## 1980 CHAPTER 20

An Act to amend the law relating to education.

[3rd April 1980]

Be it enacted by the Queen's most Excellent Majesty, by and with the advice and consent of the Lords Spiritual and Temporal, and Commons, in this present Parliament assembled, and by the authority of the same, as follows:

*School government*

Change of nomenclature.
1944 c. 31.

**1.**—(1) The members of the body constituted for a primary school under subsection (1) of section 17 of the Education Act 1944 (governing bodies of county and voluntary schools) shall be known as governors instead of managers and the instrument providing for the constitution of that body as an instrument of government instead of an instrument of management.

(2) The rules in accordance with which a primary school is required to be conducted under subsection (3)(*a*) of that section shall be known as articles of government instead of rules of management.

(3) The enactments mentioned in Schedule 1 to this Act shall have effect with the amendments there specified, being amendments consequential on the provisions of subsections (1) and (2) above.

(4) For any reference in any other enactment or document to the managers, foundation managers, instrument of management or rules of management of any primary school to which the provisions of subsections (1) and (2) above apply there shall be substituted, as respects any time after the coming into force of those provisions, a reference to the governors, foundation governors, instrument of government or articles of government of the school.

**2.**—(1) The instrument of government made for a county or voluntary school or for a special school maintained by a local education authority shall contain provisions complying with subsections (2) to (8) below.

(2) The governing body of every such school as is mentioned in subsection (1) above shall include governors appointed by the local education authority by whom it is maintained.

(3) The governing body of a county primary school or voluntary primary school serving an area in which there is a minor authority shall include at least one governor appointed by that authority.

(4) The governing body of a voluntary school shall include foundation governors and—

    (*a*) in the case of a controlled school, at least one-fifth of the members of the governing body shall be foundation governors;

    (*b*) in the case of an aided or special agreement school—

        (i) the foundation governors shall outnumber the other members of the governing body by two if that body has eighteen or fewer members and by three if it has more;

        (ii) at least one of the foundation governors shall at the time of his appointment be a parent of a registered pupil at the school.

(5) The governing body of a county or controlled school shall include at least two parent governors, that is to say persons who are elected by parents of registered pupils at the school and who are themselves such parents at the time when they are elected; and the governing body of an aided or special agreement school shall include at least one parent governor.

(6) Subsection (5) above shall apply to a special school maintained by a local education authority as it applies to a county or controlled school except that if the school is established in a hospital and it appears to the authority to be impracticable for the governing body to include parent governors it shall include at least two governors who are parents of children of compulsory school age.

(7) The governing body of a county or voluntary school or of a special school maintained by a local education authority shall, if the school has less than three hundred registered pupils, include at least one, and in any other case, at least two teacher governors, that is to say persons who are elected by teachers at the school and who are themselves such teachers at the time when they are elected.

(8) The head teacher of a county or voluntary school or of a special school maintained by a local education authority shall, unless he elects otherwise, be a governor of the school by virtue of his office and shall in any event be treated as a member of the governing body for the purposes of subsection (4) above.

(9) It shall be for the local education authority, in the case of a county or controlled school or of a special school maintained by the authority, and for the governors, in the case of an aided or special agreement school—

> (*a*) to determine any question whether, for the purposes of an election of parent governors or teacher governors, a person is a parent of a registered pupil at the school or a teacher at the school; and
>
> (*b*) to make all necessary arrangements for, and to determine all other matters relating to, any such election (including such matters as qualifying dates and any minimum number of votes required to be cast) but so that any contested election is held by secret ballot.

(10) Nothing in this section shall be construed as preventing the inclusion in the governing body of any school of governors additional to those required by this section.

(11) This section applies to an instrument of government made for a school only if—

> (*a*) the instrument is made after the coming into force of this section; or
>
> (*b*) an order is made by the Secretary of State applying this section to the school or to schools of a class or description to which the school belongs.

1944 c. 31.

(12) Sections 18 and 19 of the Education Act 1944 (composition of governing bodies of county and voluntary schools) and

1968 c. 37.

so much of section 2(2) of the Education (No. 2) Act 1968 as enables the local education authority to determine the size and composition of the governing body of a special school shall not apply to any school in relation to which this section applies.

Grouping of schools under single governing body.

**3.**—(1) Subject to the provisions of this section, a local education authority may make an arrangement for the constitution of a single governing body for any two or more schools maintained by the authority.

(2) Any arrangement under this section, other than one relating only to two primary schools neither of which is a special school, shall require the approval of the Secretary of State.

(3) Any arrangement under this section relating to a voluntary school shall require the consent of the governors or, in the

case of a school in respect of which proposals have been submitted under section 13 below and for which no governors have yet been appointed, of the persons submitting the proposals.

(4) The governing body constituted by an arrangement under this section shall include parent governors and teacher governors; and for the purposes of the election of such governors the schools to which the arrangement relates may be treated either separately or as if they were a single school.

(5) Any arrangement under this section may, if it does not relate to any voluntary school, be terminated at any time by the local education authority by whom it was made, and any such arrangement which relates to a voluntary school may be terminated by agreement between the local education authority and the governing body constituted by the arrangement or, in default of agreement, by one year's notice served by the local education authority on the governing body or by one year's notice served by the governing body on the local education authority.

(6) The Secretary of State's approval for the making of any arrangement under this section may be given subject to such conditions as he may specify; and the Secretary of State may at any time terminate any such arrangement either wholly or in relation to any school or schools to which it applies.

(7) While an arrangement under this section is in force in relation to any school—

>  (*a*) neither section 2 above nor the provisions as to the constitution of the body of governors in sections 17 to 19 of the Education Act 1944 shall apply to the school; and

1944 c. 31.

>  (*b*) for the purposes of any other enactment the governing body constituted by the arrangement and the members of that body shall be deemed to be the governing body and the governors of that school.

(8) This section applies to—

>  (*a*) schools having an instrument of government made after the coming into force of section 2 above; and

>  (*b*) schools in relation to which an order has been made under subsection (11)(*b*) of that section.

(9) The provisions of section 20 of the said Act of 1944 and section 2(4) of the Education (No. 2) Act 1968 (grouping of schools) shall not apply to any school to which this section applies; and any arrangements made under those provisions shall cease to apply to any school in relation to which an

1968 c. 37.

arrangement is made under this section or an order under section 2(11)(*b*) above comes into force.

Governors' proceedings and tenure of office.

**4.**—(1) The Secretary of State may make regulations—

(*a*) as to the meetings and proceedings of the governors of county and voluntary schools and of special schools maintained by local education authorities and as to the publication of information relating to those meetings and proceedings;

1944 c. 31.

(*b*) subject to section 21(1) of the Education Act 1944 (resignation and removal of governors), as to the tenure of office and disqualification of the governors of such schools.

(2) Regulations under subsection (1) above shall make provision for the election of a chairman by the governors of any such school.

(3) The instrument of government of any such school and any arrangement made under section 3 above may contain provisions with respect to the matters mentioned in subsection (1) above but any provision relating to a matter dealt with by regulations under that subsection shall have effect subject to the regulations.

(4) Where an aided or special agreement school has an instrument of government made after the coming into force of section 2 above, any decision taken at a meeting of the governors shall, if it is of the kind specified in subsection (5) below, require confirmation at a second meeting of the governors held not less than twenty-eight days after the first.

(5) The decisions referred to in subsection (4) above are—

(*a*) any decision that would result in the submission of proposals under section 13 below;

(*b*) any decision to serve a notice under section 14(1) of the Education Act 1944 (discontinuance of school);

(*c*) any decision that would result in an application under section 15(4) of that Act (revocation of order whereby school is an aided or special agreement school);

(*d*) any decision to request the making of an order under subsection (2) of section 16 of that Act (discontinuance of school for which another school is substituted) or as to the submissions to be made to the Secretary of State in any consultations under subsection (3) of that section;

(*e*) any decision to make an agreement under Schedule 2 to that Act (agreement for transfer of interest in school to local education authority).

(6) Section 21(2) of the said Act of 1944 and Schedule 4 to that Act (which are superseded by subsection (1)(*a*) above) shall cease to have effect; and in section 2(5) of the Education (No. 2) Act 1968 (which applies those provisions to special schools) for the words from "section 21" to "voluntary schools)" there shall be substituted the words "section 21(1) and (3) of the Education Act 1944 (provisions as to governors of county and voluntary schools)".

1968 c. 37.

5.—(1) Where a trust deed or other instrument made before the coming into force of section 2 above contains a provision whereby the persons who are for the time being governors of a voluntary school are by virtue of their office trustees of any property held for the purposes of or in connection with the school, that provision shall have effect as if the governors of the school consisted only of the foundation governors and the governors appointed by the local education authority and any minor authority.

Governors as ex officio trustees.

(2) Subsection (1) above is without prejudice to any power to amend any such provision as is mentioned in that subsection.

# Bibliography

Alexander, A., *Local Government in Britain Since Reorganisation*, Allen & Unwin, 1982.

Alford, R., *Health Care Politics: Ideological and Interest Group Barriers to Reform*, University of Chicago Press, 1975.

Archer, M.S., *Social Origins of Educational Systems*, Sage, 1979.

Archer, M.S., 'Educational politics: a model for their analysis' in Broadfoot, P. *et al.* (eds), *Political and Educational Change*, Croom Helm, 1981.

Arnstein, S., 'A ladder of citizen participation', *Journal of the American Institute of Planners*, vol. 35, 1969.

Bachrach, P. and Baratz, M.G., *Power and Poverty: Theory and Practice*, Oxford University Press, 1971.

Bacon, A.W., 'Co-management of the school system – a case study of teacher representation on school governing and managing bodies', in *Educational Studies*, vol. 3, no. 1, March 1977.

Bacon, A.W., *Public Accountability and the Schooling System*, Harper & Row, 1978.

Baldridge, J.V., *Power and Conflict in the University*, Jossey-Bass, 1971.

Baron, G. and Howell, D., *The Government and Management of Schools*, Athlone Press, 1974.

Becher, T. and Kogan, M., *Process and Structure in Higher Education*, Heinemann, 1980.

Becher, T., Eraut, M. and Knight, J., *Policies for Educational Accountability*, Heinemann, 1982.

Bennett, S. and Wilkie, R., 'Structural conflict in school organisation', in Fowler, G. *et al.* (eds), *Decision-Making in British Education*, Heinemann, 1973.

Benson, J.K., 'The inter-organisational network as a political economy', *Administrative Science Quarterly*, vol. 20, no. 2, 1975.

Berube, M. and Gittell, M. (eds), *Confrontation at Ocean Hill, Brownsville*, Praeger, 1969.

Bidwell, C.E., 'The school as a formal organisation', in March, J.G. (ed.), *Handbook of Organisation*, Rand McNally, 1965.

Bird, C. *et al.*, *Disaffected Pupils*, Brunel University, 1980.

Blau, P.M., *Exchange and Power in Social Life*, John Wiley, 1964.

Blau, P.M. and Scott, W.R., *Formal Organisations: A Comparative Approach*, Routledge & Kegan Paul, 1963.

Boaden, N., Goldsmith, M., Hampton, W. and Stringer, P., *Public Participation in Local Services*, Longman, 1982.

Brooksbank, K. and Revell, J., *School Governors*, Councils and Educational Press, 1981.

Bucher, R., 'Faculty politics and power', in Blankenship, R.L. (ed.), *Colleagues in Organisations: The Social Construction of Professional Work*, John Wiley, 1977.

Bullivant, B., *The New Governors Guide*, Home and School Publications, 1974.

*Bundy Report*, Mayor's Advisory Council on Decentralisation of the New York City Schools, Reconnection for Learning, A Community School System for New York Schools, 1967.

Burgess, T. and Sofer, A., *The School Governor and Managers Handbook and Training Guide*, Kogan Page, 1978.

Bush T. and Kogan, M., *Directors of Education*, Allen & Unwin, 1982.

Child, J., 'Organisational structure, environment and performance: the role of strategic choice', *Sociology*, vol. 6, no. 1, 1972.

*Children and their Primary Schools*, Report of the Central Advisory Council for Education (England) *Plowden Report* HMSO, 1967.

Collins, C.A. *et al.*, 'The officer and the councillor in local government', *Public Administration Bulletin*, December 1978.

Darke, R., 'Attitudes towards public participation', *Local Government Studies*, vol. 7, no. 3, May/June 1981.

Davies, B., 'On the contribution of organisational analysis to the study of educational institutions', in Brown, R., *Knowledge Education and Cultural Change*, Tavistock Publications, London, 1973.

Dearlove, J., *The Politics of Policy in Local Government*, Cambridge University Press, 1973.

Dennison, W.F., *Education in Jeopardy: Problems and Possibilities of Contraction*, Blackwell, 1981.

Derr, D. and Deal, T., 'Towards a contingency theory of change in education: organisational structure, processes and symbolism', in King, E.J. (ed.), *Education for Uncertainty*, Sage Annual Review of Social and Educational Change, vol. 2, 1978.

DES, *Circular 14/77, Local Education Authority Arrangements School Curriculum*, HMSO, 1977.

DES, *Circular 15/77, Information for Parents*, HMSO, 1977.

DES, *Education Act 1980: School Government*, Circular No. 4/81, June 1981.

DHSS, *Health Care and its Costs*, HMSO, 1983.

Dunleavy, P., *Urban Political Analysis*, Macmillan, 1980.

Dunleavy, P., *The Politics of Mass Housing in Britain*, Clarendon, 1981.

Education (School Governing Bodies) Regulations, 1981.

Elger, A., 'Industrial organisations: a processual perspective', in McKinlay, J. (ed.), *Processing People: Cases in Organisational Behaviour*, Holt, Rinehart & Winston, 1975.

Elliott, J., Bridges, D., Ebbutt, D., Gibson, R. and Nias, J., *School Accountability*, Grant MacIntyre, 1981.

Elmore, R.F., 'Backward mapping: implementation research and policy decisions', in Williams, W. and Elmore, R.F., *Studying Implementation. Methodological and Administrative Issues*, Chatham House Publishers, 1982.

Etzioni, A., *The Semi-Professions and Their Organization*, Free Press, 1974.

George, A., *Resource-based Learning for School Governors*, Croom Helm, forthcoming.

Gross, E., 'The definition of organisational goals', *British Journal of Sociology*, vol. 20, no. 3, 1969.

Hall, R.H., 'The concept of bureaucracy: an empirical assessment', *American Journal of Sociology*, vol. 69, no. 1, 1963.

Halmos, P., *The Personal Service Society*, Constable, 1970.

Ham, C., 'Community Health Council participation in the NHS planning system', *Social Policy and Administration*, vol. 14, no. 3, Autumn 1980.

Hampton, W., 'Research into public participation in structure planning', in Sewell, W.R.D. and Coppock, J.T. (eds.), *Public Participation in Planning*, John Wiley, 1977.

Harding, P. and Scott, G., 'Management structures in colleges of further education', *Educational Management and Administration*, vol. 10, no. 1, February 1982.

Hinings, C.R. *et al.*, 'The organisational consequences of financial restraint in local government', in Wright, M. (ed.), *Public Spending Decisions*, Allen & Unwin, 1980.

Howell, D.A., 'Corporate management in English local government and the education service – An interim report', *The Journal of Educational Administration*, vol. 17, no. 2, October 1981.

Howell, D.A., 'Problems of school government', in Simon, B. and Taylor, W. (eds.), *Education in the Eighties: The Central Issues*, Batsford, 1981.

Howell, D.A. and Brown, R., *Educational Policy-making: An Analysis*, Heinemann, 1983.

Hoyle, E., 'Leadership and decision-making in education', in Hughes, N. (ed.), *Administering Education*, Athlone Press, 1975.

Hoyle, E., 'Micropolitics of educational organisations', *Educational Management and Administration*, vol. 10, no. 2, June 1982.

Hunter, C., 'Education and local government in the light of central government policy', in Ahier, J. and Flude, M. (eds.), *Contemporary Education Policy*, Croom Helm, 1983.

ILEA, *The Report of the William Tyndale Junior and Infant Schools' Public Inquiry* (Auld Report), ILEA, 1976.

Illich, I., *Medical Nemesis*, Calder & Boyars, 1975.

Jennings, R.E., *Education and Politics: Policy-Making in LEAs*, Batsford, 1977.

Johnson, D. and Ransom, E., *Family and School*, Croom Helm, 1983.

Johnson, D. *et al.*, *Secondary Schools and the Welfare Network*, Allen & Unwin, 1980.

Johnson, T., *Professions and Power*, Macmillan, 1972.

Jones, G.W., 'Varieties of local politics', *Local Government Studies*, vol. 1, 1975.

Kimberley, J.R., 'Organisational size and the structuralist perspective: a review, critique and proposal', *Administrative Science Quarterly*, vol. 21, December 1976.

King, R., *The Sociology of School Organisation*, Methuen, 1983.

Kogan, M., *Educational Policy Making: A Study of Interest Groups and Parliament*, Allen & Unwin, 1974.

Kogan, M., 'Institutional autonomy and public accountability', *British Educational Administration Society Journal*, Winter 1975.

Kogan, M., *The Politics of Educational Change*, Fontana, 1978.

Kogan, M., *Should Governors Govern?*, Address to Annual Conference of NAGM, 1981.

Kogan, M., 'The central–local government relationship: a comparison between the education and health services', *Local Government Studies*, January/February 1983.

Krause, E.Q., 'Functions of a bureaucratic ideology: citizen participation', *Social Problems*, vol. 16, 1968.

Lawrence, P.R. and Lorsch, J.W., *Organisation and Environment*, Harvard University, 1967.

Lawton, D., *The Politics of the School Curriculum*, Routledge & Kegan Paul, 1980.

Leach, S., 'County-district relations in town planning', in Leach, S. and Stewart, J., *Approaches in Public Policy*, Allen & Unwin, 1982.

Lewis, J., 'Variations in service provision: politics at the lay–professional interface', in Young, K. (ed.), *Essays on the Study of Urban Politics*, Macmillan, 1975.

Lukes, S., *Power: A Radical View*, Macmillan, 1976.

Macbeth, A., Mackenzie, M. and Breckenridge, I., *Scottish School Councils: Policy Making, Participation or Irrelevance?*, HMSO, Edinburgh, 1980.

Maddison, D., 'Professionalism and community responsibility', *Social Science and Medicine*, vol. 14A, 1980.

March, J.G. and Olsen, J.P., *Ambiguity and Choice in Organisations*, Bergen, 1976.

McCormick, R., *Calling Education to Account*, Heinemann, 1982.

McGrew, A.G. and Wilson, M.J., *Decision-Making Approaches and Analysis*, Manchester University Press, 1982.

Meyer, J. and Rowan, B., Institutionalised organisations – formal structure as myth and ceremony', *American Journal of Sociology*, vol. 83, no. 2, 1977.

Ministry of Education, *Education Act 1944*. Schedule to Administrative Memorandum No. 25 issued 26 January 1955. Model Instrument of Government for a County Secondary School, Clause 4.

Morgan, C. *et al.*, *The Selection of Secondary Headteachers*, Open University Press, 1983.

National Union of Teachers, *Teacher Governors*, 1982.

Newton, K., *The Theory of Pluralist Democracy*, Oxford University Press, 1976.

Open University, *Governing Schools*, Course No. P.970.

Open University, Governing Schools Course Team, *Governing Schools Training Manual*, Open University, 1981.

Packwood, T., 'The school as a hierarchy', in Bush, T. *et al.* (eds.), *Approaches to School Management*, Harper & Row, 1980.

Parry, G., and Morriss, P., 'When is a decision not a decision?', in Crewe, I. (ed.), *Political Sociology Year Book*, Croom Helm 1974.

Parry, N., and Parry, J., 'Social work, professionalism and the state', in Parry, N., Ruston, M., and Satyamurti, C., (eds), *Social Work, Welfare and the State*, Edward Arnold, 1979.

Pateman, C., *Participation and Democratic Theory*, Oxford University Press, 1970.

Peters, B. Guy, 'Insiders and outsiders: the politics of pressure-group influence and bureaucracy', *Administration and Society*, Sage Publications, 1977.

Pettigrew, A.M., 'On studying organisational cultures', *Administrative Science Quarterly*, vol. 24, December 1979.

Pitkin, H., *Representation*, University of California Press, 1967.

Potter, A., *Organised Groups in British National Politics*, Faber, 1961.

Pugh, D.S. *et al.*, 'Dimensions of organisation structure', *Administrative Science Quarterly*, vol. 13, 1968.

Ranson, S., 'Changing relationships between centre and locality in education', *Local Government Studies*, vol. 6, no. 6, 1980.

Ranson, S. *et al.*, 'The structuring of organisational structures', *Administrative Science Quarterly*, vol. 23, March 1980.

Regan, D.E., *Local Government and Education*, Allen & Unwin, 1977.

Regan, D. and Stewart, J., 'An essay in the government of health: the case for local authority control', *Social Policy and Administration*, vol. 16, no. 1, Spring 1982.

Richardson, E., *The Teacher, The School and the Task of Management*, Heinemann, 1973.

Richardson, E., *Authority and Organisation in the Secondary School*, Macmillan, 1975.

Richardson, J.J. and Jordon, A.G., *Government Under Pressure*, Martin Robertson, 1979.

Robinson, T., *In Worlds Apart*, Bedford Square Press, 1978.

*Royal Commission on the Elementary Education Acts, England and Wales* (Cross Commission), HMSO, 1888.

*Royal Commission on the Revenue and Management of Certain Colleges and Schools and the Studies Pursued and Instruction Given Therein* (Clarendon Commission), Eyre & Spottiswoode for HMSO, 1864.

Sainsbury, E., *The Personal Social Services*, Pitman, 1977.

Salaman, G., *Work Organisations: Resistance and Control*, London, 1978.

Sallis, J., *Taylor and After*, Ward Lock, 1977.

Saunders, P., *Urban Politics: A Sociological Interpretation*, Penguin, 1980.

Silverman, D., *The Theory of Organisations: A Sociological Framework*, Heinemann, 1970.

Socialist Educational Association, *Handbook for Labour Governors*, 1982.

Taylor, F., *Accountability in Education: the role of elected parent and teacher governors of schools, and their relationship with their constituencies*, CIS Commentary Series, NELPCO, 1983.

Taylor Report, *A New Partnership for our Schools*, HMSO, 1977.

Turner, C., 'Organising educational institutions as anarchies', *Educational Administration*, vol. 5, no. 2, Spring 1977.

Tyler, W., *The Sociology of the School: A Review*, Tyler, Kent, 1982.

Walsh, K., 'Power and advantage in organisations', *Organisation Studies*, vol. 2, no. 2, 1981.

Walton, R.E. and Dutton, J.M., 'The management of interdepartmental conflict – a model and review', *Administrative Science Quarterly*, vol. 14, 1969.

Warwick, D., 'The local government of middle schools: governing bodies and the problems of middle school identity', in Hargreaves, A., and Tickle, L. (eds.), *Middle Schools: Origins, Ideology and Practice*, Harper & Row, 1980.

*Weaver Report on the Government of Colleges of Education*, DES, 1966.

Weick, K.E., 'Educational organisations as loosely-coupled systems', *Administrative Science Quarterly*, vol. 21, no. 1, 1976.

Williams, G., 'Educational planning: past, present and future', *Educational Policy Bulletin*, vol. 7, no. 2, 1979.

Wirt, F., 'Professionalism and political conflict: a developmental model', *Journal of Public Policy*, vol. 1, part 1, February 1981.

Wragg, E.C. and Partington, J.A., *A Handbook for School Governors*, Methuen, 1980.

# Index